1, 2 and 3 JOHN

John Hannah has the mind of a scholar and the heart of a pastor. In this thoughtful and practical exposition of the Johannine Epistles, Hannah carefully explains the text and skillfully applies its message to our contemporary world. If you want to see afresh the beauty of Christ and grow in your love for Him and His people, this book is for you.

Matthew S. Harmon
Professor of New Testament Studies
Grace Theological Seminary, Winona Lake, Indiana

Of all my teachers, Dr. John Hannah has been one of the most beloved. From a rigorously reformed perspective, Dr. Hannah daily communicated to me and countless other students a warm-hearted affection for the Savior. That is why I am so grateful to have a commentary from him that communicates that same theological rigor and devotional depth. I am delighted to recommend this commentary on the Johannine epistles. It is a beloved message from the beloved disciple expounded by a beloved professor. Highly recommended.

Denny Burk,
Professor of Biblical Studies,
Boyce College, Southern Baptist Theological Seminary,
Louisville, Kentucky

1, 2 and 3 JOHN

Redemption's Certainty

John D. Hannah

CHRISTIAN
FOCUS

John D. Hannah is Research Professor of Theological Studies and
Distinguished Professor of Historical Theology at Dallas Theological
Seminary, Dallas, Texas.

Copyright © 2016 John D. Hannah

ISBN 978-1-78191-771-8

10 9 8 7 6 5 4 3 2 1

Printed in 2016
by
Christian Focus Publications Ltd.,
Geanies House, Fearn, Ross-shire,
IV20 1TW, Scotland, U.K.

www.christianfocus.com

Cover design by Daniel van Straaten

Printed and bound by
Bell & Bain, Glasgow

Contents

Dedication

I affectionately dedicate this volume to the adult class, 'A Grace Gathering,' that it is my privilege to teach at Stonebriar Community Church, Frisco, Texas.

This comes with the prayer that our fellowship in Jesus Christ may continue to be rich as we seek to conform to the truth of the apostle's teachings, grow in devotedness to the object of our affections, express it in love for others, and echo His message together throughout the world.

May our love for God increase.
May our knowledge of God deepen.
May our hearts with care for others enlarge.
May our passion to speak of Christ burn within us.
May God allow us to walk together in truth and love.
May we learn each day more of the love that God has for us.
May the atoning Lord both delight and humble us.
May the Spirit of God guide and nourish us.
May the beauty of God ravish our souls.
May we think much of His coming.
May we live together in hope.

Throughout the commentary, the author has provided individual application questions for personal reflection. At the close of the commentary, there are Group Study Questions for Bible Study Groups.

Preface

As I think about approaching the Holy Scriptures with the intent of writing an explanatory synopsis of John's letters, I do so with a degree of fear as well as delight. Delight because the Bible is the Word of God; it is the written revelation of the mind of the infinitely wise, all knowing, and omnipotent of Beings. To read it seriously is to come into the presence of God, an experience that transcends the collectivity of all other human experiences for its depth of wisdom and durative pleasures. Further, since the Bible is of divine origin, unquestionably trustworthy, any attempt to explain the meaning, as a finite, fallible being, of what the infinite God has made available to us should cause trembling. In a sense, it is the passion of fools!

As I read John's first letter, the problem he seems to address is human confidence in claiming that we know God when our lives are not all that they should be, when God is unflinchingly holy and His demands are conformity to His character (God's character is the criteria of human ethics and to say we know God is to possess His life, which is His character). As a religious historian by profession, a career invested in a theological institution, I find it a heavy task at times to stand before students in my professional capacity realizing that I am seeking to explain the meaning of temporal as well as ultimate realities. With a finite mind that has become twisted through inheritance, as evidenced by intellectual misperception and moral blindness, with the distance of centuries that makes the past blurry and incapable of replication, and with human biases that are only somewhat ameliorated through diligence of study, the task is not only made more complex, it is daunting.

As I thought about my future life as a pastor-teacher in the early years of ministerial preparation, I actually wondered if I might not get bored, thinking once I preached through the Bible I would have little further to offer and decades to do it. I have come to realize that this great book is beyond my ability to mine the enormity of its riches, and that a life spent in diligent study would only scratch the surface of its profundity. The task of pastors, as faithful under-shepherds, is to explain the meaning of the words of the Great Shepherd. This should not only drive them to their knees in supplication for guidance and clarity, but also for mercy for themselves and for their hearers as they pursue their divinely appointed task as students of the Bible and disseminators of its message.

The stark simplicity of some of John's statements lends to an understanding of the drift of his thought that is generally grasped by commentators. Such ideas as the unity of truth and love, the coherency of Jesus Christ's redemptive mission as an earthly reality but with heavenly origin, the perception that the infinite and invisible can be discerned through the finite and visible, and the acknowledgement that a spirit of deception can masquerade in the strappings of helpfulness are lessons easily discernible as one even reads the letters in a cursory manner. However, it does not take a deeply insightful person to come to the realization that our best scholars find the letters perplexing and the outline of John's thought difficult to follow at times. Beyond the linguistic issues, raised by John's grammatical and literary style, are several theological conundrums, none so perplexing as the notion that believers do not sin (3:6, 9; 5:18), when John makes the clear statement that they do (2:1-2).

An issue that affects how one approaches these writings concerns the relationship of the definitive, non-repetitive redemptive experience to the progressive nature of growing in the knowledge of Jesus Christ and conformity to Him. Are the two organically interconnected or are they separable? Is 'abiding' a temporal experience somehow dependent on obedience or is it a synonym for the redemptive state? Does not John's instruction indicate something about the danger of separating the redemptive experience from progressive sanctification?

Still another question concerns the theological error that created the crisis that the writings address. Are John's opponents in denial of Jesus' humanity or was it that they denied His deity, His role as the anointed one, the atoning Savior, the Christ? Is the theme that John addresses the product of Christological error that has moral and intellectual ramifications (a valid maxim, I propose, is that every theological error has ethical implications)?

What follows is an attempt to help pastors and teachers of the Bible to understand John's letters; it is not an attempt to speak to the world of the academy, but to the church. While it is hoped that scholarly research will not be lacking, the rationale for exegetical decisions will not be detailed, though conversation with the academy will underlay and undergird the argument of the books as they are set forth in the pages that follow. Further, the rehearsal of background materials to facilitate an understanding of the books will be limited with a reliance, as far as possible, upon the information available from the texts themselves, as well as any relevant collaborative New Testament materials. For example, it is not uncommon for writers approaching these books to comment, sometimes in lengthy fashion, on such matters as authorship, date of writing, historical setting, and textual integrity. It is the assumption of this writer that the son of Zebedee, the 'beloved disciple', the brother of James, one of the earliest disciples of Jesus, the Apostle John, wrote the letters. Also, it is my conviction that the words in these letters are simply and unquestionably true, not merely the ideas expressed (how can the two be separated?), having been originated in the mind of God, who is incapable of deception or being deceived, then conveyed and preserved through supernatural care by the Spirit of God, and structured by the literary talents and acumen of the apostle. Further, it is assumed that John wrote these letters in the later decades of the first century in Asia Minor, most likely from Ephesus, to a church or group of churches nearby that he had more than a casual interest in and, therefore, felt compelled to strengthen in a troubling time.

The particular approach to this commentary will be grammatical, biblical, theological, and practical. An overarching assumption concerning the question that John is addressing will be presented, hopefully warranted from the data of the texts (parallel constructions, dependent clauses, main verbs, verb tenses), to discern the apostle's argument and formulate the outline of the books, all of this with the goal of aiding in the accurate preaching and teaching of the text. In citing texts from the Bible throughout the study, the New American Standard Bible (NASB), unless otherwise cited, published by the Lockman Foundation, will be used for no other reason than it is the translation that has been my companion since its original publication.

Though this writer admits his frailties to execute the task before him, likely exposing his ignorance to public scrutiny, and assuming responsibility for any inaccuracies of thought or expression, he nevertheless does so with the plea, expressed to God in prayer, that what is written would somehow be used by our merciful redeemer and great God to promote the interests of His kingdom.

JOHN D. HANNAH
September 2016

The Setting of John's Letters

While John's letters are some of the easiest first-century literature for contemporary students of the language to read (that is why this was the first book most of us worked through in learning the language), the vocabulary rather common, and the grammatical constructions straightforward in most cases (I recognize that this is not the case in 1:1-4, for example), they have proven among the most difficult to interpret from the perspective of grammar because contextual clues are often sparse, referent of pronouns unclear at times, and finding parallels in later literature methodologically suspect. Perhaps, the latter can be illustrated by the propensity of earlier interpreters to find similarities between the writer's opponents and the later church's grappling with the docetic affirmations of Gnosticism, a view not entirely without some support, but one entertained with suspicion when evaluating the meager data that John provides for us. Further, reviewing scholarly attempts to outline the book reveals the difficulties of interpreting it; there is little agreement about the structure of the contents of John's first letter, for example (the other two letters are quite common in structure with contemporary letter-writing style). That the letters are jewels in the treasury of the church is without question.

Though there is no explicit statement that the Apostle John composed the letters, it is an assumption that undergirds the study of this small trilogy of writings (this is said to indicate that these writings were not, in this writer's opinion, the product of a 'Johannine community' acquainted with John). Johannine authorship had not been challenged from the time of the earliest churchmen until the emergence of skeptical religious scholarship some centuries ago (again, in assigning authorship to other than John is not necessarily a denial of the integrity of what has been written; it is simply the opinion of some conservative scholars).

John grew to adulthood in the Galilean town of Bethsaida (John 1:44) with his father Zebedee, his mother Salome, and at least one sibling, James (together Jesus called them the 'Sons of Thunder' [Mark 3:17], perhaps an indication of their emotional makeup, being men of quick decision-making and non-negotiable convictions, as can be seen, for example, when Jesus was refused hospitality from the Samaritans. The brothers were so offended that they responded to the insult by asking Jesus if they should call down fire from heaven in judgment [Luke 9:51-55]!).

John seems to have been a man of clear doctrinal com-mitments and feelings, a man living in a world of sharp antitheses. One so convinced of truth than he could be blunt, even stark, and yet motivated by a deep encounter with the love of God revealed through the life and ministry of Jesus Christ (John's confession was that 'in Him was light...' [John 1:4] and that 'He explained Him' [John 1:18]).

The family appears to have had wealth and influence. The sons of Zebedee joined their father plying the riches found in the Sea of Galilee. If 'that disciple' (John 18:15) was indeed John, as most believe, he was known to Joseph Caiaphas, the high priest, and witnessed the early phase of our Lord's trials, whereas Peter was permitted only into the courtyard of the enclave. Another indication of financial security of sorts, as well as Jesus' trust in him, was that shortly before His death, and while upon the cross, Jesus committed the care of His mother Mary to John (John 19:25-27). It is probable that Mary and Salome were sisters, so making John and Jesus cousins.

Originally a follower of John the Baptist, John was an early disciple of Jesus, within the inner circle of the twelve, and denominated as the 'disciple whom Jesus loved' (John 20:2; 21:7). Within the inner core of the disciples, composed also of his brother James and Peter, John witnessed the miracle of the raising of Jairus' daughter in Capernaum (Mark 5:37; Luke 8:51), observed the Transfiguration (Matt. 17:1-2), sat nearest Jesus at the Last Supper, which he was appointed to prepare (Luke 22:8), was the first to observe the empty tomb from within it (John 20:4-5), and was the first to recognize the resurrected Lord in the context of the miraculous catch of fishes (John 21:1-7). He appears four times in the Book of Acts, in a leadership role in the Jerusalem church. For example, and in addition to being on the scene in the events of Acts 2, he was with Peter at the miracle of the healing of the lame man (Acts 3) and, subsequently, experienced imprisonment by the Jewish hierarchy (Acts 4). Following the dispersal of the apostles from Jerusalem (Acts 8:4), second century sources indicate that John came to reside in Ephesus where he sustained an influence on nearby churches (Rev. 2–3). This area, western Asia Minor, seems to have been the context out of which he composed the three letters, as well as the Revelation (some date the gospel late in the first-century as well, though the recent trend in scholarship is to place it in the early 60s, in the period of the martyrdom of Peter [thus providing the context of the gospel's epilogue which seems to have been an addendum]).

Roman legions entered the continent of Asia, actually the western portion of modern-day Turkey, naming it Asia Minor, in the second century B.C. With the passage of time the province offered enormous economic wealth to the empire and became a robust center for the propagation of Greco-Roman culture. Christianity was brought by missionary teams into Asia Minor, chronicled in part in the Books of the Acts by Luke, the letters of Paul and Peter, and the writings of John. As stated above, the earliest Christian writers, such as Papias and Irenaeus, provide uniform testimony that John the Apostle lived in Ephesus in his later years and sustained ministry in the churches of the area.

The Context of John's Letters

The issue that John addresses in his letters was a specific one that was ongoing and seems to have had the potential of increasing, creating further destruction and disturbance. In essence, the disruption in the churches to which he writes is an internal division of opinion that has resulted in controversy, turmoil, and fracturing. The least that can be said is that the harmony and unity of the churches had been threatened by what the apostle conceives to be a mounting crisis. This seems to be indicated by the introductory statement of purpose (1:1-4); the true message that Jesus passed on to the apostolic band (five occurrences of the plural pronoun 'we') concerning His claims about Himself, and with a view to the creation of Christ-following communities characterized by love, a unity focused outwardly of delight in the Savior, and affectionate regard and harmony among the saints ('that you also may have fellowship with us, and indeed our fellowship is with the Father, and with His Son Jesus Christ', 1:4).

The threat to the unity of the assembly of the saints had progressed to the stage that some were teaching what was labeled by the apostle as non-apostolic, meaning that those who did so were without authority or sanction for their actions. The terms that John uses to describe the perpetuators of the errors are emotional and graphic (he does not write from the perspective of an observing bystander, but as a gravely concerned participant). The errorists who are promoting false teaching and improper behavior are denominated as false teachers ('… many false prophets have gone out into the world [4:1]), antichrists ('…you heard that antichrist is coming, even now many antichrists have arisen' [2:18]), liars (2:22), and deceivers (II John 7). Perhaps the most chilling comment concerning the gravity of the error of the false teachers is that they are unbelievers ('Any one who goes too far and does not abide in the teachings of Christ, does not have God…' [II John 9]). Clearly John has opinions that he is unwilling to compromise and his manner of addressing the issues at hand is forthright and blunt with regard to the disturbers, yet gentle and instructive with the disturbed.

In this regard, a clue emerges from the first letter that the controversy is ongoing and the consequence of the defection has affected only some of the churches. John gives evidence of writing to a group that agrees with his views on the matter though they need reassurance that they are right in their stance. This is evident by the use of pronouns such as 'we,' 'you,' 'us,' and 'they.' The 'we,' 'you,' and 'us' is juxtaposed against the other types of 'they' at times. '…*you* have fellowship with *us*… (1:3). '*They* went out from *us*, but *they* were not of *us*…. But *you*… (2:19-20).' '*They* are from

the world.... *We* are from God; he who knows God listens to
us...' (4:5-6).

The trouble in the church has progressed to the point that
the unity of the churches is threatened with schism, parties
were dividing and new churches formed. This is evident
when John writes, 'They went out from us, but they were
not *really* of us...' (2:19). From this comment several things
become apparent: first, the controversy in the churches over
what is apostolic teaching has gone beyond the boiling stage;
it has spilled over into the fire of separation and ecclesiastical
disunity. New gatherings of 'believers' have formed around
teachers who have convinced some that they were the correct
interpreters of Christian truth. Second, the false teachers
were once participants in the local assemblies that they have
disturbed (2:19). They appear to have been welcomed into
the outward manifestation of Christ's body, symbolic of
their oneness with God in ownership and confidence, but,
persuaded by unrevealed circumstances and undisclosed
motives, they drifted from apostolic instruction, increasingly
becoming assured and vocal with new insights to the point
that they usurped their place, divided the assembly over the
propriety of their views, started a schismatic assembly, and
were now exporting their teaching to other churches, possibly
creating a movement.

If this reconstruction of the context is valid, it would seem
to tie together John's two very brief letters with his first one.
Would it not be reasonable that John's second letter was
written as a warning to a church about the spreading of error,
and that the church should be cautious about whom they listen
to and support? 'If any one comes to you, and does not bring
this teaching, do not receive him into your house, and do not
give him a greeting' (v. 10). Traveling teachers or itinerants
composed a recognized service in the earliest churches. These
churches were led by a plurality of elders with the duties
of admonition, instruction, and governance, but in addition
prophets traveled among the churches ('And He gave some
as apostles, and some as prophets, and some as evangelists,
and some as pastors and teachers' [Eph. 4:11]) also. I take it
that three of the offices were exercised without geographic
limitations and the latter two were localized offices.

Further, could it be that John pens a letter to Gaius, and indirectly to the church that he attends, perhaps in his home or nearby, where the disturbers already manifested a threatening influence? The fellowship had correctly responded to the errorists by refusing to countenance their teaching, but under the heavy hand, or domineering spirit, of Diotrephes have gone too far in their reaction. By refusing the false teachers, he seems to have closed the door to all itinerant teachers entering the assembly, refusing all aid to any in that work, and thus was a threat to the unity of the church by casting out those who disagreed with his high handed approach (III John 9-10). Demetrius, however, is an example to John of a worthy itinerant prophet/teacher (v. 12) and Gaius should not withhold support from such (vv. 5-6), though Diotrephes is acting in an autocratic manner. The point of the letter being that the common crisis of false teaching had caused another problem, one of overreaction.

The Teachings of John's Opponents

There is little disagreement among students of John's writings that his intent in writing his letters was pastoral and polemical. However, the nature of the apostle's polemics is disputed because the teachings of his opponents have not been identified with any unanimity. Generally speaking, the tendency of scholarship has been to identify John's adversaries in light of the development of Gnosticism, at least in its incipient stages, though there is little agreement between Gnostic teachings and John's opponents other than a willingness to reject the preexistence and, thus, the deity of Jesus Christ, God in human fleshly existence. It seems that the data John provides is vague and to seek clarification of it by reading developments decades after his death is, in the least, questionable methodologically. Edwards simply says that 'Gnosticism is vast and complex, and quite alien to I John's.... Rather than being a source of Johannine thought, these texts (meaning latter Gnostic assertions) were likely influenced by it' (138).

Two additional comments are worthwhile in rejecting a Gnostic or proto-gnostic background to John's writings: first, it is clear that the historical, material existence of Jesus was not questioned by John's opponents, but His deity and redemptive role was the issue; second, the dualism in these writings seems to be ethical in nature, not cosmic (i.e., the spiritual versus the material). In regard to the latter insight, Smalley writes: 'If the thought of this verse [4;4], with its allusion to the battle between spiritual truth and error, God and the evil one, grazes the edge of dualism, this dualism is ethical and not cosmic… Jewish not Greek' (227). Previously, Smalley noted on another seemingly dualistic verse (2:15): 'The injunction to resist worldliness, to choose light rather than darkness, presupposes a background of dualism: the struggle between good and evil. There is, however, no need to locate the dualism in Hellenistic, gnostic thought…. Given that the basic indebtedness of the Johannine church and its tradition was Jewish, rather than Greek…' (81).

Thus, it would seem that whatever one can argue about John's opponents, it should be derived from his writings themselves and not imported through the grid of subsequent centuries (it is more reasonable to believe that itinerants twisted the apostles' instructions from the earliest inception of the movement which gradually mutated into what became Gnostic tenets, borrowing selectively from Christian faith, mixing in components of various mystery religions but twisting its redemptive message into a gross, grotesque remnant of it).

As I reflect on the error that John seeks to address, it seems that it resided in three misconceptions of Jesus' life and ministry and one concerning its implication. The four are not only interconnected and inseparable; there is a logical sequence, one leading to another.

The first concerned the person of Jesus. Was He the Christ, God's anointed one, whose very origin was from the very presence of God or was He merely a wise sage, a prophet-like figure, upon whom God's unique blessing rested? What seems denied by John's opponents is not Jesus' humanity (a clear Gnostic tenet. They embraced His humanity, but denied His role as the Christ, the divinely sent-from-heaven one), but His divinity.

Second, the issue of Jesus' identity is not an idle one because it is related to the need that He addressed. Though only indirectly considered, what was the need that Jesus came to ameliorate? Was it that Jesus was an educator because the nature of the human dilemma was intellectual ignorance and insufficient corrective programming or was the problem a need so deeply rooted in the perversity of human nature that it requires neither instruction to learn nor mere instruction to adjudicate?

Third, Jesus did tell us much about the needs He met and the person that He was; the two are interconnected. What did Jesus do to ameliorate the plight of those He came to 'save'? Was it that Jesus came to instruct us, to enlighten our minds, to show us the correct set of assumptions to pursue, because all we need is intellectual insight or did He come to be our atoning, substitutionary sacrifice? Did Jesus come to show us the way or to be the way into the presence of God? If Jesus was not God-in-the-flesh, how could a mere creature bring us into the presence of God? His deity, our profound impossible-to-remediate need and His atoning death are inseparable. Brown is rather to the point when he writes: 'If I am right in diagnosing the point of difference between the secessionists and the epistolary author to be the salvific value of Jesus' career in the flesh and the degree to which that career was part of His identity as the Christ, inevitably the attitude toward His death will be crucial' (77).

I have come to the conclusion that John battled against the tendency in the churches through the centuries to disparage the identity and accomplishments of Jesus Christ because of a presuppositional unwillingness, a constitutional bias, to embrace human frailty and spiritual bankruptcy. When the Christian faith is defined by only what can be gained through the intuitive or sensory perception, it ceases to be Christian at all (what remains are baseless moral codes). Simply put, you cannot have Christianity without the God who became man, a God/man who can alone lift humankind out of its human dilemma to the heights of truth and the experience of reality that is only momentarily shadowed in this realm of life. In essence, John was fighting against an effort to maintain the importance of Jesus in Christianity without embracing His absolute deity, making him a mere symbol or idealization of the best that we can self-discover by an inward journey of self-resolve, self-realization, and self-esteem. With a Jesus who is not the Christ, or the atoning sacrifice, we can perpetuate the false message of self-redemption through self-effort, but it does not resolve the issue of human brokenness. False ideas of salvation can be, at best, a bandage approach to a rapidly aggressive cancer.

The fourth point concerning the troubling and contrary teachings of John's opponents was the coherency of their argument about God, which seems to encompass a certain rational plausibility. If God is absolutely perfect, and the criteria of knowing Him is to share in His holiness (I John 1:5), then we must be holy. While this might make some sense, the reality is that such a condition of comparable holiness in the temporal state is not what John's readers received from apostolic instruction. If the opponents' teachings are unfounded, then their solution was a matter of psychological delirium and heterodoxy. However, how can you say that you know God when you are not like Him? This seems to be the question that John is addressing. His answer is that the apostolic instruction is correct, that fellowship with God, knowing God, is through sharing in the divine nature. This is possible only through God's anointed Son, Jesus Christ, who came from the very presence of God to live and die for us, that His atoning sacrifice has resolved the dilemma of human sinfulness, the criteria of holiness, and divine salvation. Thus, John's point is that though sin remains in us, righteousness does also ('we know that, when He appears, we shall be like Him, because we shall see Him just as He is' [3:2]). Christianity is the religion of sinners who sadly reveal the blight on their souls all too often, but by the grace of God have come to know that divine love has justly trumped human failure. This seems to have been the point at which the opponents of John gained an inroad into the churches. They promised a 'now' salvation without the realities of a 'not yet' salvation; they separated the two, rejecting the second, to live in a myth of false Christian fantasy and mysticism. It is consistent with apostolic teaching that God is our righteousness through Christ and that we now are seen by God as sharing in the fruit of Jesus' cleansing sacrifice, it being substitutionary in nature. To his readers, John's message is that, in spite of human imperfection, believers in Jesus can know that they know Him. These believers need not be shaken by the evidence of the remnants of sin's once universal grip on their lives; there is no solution in finding Jesus to be a wise instructor of self-potential through denial; only the apostles' teachings puts human sin in its place through the conquest by the Christ, God's chosen servant, our atoning sacrifice. There is no need to live in a fantasy world concerning our sin; it is real, it lingers though debilitated, and one day, in the final judgment, we, as well as the earth, shall be completely purged of the effects of it.

The poet Horatio Spafford penned the words of the hymn, 'It is Well with My Soul,' in 1876, expressing the harsh realities of life and yet the hope that we have that Jesus has crushed the last enemy of our souls. We await the fruition experientially of all of its implications, the point being that imperfection and disappointment is our lot at times now, but a wonderful future awaits us. As we wait, we do not need to delude ourselves that struggles have ended; instead we must focus on the attainments of the one that John says came from the Father, Jesus who is the Christ.

> When peace, like a river, attendeth my way,
> When sorrows like sea billows roll;
> Whatever my lot, Thou has taught me to
>   say,
> It is well, it is well, with my soul.
>
> Though Satan should buffet, though trials
>   should come,
> Let this blest assurance control,
> That Christ has regarded my helpless
>   estate,
> And hath shed His own blood for my soul.
>
> My sin, oh, the bliss of this glorious
>   thought!
> My sin, not in part but the whole,
> Is nailed to the cross, and I bear it no more,
> Praise the Lord, praise the Lord, O my soul!

> For me, be it Christ, be it Christ hence to
>   live:
> If Jordan above me shall roll,
> No pang shall be mine, for in death as in
>   life
> Thou wilt whisper Thy peace to my soul.
>
> But, Lord, 'tis for Thee, for Thy coming we
>   wait,
> The sky, not the grave, is our goal;
> Oh trump of the angel! Oh voice of the
>   Lord!
> Blessèd hope, blessèd rest of my soul!
>
> And Lord, haste the day when my faith
>   shall be sight,
> The clouds be rolled back as a scroll;
> The trump shall resound, and the Lord
>   shall descend,
> Even so, it is well with my soul.

Let me elucidate upon the above four assertions. From the comments of John, it is clear that the secessionist party had a deviate, hence non-apostolic, understanding of Jesus Christ. From the fragmented data provided in the letter, what is revealed is that the content of the false teaching concerned the person of Christ as it relates to the incarnation as God's divinely appointed messenger. In this regard there are at least three instances that suggest a denial that Jesus was God come in the flesh, hence denying the incarnation of God:

> '... every spirit that confesses that Jesus Christ has come in the flesh is from God and every spirit that does not confesses Jesus is not from God...' (4:2-3);

> 'This is the one who came by water and blood, not with water only, but with the water and the blood' (5:6);

> 'For many deceivers...who do not acknowledge Jesus Christ *as* coming in the flesh' (II John 7a).

The sense in which they denied His humanity relates to the role of Jesus as the Christ, the redeemer figure. 'Who is the liar but the one who denies that Jesus is the Christ?' (2:22). It is Jesus' capacity as the divine savior, the promised one, which seems to be the issue. The first letter begins with the interconnection of Jesus as the life-giver – 'Word of Life' (1:1) and eternal life (1:2); it ends with a similar comment, a summary of the apostle's argument (5:13-20). Further, we have statements by John such as these: '… God sent forth His only begotten Son into the world so that we might have life through Him' (4:9); 'And we know that the Son of God has come, and has given us understanding…. This is the true God and eternal life' (5:20); 'And He has borne witness concerning His Son…. And the witness is this, that God has given us eternal life and this life is in His Son' (5:9, 11). It seems probable that John's opponents are not rejecting apostolic teaching about Jesus as it relates to His humanness, though that cannot be discounted because an ontological unity exists in the incarnate Jesus, being perfect humanness and deity in one being. What the false teachers rejected of apostolic instruction was not so much the humanity of Jesus, but the eternality of Jesus, the interconnection of preexistence with human existence. They would have accepted the earthliness of Jesus, but not His divinity. As Brown suggests: 'Thus, not the fact but only the manner of the coming is the subject of the debate between the epistolary author and the secessionists' (76). John's protagonists were willing to grant specialty to Jesus, a prophet-like figure, but not eternality, not the status of deity in the flesh. This is the reason that John repeatedly makes the point that Jesus is the Christ, God's appointed one, sent from His very presence to reveal God to us: '… the eternal life, which was with the Father and manifested to us' (1:2); '…God sent His only begotten Son into the world…' (4:9); 'And we have beheld and bear witness that the Father has sent the Son to be the Savior of the world' (4:9). The truth of the deity of Jesus Christ is inseparable from the apostolic witness to His accomplishments.

An integral correlate of the person of Jesus Christ is the matter of our redemption; this Brown has denominated as the 'cornerstone of Johannine soteriology' (74). The procurement of redemption would be impossible if Jesus was not human because the Bible teaches that He took upon Himself the debt of human sin, a burden no human could adjudicate (finitude cannot appease infinitude if the criteria is infinite), that He became sin for us, and that He could not have satisfied divine wrath for our offenses had not the quality of His sacrifice been infinite, and thus pleasing to God. If He were merely human, that is all and nothing more, even though He might have been the most insightful and self-sacrificing among us, human redemption would remain an impossibility.

This nuance seems sustained by John's detailed emphasis on the accomplishment of Jesus' mission to obtain eternal life for sinners. The repetition of the mechanics of the procurement of life for us seems to highlight the emphasis that the incarnation was integral to the accomplishment of salvation, not an end in itself. 'He Himself is the propitiation for our sins...' (2:2, also 4:10). 'He appeared to take away sins, and in Him there is no sin' (3:5). 'He loved us and sent His Son to be the propitiation for our sins' (4:10). This seems to be the point in that John in his writings connects the mission of Jesus with the acquisition of eternal life for sinners. John's claim in the gospel is that Jesus was sent from God to this world in the capacity of its redeemer. It may be that the false teaching did not include a denial of our Lord's specialty, certainly not that He came among us; however, the error seems to have been a misunderstanding of His true identity and, consequentially, the manner and nature of His accomplishments, going beyond the warrant of the apostolic teaching. While we are not privy to how the errorists taught it, they seem to claim that Jesus eradicated sin from the Christian's experience entirely in this present life and did so in other than by an atoning sacrificial death. If Jesus was a human prophet, the most rational response to the issue is that He provided a superior example that should be emulated, a truth that should be imagined by faith and acted out. This approach seems consistent with John's insistence that 'any one who goes too far, and does not abide in the teachings of Christ, does not have God...' (II John 9).

It would appear that the issue posed by the disturbers of the church is the claim that the redemption procured by Jesus is a past event without ongoing consequences; that is, Jesus obtained the divine right of our forgiveness, that His death brought about a state in us, through His teachings and life-modeling, requiring no further application. To unpack this even further, the opponents appear to be saying that Jesus, a prophet-like teacher of morality, has brought us to a state equal to His own: 'If we say we have no sin...' (1:8) and 'If we say we have not sinned...' (1:10). John's answer to their error is they have confused the present experience of the new life through Christ with the ultimate experience of the life in a later day. He makes the point that Christ's atoning death has an ongoing dimension ('... and the blood of Jesus His Son cleanses us from all sin' [1:7]) and that Jesus functions presently for the believer as their advocate, suggestive of the need thereof ('And if any one sins, we have an Advocate with the Father, Jesus Christ the righteous...' [2:1]). The 'now and not-yet aspects' of our redemption are brought out later in his letter when he writes, '... it has not yet appeared what we shall be. We know that, if He should appear, we shall be like Him, because we shall see Him just as He is' (3:2).

The foundational error of the false teachers was to reject Jesus' deity while affirming His humanity. Jesus, to them, was only one in a long line of instructional prophets who taught and served as spokesmen for God. Based upon a denial of Jesus' divine origin, they rejected the notion of a divine substitutionary sacrifice, while embracing the notion that Jesus' moral success in emulating the life of God was the 'real' message. Sin was not the issue that Jesus came to resolve; it was moral ignorance. Ignorance of the fact that sin does not really matter in claiming a relationship with God. This could lead to license, freedom from the necessity to manifest the presence of God in the life of the believer by conforming to the character of God revealed in love for others. Thus, the issue that the apostle addresses, though the particular context has obviously changed through the centuries, is that of the relationship of divine salvation to sanctification; it is about the change that God initiates when He redeems. It answers the question posed throughout history many times: what degree of change has Christ brought to us and how can that change help us to understand our struggles as Christians in following Him? The timeless subject of John's writings is Christian spirituality.

A primary reason for the above assessment that the errorists rejected the deity, the divine origins of Jesus, and His earthly mission was because they did not connect His coming with redemption from the penalty of sin. There is no clue in the letters that they rejected His historical, physical existence. The error of the secessionists was over the actual identity of Jesus and, consequently, the implications of His coming, rooted in a misunderstanding of His redemptive mission. It seems that the secessionists had an alarming point that made their teachings appear valid: if the standard of standing before God is absolute perfection (1:5), is it not ludicrous to claim that we know Him who is Light since we all evidence a blighted lifestyle? Since there does not appear to be a denial that Jesus existed, the error must be relative to His accomplishments or mission. Refusing to accept His divine origin and character, they denied His true purpose in coming. John connects sin and the need for cleansing with the work of Christ, so the false teachers are likely denying the salvific dimensions of the incarnation because they are unable to connect the absolute perfections of God with the Christian profession that struggle with sin is a constant until glorification and that human perfection is not a prerequisite for the possession of the life of God because of our divine substitute, Jesus Christ. The errorists could not grasp the insight that sinners can stand before a righteous God, clothed in righteousness, yet blighted in actions and sullied in soul.

Assuming that John is stating the claims of the false teachers,[1] and making the same judgments of them as he does in his letters,[2] the answer to their message is found in Christ's redemptive mission.[3] The opponents could not

---

1. 'If we say that we have fellowship...' (1:6); 'If we say we have no sin...' (1:8); 'If we say we have not sinned...' (1:10).

2. 'yet walk in darkness' (1:6); 'we are deceiving ourselves, and the truth is not in us' (1:8); 'we make Him a liar...' (1:10).

3. 'the blood of Jesus... cleanses us from all sin' (1:7); 'He is faithful and righteous to forgive us our sins, and to cleanse us from all unrighteousness' (1:9); 'He Himself is the propitiation for our sins' (2:2); and 'He laid down His life for us' (3:16).

grasp the reality that God saves sinners, not the 'righteous', by seeing them through Christ as righteous. In essence, they had a faulty understanding of Christ and His mission! Their answer was to claim that sin no longer matters, that Jesus, this great and, perhaps, final prophet, came to show us this profound insight.

Believing that the Christian life is not incompatible with struggles with sin as an ever-present reality, John sees their behavior as worldly. It is not that he claims that they are denying the reality of the commandments of God; it is that they do not grasp the depth of human sin, thus leaving them with 'rose-colored' glasses to explain the twistedness of the world while they live in the denial of their own prevarications. In John's judgment, they have adopted the ways of the world, salvation through self-realization, self-discovery. 'Do not love the world, nor the things in the world,' wrote the apostle (2:15). The particular evidence that the disturbers should be abandoned as dangerous is that they do not practice what they teach. They claim a right standing before God, that being a Christian means that the sin which once blocked access to a holy God no longer exists, that they are standing before God as holy. Yet their conduct belies their profession, so exposing their erroneous view of the nature of redemption. A divisive, disruptive spirit that stands averse to apostolic teaching and destroys the moral and doctrinal harmony of the churches is sinful, writes John. The errorists claim truth and love, but they possess neither! 'The one who says he is in the light, and *yet* hates his brother, is in the darkness until now' (2:9). 'If any one says, "I love God," and hates his brother, he is a liar; for the one who does not love his brother whom he has seen, cannot love God whom he has not seen' (4:20).

It seems also from the data John provides that the error of his opponents did not lead to any serious moral perversion; at least he does not make mention of any derelictions of this kind. In this regard, John's charge seems to be a lack of brotherly love resulting from allowing disagreements to cause division in the churches alongside an aggressive approach to perpetuating them. It seems that what they were saying is that sin in the believers' lives did not matter in light of the new life that they had in Christ. Their moral error seems to be one of arguing that disobedience or obedience is inconsequential in the Christian life. 'The one who says, "I have come to know Him," and does not keep His commandments, is a liar...' (2:4). They seem not to have taken a low view of the place of the law in sanctification; instead the law is value-neutral. Thus, they could fail to act in Christian love and feel at the same time theologically justified in doing so. It seems that for them some sins were unimportant while others, such as failure to accept their views on certain matters, was far more serious. Loyalty to their own ideas took priority over the value of community harmony among the faithful or over the instruction of the apostles. To John, the center of the apostolic message is that God sent His only begotten Son to become our redeemer through His atoning death. The essence of Christianity revolves around a litany of inseparable concepts: God's existence, the deity and incarnation, blood atonement, and a present redemption that is incomplete but ultimately assured because the curse of death is removed by the death of Jesus.

The Theses of John's Letters
If the above discussion of the views of John's opponents is valid, it would seem that John's point in the letter is to address the assertion that the Christian redemptive message requires not only perfection, but constancy thereof. The errorists have come to this conclusion based upon a valid insight, that to profess to have intimacy with God requires sinless perfection. This apparently led the secessionists to define away the existence of sin, obliterating the now and not-yet dichotomy of deliverance from sin. To buttress their claim they implied that they possessed apostolic authority for their teaching. In so doing, they distorted the earthly life of Christ, particularly the reality of His atoning death, because they perceived that Jesus accomplished more than what the churches had been led to believe. The root of the problem, then, is a distortion of the accomplishments of Christ, leading to a non-apostolic understanding of His triumph in the believer's daily struggle with the remnants of sin's once universal reign. In so doing, they believed that they had justification for disrupting the

peace and tranquility of the churches in order to teach the good news of Christ's accomplishments more accurately. However, what they actually accomplished was sowing seeds of heresy that threatened the vitality, if not the existence, of the Christian Faith.

The secessionists' perversion seems to have been the occasion for turmoil in the church or churches to which John writes because the health and spiritual maturity of the believers had been rattled, their confidence shattered, and their minds confused. The context into which the apostle speaks seems twofold: first, to reveal the erroneous teaching of those creating havoc in the churches and, second, to reassure and reestablish troubled saints in the apostolic gospel. As believers in John's acquaintance looked into their oft-imperfect lives their confidence was shaken. Maybe these teachers are right. Could this be apostolic teaching? The net effect was troubled saints. If I do things that I should not and God's standard of acceptance is His own perfect character, how can I be a Christian? How can we know this? If knowing God is not about getting it right, what is it about?

The question he addresses is, therefore, one of Christian certainty. If God is absolutely holy and His perfections are the criteria of knowing Him, how can troubled, struggling saints have assurance that they know God? How can a claim of being in possession of the divine life be possible when the struggle with sin seems so real? If God is absolutely holy, and in Him is no darkness at all (1:5), how can it be true that sinners can truly be in Him? If I do things that I should not and God's standard of acceptance is His own perfect character, how can I be a Christian? John's answer is that a saint can have certainty of life in God, not by perfectionism, but by the change that redemption has occasioned (the shift in priorities and values toward a new object). To formulate the question another way is to say it in this manner: How can we have assurance that we are God's children since we are imperfect creatures? How can we know this? If knowing God is not about getting it right all the time, what is it about? Assurance of knowing God is not in our perverted dreams of illusive obedience; it is in the object of our faith and in the fact that we are not what we were even though there is room to grow.

A clue to this approach in understanding the letters of John is found in the occurrence of the word 'know'. In I John, a letter composed of 104 verses, the term is found numerous times (two Greek words are used to convey the concept, but the lines of distinction between them are not clear). In addition, the phrase 'by this we know' is found seven times.

> 'And by this we know that we have come to know Him...' (2:3).

> 'By this we know that we are in Him' (2:5).

> 'We shall know by this that we are of the truth' (3:19).

> 'And we know by this that He abides in us' (3:24).

> 'By this we know the Spirit of truth from the spirit of error' (4:6).

> 'By this we know that we abide in Him and He in us' (4:13).

> 'By this we know that we love the children of God...' (5:2).

There are, also, several key concepts in the book that often appear in a cluster of synonyms. These concepts are 'life' (1:2; 3:14; 5:12), 'Word of Life' (1:1), and 'eternal life' (1:2; 2:25; 3:15; 5:11,13, 20), 'abides' (2:6, 10, 14, 24, 27, 28; 3:6, 9, 14, 15, 24; 4:12, 13, 16; II John 2, 9), 'fellowship' (1:3, 6, 7), 'light' (1:5, 7; 2:8, 9), 'believe' (3:23; 4:1; 5:1, 5, 10, 13); and 'darkness' (1:5, 6; 2:8, 9). These will be unpacked in the commentary that follows.

It is for these reasons that the first letter of John has been dubbed by more than one of our scholars as 'The Epistle of Christian Certainty'. Perhaps the text that summarizes the intent of the letter is found in 5:13: 'These things have I written unto you who believe in the name of the Son of God that you may know that you have eternal life,' though it may also be found as well in 5:20: 'And we know that the Son of God has come, and has given us understanding, in order that we might know Him who is true, and we are in Him who is true, in His Son Jesus Christ. This is the true God and eternal life.'

I JOHN

Prologue
(1 John 1:1-4)

The prologue, though a single sentence, presents a literary conundrum. It contains a litany of dependent clauses (five in all), three parentheses, a main verb that appears late in the section, and a purpose statement. It is one long, convoluted sentence. What can be said about the structure of the sentence is as follows:

(1)   most of verse 1 consists of four dependent clauses beginning with the word 'what';

(2)   these dependent clauses are followed by a parenthesis or digression that functions to describe the subject of the testimony of the apostles at the end of the verse (the content of 'what'). The second verse is an expansion of the digression, explaining the meaning of 'word of life', consuming all of verse 2 (it specifies the content of the 'what');

(3)   the third verse advances the thought of verse 1 with a dependent clause repeating two phrases from verse 1, the main verb, and a third digression (this time nuancing 'fellowship' in the verse). Thus, the main verb of the sentence is found in verse 3. Verse 4 presents John's purpose for writing the prologue. It is important to know that themes introduced here, such as 'life' and 'fellowship', are more fully developed in the letter.

Many scholars make the point that the beginning of this 'letter', some call it an address, and of the gospel by the same author have significant similarities in structure and content (repetition of phrases, digressions, themes introduced and later developed [e.g., life]), though the gospel introduces us to a person while 'the letter' introduces us to something about that person. Like the Letter to the Hebrews, both the gospel and the 'letter' of John begin with a prologue rather than with what would be expected in a first century Christian letter, thus suggestive, in the cases of I John and the gospel, that they were intended for a broader audience than a single gathering of people. In structure, I John can profitably be conceived as a treatise more than a letter, though it is difficult to find a designation that fits all the characteristics of this writing.

1. The testimony of the apostles' preaching (vv. 1a-d)

The four relative or dependent clauses here are connected to the main verb ('we proclaim') that is found in verse 3. The clauses function to emphasize the authority behind the content of the proclamation; it is apostolic. The fourfold repetition of 'we' indicates that John is presenting testimony. However, what is the referent of the plural pronouns? The most probable answer seems to be that the pronouns relate to a group of people who experienced firsthand, sensual knowledge of the giver of life, Jesus Christ. Thus, the 'we' are the original apostles and the point is that John is writing from the perspective of collective apostolic authority. When John refers to himself, he uses the first person singular (2:1, 7, 8, 13, 14, 21, 26; 4:20; 5:13); thus here he identifies himself with the apostles in writing the letter. John is telling us that what he will communicate is the collective testimony of the original apostolic band.

The four clauses have reference to the earthly ministry of Christ; John is describing what they saw in Him by emphasizing their personal contact with Him (see 4:2; II John 7). The pronoun translated 'what' is neuter; thus it does not point to a person, but to something about that person. A further evidence that this is the way to read the sentence is that John tells us that the content of what the apostles perceived is the message (1:5) that he desires to declare (the verb 'declare' in verse 5 shares the same verbal root with 'proclaim' in verse 3). Scholars have pondered the significance of the verbal tense changes in this verse; I am inclined to credit it to John's literary style.

The phrase 'from the beginning' has caused considerable discussion because of the occurrence of it in John 1:1, there a reference to Christ's pre-incarnate existence, and John clearly has the prologue to the gospel in mind as he writes. The phrase appears seven additional times in the letter. Four of the occurrences suggest temporal beginnings (2:7, 24 [2x]; 3:11); two may more likely refer to eternality (2:13, 14). However, the other clauses of the verse have a temporal nuance ('heard,' 'seen,' 'beheld… hands have handled'). John is stating that what they observed from Jesus throughout His life was consistent with the day they encountered Him initially. In the gospel, John does use the phrase for the temporal beginnings of Christ, for example in John 2:11, the first of His miracles. As stated above, the purpose of the gospel is to introduce its readers to a person through his claims and demonstrations, words and works; the purpose of this writing is to assure a troubled audience about an aspect of the Christian life. The gospel declares God's message revealed through His Son to the world; the purpose here is to apply the implications of that message to a group of believers torn apart by false teachings concerning the person and accomplishments of Jesus Christ as it relates to the spiritual life.

Thus, John is describing something about Jesus that the apostles observed from the beginning of their acquaintance with Him. 'Heard' suggests the many conversations, discourses, and dialogues Jesus had throughout His earthly ministry, recorded in part by the four gospel writers. In the gospel, John has recorded for us the defense of the temple soldiers who failed to arrest Jesus: 'Never did a man speak as this man speaks' (7:46).

'Seen' would suggest the observation of His many miracles, culminating in the resurrection. This particular word for the act of perception[1] is used of the experience of Peter and John at the empty tomb (John 20:1-10). One of the words used in that narrative as well as the one used here three times means

---

1. John uses three different Greek words for seeing.

to see with understanding (20:8), the text stating, 'They saw and believed.'

'Hands have handled' implies intimacy of physical contact; the term means 'to grope' or 'to feel'. Generally speaking, one would think of the instruction in the Upper Room (John 13–16), the washing of the disciples' feet (John 13:1-11), or the apostles' contact with Jesus after a failed night of fishing, Jesus having prepared a breakfast for them (John 21:1-13). The point is that John is claiming, with the other apostles, firsthand knowledge of Jesus Christ. Interestingly, as the verses unfold, it is not so much about the earthly, material existence of Jesus that is the topic, nor His divine origin as expressed in the gospel prologue, as it is His spiritual mission, which is expressed in the prologue to John's gospel (1:4, 18). As one has stated, 'The neuter gender of "that which was from the beginning" points to the gospel rather than to the personal Christ' (Bruce, 35).

The prologue can be conceived as an indirect, opening shot at the perversity of those troubling the church. The fact that none of John's opponents could claim such intimacy with Christ as that experienced by the apostles is a powerful argument, though admittedly subtle, for the falsity of their claims. The argument would be simply this: those with direct, intimate information about a subject are more likely correct in their perceptions than those only having second-hand knowledge. Hence, the reason for John's references to the material, earthly beginnings of the identity of Jesus is to drive a wedge between the apostolic teachings concerning Jesus and those of His opponents. His opponents embraced the idea of a historical Jesus, but in the end He was little more than another insightful prophet-like figure. It is interesting that John does refer to God's Son as Jesus Christ, not as Jesus only. He is making the point that the apostolic witness is to the one who came to reveal the Father. It is in His role as deity, deity incarnated, that He is the purveyor of the life of God, eternal life. John is confronting the repeated error observed through the centuries of misunderstanding the identity of Jesus and, as a consequence, distorting the meaning and nature of salvation. The opponents of John today are masquerading with much of the religious nomenclature used by the apostles, but denying their content. John would say of these false interpreters of Jesus Christ that 'they went out from us...' (2:19) and 'Anyone who goes too far and does not abide in the teachings of Christ does not have God...' (II John 9).

2. The subject of the apostles' preaching (v. 1e)

At the end of the initial verse is a parenthesis that tells us what the apostles saw in the life and ministry of Jesus. It is evident by the dependent clauses that John is not seeking to call attention to Jesus as a person (it is not possible to 'see' or 'touch' life, though the effects of life can be observed) but something about Him. The phrase before us is 'concerning the word of life'.

The first term to decipher is 'word', a designation of Jesus' identity that is the focus of John 1:1. However, the word occurs five other times in the letter (1:10; 2:5, 7, 14; 3:18), each with the meaning of message or verbal content; 'word' does not seem to refer to Jesus *per se*, but to His message. The 'word' here is parallel to 'we proclaim' (v. 3) and is continued in 'announced' (v. 5). In the gospel, John's focus is upon the unique personhood of Jesus, His heavenly origins and divine character; in this letter John's point is upon the redemptive accomplishments of Christ. Further, the proposition 'of,' being a genitive, denotes content (the content of the word is about life). The word, 'word,' then refers to Jesus' revelatory ministry; He came to show us life, eternal life, life in the Father and the Son. 'Word' is connected to what John is reporting about what they perceived in Jesus, which fits the immediate context (1:1-4). Boice has made the point succinctly: 'In other words, it is not the "Word" that is proclaimed, but Christ who is the content of it' (22).

The second term is 'life'. In the letter, the term is found four other times (1:2; 3:14; 5:12 [twice]). In 1:2, it is 'life' revealed or disclosed; in 3:14, 'life' is juxtaposed against death; and in 5:12, 'life' is defined as possessing the Son. Additionally, John uses 'life' and 'eternal life' synonymously (1:2; 5:11). On three other occasions, he speaks of 'eternal life' (2:25; 5:13, 20). Thus, to bring out the nuance of the phrase, we might translate it this way: 'concerning the life-giving message or report.' Calvin clarifies the phrase by stating: 'The genitive here is used adjectivally – "vivifying" or "life-giving," for in him, as it says in the first chapter of John's Gospel, was life' (17). Again, this seems consistent with the import of the four dependent clauses that precede it (the repeated word is 'what', not 'who' or 'the one who'), suggestive of something observed in the apostles' contact with Jesus. The apostles caught Jesus' comment when He said, 'I am… the life' (John 11:25; 14:6). What will become more apparent as the letter unfolds is that John is concerned with a secessionist faction that has rejected the apostles' teaching concerning the person of Christ and His redemption. A writer has summarized the thought quite well: '…John is fighting a Christological heresy that involved the incarnation of deity, that is, the denial that the Christ was the historical Jesus' (Akin, 55).

3. The elucidation of the apostles' preaching (v. 2)

This verse is a second parenthesis further explaining the life-giving message. John reveals three things in this verse about the life-giver. First, it was a message revealed by Jesus. John's salient point in the gospel is that Jesus made the claim that He was God-sent from heaven to declare and explain the life of God and how to possess it. John emphasizes the term 'life' rather than 'word' to make the point that he is writing about something in Jesus' life; that is, that He brought life from heaven to us (He is life revealed!). Hence, the emphasis here is on the earthly life of Jesus rather than on His heavenly origins ('manifested' is repeated in this verse for emphasis). John uses the verb 'manifested' in the gospel (21:1, 14) with this nuance; that is, the disclosure of Jesus to the disciples after the resurrection. The term appears three additional times in the letter (2:28; 3:5, 8) with the same meaning.

Second, it is to this life that the apostles bear witness through their personal experience. The repetition of 'seen' and 'heard' signifies emphasis. This is extended with the further insight that His message is now their message ('we', 'us'). The verb translated 'proclaim' conveys the notion of reporting something.

Third, this message of life, the subject of John's passion, is the very life of God, designated as 'eternal life'. It is interesting that the definite article appears before 'life' and 'eternal' in John's writings only here and in I John 2:25. Whether or not it is another evidence of John's literary style, the life that John speaks of is always eternal life!

Contrary to Calvin and some recent commentators, the phrase 'with the Father' is not a statement of Jesus' preexistence, though that is certainly a truth. The word is not 'who was from the beginning', but 'that' or 'what'. The immediate subject contextually is life, the life that Jesus revealed in His earthly ministry, the life possessed of the Father that the Son came to reveal, eternal life. Calvin understood 'in the beginning' in light of John 1:1, not uncommonly so, as a statement of His deity and carried the thought into his interpretation of 'with the Father' (16).

4. The fact of the apostles' preaching (v. 3a)
Here we encounter the main verb of the paragraph; it is a message, the message of life in the one they had witnessed during Jesus' incarnation. For the third time the themes of 'seen' and 'heard' are repeated, the idea of proclamation twice.

5. The consequence of the apostles' preaching (v. 3b)
The purpose of this life-giving message is now stated, 'that you may have fellowship' in the circle of apostolic witness. The term translated 'fellowship' is difficult to capture in English, having no exact equivalent in the language. It is found four times in John's first letter, twice in verse 3 (also in 1:6 and 7), but not elsewhere in John's writings. In these occurrences, the nuance seems to be a harmonious, communal relationship between parties, the emphasis being on the union itself and not upon the consequences of it (as in Philippians). In verse 3, it is the apostles ('our') who have intimacy with the Father and the Son. It is interesting that John speaks of Jesus as the 'Son' (seven times) or 'Son of God' (seventeen times), collectively twenty-four times in this letter; it is a strong affirmation of what John's opponents denied. Jesus is more than a prophet; He is deity in flesh. Further, He is Jesus Christ, God's Anointed One. John identifies Jesus as God's Son four times in his letters (1:3; 3:23; 5:20; II John 3). John's

opponents embraced the historical, merely human Jesus, but not His deity!

Parenthesis 1: A clarification
The term 'fellowship' has occasioned considerable discussion, even division, among some Christians. Is 'fellowship' a synonym for a living relation with others in the gospel and, therefore, a permanent state for all Christians or is it a temporal state of the enjoyment of the benefits of the gospel? Is 'fellowship' a steady state or potentially a temporal one, though those on either side of the question, as currently expressed, would not deny the eternal security of the believer? Is 'fellowship' a category of Christians, meaning that some walk in greater intimacy than others? Or, is it a reality for all Christians regardless of spiritual maturity, even of degree of moral obedience?

While it seems precarious to deny that Christians experience the sanctifying work of the Spirit in varying portions according to their circumstances of life experience, the biblical teaching of sanctification does not appear to be the topic of John's letter, though no one should fail to see significant implications in it of one's walk with God.

I take it that such terms as 'life,' 'eternal life,' 'light,' and 'abides', like 'fellowship,' are descriptive of a state experienced by all believers regardless of educational advantages, or lack thereof, derelictions, triumphs, giftedness, or disappointments. 'Fellowship' is the consequential experience of all of God's children through the life-giving gospel revealed to them by the Spirit in His witness to the person and work of Jesus Christ. It is, as one has written: 'Kioinonia [fellowship]… appears to denote a personal relationship with the author or with God, and may in 1:3 in particular, include the idea of a commitment to a common task, that of the proclamation of the Word of life' (Kruse, 60-61). By simple definition, a Christian is one who is in the permanent state of fellowship with God, or life in God, and consequently with those of like commitments!

To be more specific, the term appears four times in this letter (1:3 [twice], 6, 7), all in the first chapter. What is shared in common is salvation or the very life of God. Simply put, it means to know God. To make the point even stronger, John connects the term with other verbs and phrases that function as synonyms. In 1:6 the claim to 'fellowship' is evidenced by a moral lifestyle; in 2:4 the claim 'to know' God is evidenced by the same criteria. As Marshall states: 'The Christian's relationship to God, which was expressed earlier in terms of fellowship with him, is now [2:3] spoken of as knowledge of God living (literally, "abiding") in him.... [the two terms are] alternative ways of expressing the same reality' (121). As hinted by Marshall in the above citation, the term 'abiding' is equivalent to knowing God and having fellowship with and in God. This is most evident in comparing 2:3 and 3:24, for example. 'Fellowship' with God is the same as salvation; to say we have fellowship with God is to say that we are in the family of God through the mercies of God's anointed one, Jesus who is the Christ. Henry says fellowship means 'communion with heaven' (1061).

● ● ● ● ●

6. The purpose of the apostles' preaching (v. 4)

The words, 'these things,' take the reader back to the testimony of the apostolic community providing the reason for the letter; it very much aligns with John's statement in 5:13, even forming bookend-statements, where he speaks of assurance of eternal life as the purpose for writing. The 'we' is John writing as part of the community of the apostolic witness. The verb 'write' is the second main verb in the sentence, the other being 'proclaim' (v. 3). We could simplify the sentence by removing the dependent clauses and digressions and it would read, 'We proclaim (v. 3) and write (v. 4) these things...' the latter confirming and affirming the former.

The joy that John expresses is the delight that the apostles experience when true fellowship becomes the experience of those to whom they have proclaimed the message of life through Christ, joining with them in a community of unity and focus. John, speaking of 'joy', comments to Gaius, 'I have no greater joy than to hear of my children walking in the truth' (III John 4). The consequential purpose of the proclamation of life through Christ is the enlargement of the community of faith in truth; that community is the source of biblical delight for those who participate in it. Stott seems quite to the point when he writes: 'The purpose of the proclamation of the gospel is, therefore, not salvation, but *fellowship*. Yet, properly understood, this is the meaning of salvation.... "Fellowship" is a specially Christian word and denotes that common participation in the grace of God, the salvation of Christ, and the indwelling of the Spirit which is the spiritual birthright of all Christian believers' (63). Smalley nuances the term negatively to explain the concept: 'Christian fellowship is not the sentimental and superficial attachment of a random collection of individuals, but the profoundly mutual relationship of those who "remain" in Christ, and therefore belong to each other...' (12).

How can we apply the prologue?
The essence of these verses appears to be based on the content of the gospel account that John had written. Jesus Christ was sent as God's heavenly ambassador to reveal the Father to us, not only His character but also His life (a life made available through the rending of the 'veil' of Christ's flesh, so gaining entrance for us through Him into the very presence of God [John 1:14]). That very message, the apostles were eyewitnesses of it and by Christ's authority had been designated as proclaimers of it. John writes as part of that original community in order to announce that message to his readers, though in this instance they are threatened by non-apostolic teachings.

The message that Christ announced through His incarnate life and atoning death was life, eternal life. Further, the experience of that life creates a new community of harmonious delight and joy for all who are gathered into it.

First, it tells us that Jesus Christ was a real, historic person; He is not a mythological figure created by well-meaning, but empty people, to fill some kind of void in their lives.

Second, it tells us that Jesus Christ is more than a wise moralist or intellectual sage; He came to bring us life, eternal life, through the procurement of divine forgiveness for us. Forgiveness and relationships are the two greatest human needs; He came to meet them through an atoning, substitutionary sacrifice that has brought us into a new community. If our greatest need were financial, God would have sent us an economist. If our greatest problem was gross human ignorance, He would have given us an educator. If our greatest threat was geo-political, He would have provided for us a governmental strategist. Since He sent us an atoning redeemer, then we must know that our greatest need is a sin problem since that is what He addressed.

Third, it tells us that the message Jesus embodied is to be proclaimed because He left instructions in that regard. The apostles taught it and so should their followers as Christ-followers.

Fourth, it tells us that true joy in knowing Jesus Christ comes from being placed in a new community where joy, contentment, and delight are the consequential effects. True satisfaction for the Christian is derived from being in the family of God. It is interesting how many of us find our joy and contentment in material things more than in spiritual privileges, the temporal domain as opposed to the eternal. What do you count as most important to you? How do your values shape the content of your prayer life?

Fifth, it tells us that the joys of life, often determined by popular culture and the media, should be questioned. If fullness of what we as humans crave is found only in the life-giving experience of encountering the Christ, how should we look upon other joys? It is not necessarily an issue of denigrating temporal things – after all, this world is a divine gift to us composed of many legitimate delights; instead it is a matter of correct perspectives and priorities.

Sixth, in a culture that is increasingly self-oriented, John would tell us that we are walking down the road of disappointment and emptiness. The personal desire for significance and self-identity is valid; however, it is not found in the pursuit of self-interest. For believers, contentment and self-worth is found in desiring for others what God has so graciously bestowed upon them, participation first in the life of God and then in the family of God. Their delight, their goal in living, is in declaring to others that they can join this unique family as well. Are you seeking meaning on the road that leads to disappointment?

I

The Reality of Life in God Stated
(I John I:5–2:2)

The main body of John's letter has two major parts. After introducing the subject of the life that Christ disclosed (1:1-4), John argues that imperfect people can possess the life of God (1:5–2:2) and can be assured of it (2:3–5:12). The secessionists seemingly argued that God is absolute perfection and to say that we know God through Jesus is to share in that perfection. The point is obviously a valid one; however, the disturbers have erred in that Christ is our perfection (He is our atoning sacrifice and our righteousness); it is our status in Christ that is at issue, not a state of being! One does not need to minimize or ignore the reality of sin in the believer's experience. The false teachers seem to have conceived of Jesus as a moral prophet-like figure who was an insightful educator and self-help theorist rather than a God-sent redeemer. A proper understanding of the accomplishments of Christ, as well as insight into His divine personhood, involves an understanding of the devastation caused by the fall of man. If mankind's greatest needs are not found through the cleansing of the heart, we should find an instructor in moral guidance, a master of behavior modification technique, the merely sincere impetus to think positively, or the promotion of self-esteem. John's opponents are proclaiming salvation without a substitute, redemption without a cross! It is a message that we hear every day in the social media; unfortunately, it can be heard in many churches.

Thus in this section, the apostle explains the basis of fellowship with God (1:5) and eliminates misperceptions about our relationship or fellowship with Him (1:6-2:2). Though God is perfect and communion with Him, eternal life in Him, requires perfection, believers need not delude themselves about the reality of and seriousness of their sinfulness. Believers are not perfect people; they have been placed in the perfect one! Christ is our righteousness; we possess none of our own and we should not deceive ourselves about it. This passage tells us how imperfect people can know a holy God. Christ is the perfect one, not us!

Parenthesis 2: The inseparable gospel of deity in human flesh, substitutionary atonement, and the human dilemma.
What seems clear is that these opponents of John taught that believers embraced not only a faulty understanding of Christ and the redemption that He procured, they also redefined the problem of the human soul, that is the blight and devastation that sin has occasioned. In other words, a proper understanding of Christ's person, Christ's redemption, and sin's perversion are intertwined organically, being inseparable. Christ's deity, Christ's atoning mission, and human inability must never be separated, which neither John nor his opponents did exactly. However, because of a misunderstanding of sin, his opponents misunderstood the person of Christ and His accomplishments. The false teachers, since for them the human dilemma was perceived as such that knowledge could rectify, saw Jesus as a prophet declaring a moral message of victory, redemption through advanced knowledge. Says Marshall: 'Very probably the false teachers claimed a deeper knowledge of God than ordinary Christians (2:20, 27); theirs was an "advanced" understanding of religion (II John 9). It was apparently based on prophetic revelation which they claimed to be inspired by the Spirit (4:1)' (16). They denied that Jesus Christ, not Jesus merely, possessed humanity; they denied that Jesus was the Christ, the promised anointed deliverer; they taught salvation through insight rather than through an atoning sacrifice! John is arguing that Jesus Christ, grace, and sin are a single

cloth, the inseparable wonder of divine salvation! It is an old message and yet ever new!

• • • • •

1. The Criteria of life in God: Divine disclosure (1:5)

The 'and' that introduces the verse takes up the theme of the main verb ('announce' or 'proclaim,' v. 3). With the repetition of 'heard' and 'announce' we have the sense that John is elongating his argument from the prologue. The word translated 'message' is unique to John (1:5; 3:11). It is interesting that he now tells us that the substance of the witness and proclamation of the apostles is literally the message (gospel or good news) that he subsequently delineated beginning with 'that'. The term appears only once more in the letter (3:11); in both cases it has to do with the content of proclamation; the message is that God has revealed himself through Jesus Christ. The word translated 'message' comes from the same root as the verb, 'we proclaim.'

Scholars have differing opinions as to the referent of the pronoun 'him' in the verse (the referent of pronouns is often difficult to discern in John's letter). Does it refer to God the Father or to Jesus Christ? It would seem that there is more contextual evidence for the latter. The verb 'heard' would naturally take the reader to the previous occurrences of the verb (vv. 1, 3) where the subject is the eyewitness of the apostles ('we heard') to Christ. The apostles heard of God through Jesus (John 1:18).

The key phrase in the verse is 'that God is light' (I take it also to be the basic assumption that undergirds the entire letter). Since 'light' is not preceded by a definite article, we do not have a definition of God; it is a declaration or description of God. God possesses the attributes of holiness, goodness, purity, and love; He is the life that the life-giver came to reveal (1:1-3)! This is the first of four statements concerning God; the others are 'God is righteous' (2:29), 'God is love' (4:6), and 'God is life' (5:20). That God has revealed Himself is the foundation of any knowledge or intimacy with the divine being; the essence of that light (revealed through Jesus Christ) is righteousness and love; and the end of that disclosure is the life of God in those whom Christ illumines to behold and possess that light. That God is light means that He reveals himself to His children; that God is life means that He imparts Himself to His children; and that God is righteousness (unfailing self-consistency) and love (righteousness expressed) is what is imparted to His children and is the evidence that they are indeed His! The fact of life intrinsically produces the fruit of life; like begets its kind.

Light in the Old Testament is often associated metaphorically with the presence of God (Ps. 36:9) as it relates to salvation. 'That God is light' seems, therefore, to suggest that God is self-revealing; the essence of the revelation of God is salvation revealed or disclosed by Christ. Says Boice: '…light seems to be strikingly appropriate as an image of God, for it points to God as the true source of revelation, intelligence, stability, ubiquity, excellence, vision, and growth' (29). Through the disclosure of light, the darkness of man's blight is revealed. Christ came to reveal the character of God, but in the process disclosed the darkness of the human soul (John 1:4-5), revealing shortcomings as well as teaching the right way. This interpretation of 'light' seems contextually warranted since 1:1-3 speaks of the eyewitnesses' message concerning the ministry of Jesus Christ as revealing to us the life of God, which when possessed is true life. The life of which John speaks is the apostles' message, the word the readers heard through those who communicated to them the apostolic message! Using a stark contrast, a common literary device for John, light (the revealed perfection of God) is the opposite of darkness, the two being incompatible as is the confession of knowing God and possessing a habitual lifestyle of unlikeness to God. Thus, it would seem, John's reference to light entails the disclosure of God as it relates to his moral qualities, such qualities being the focus of the writing. Explaining the meaning of light in this passage, Henry writes: '… what is usually called the moral perfection of the divine nature, what we are to imitate, or what is more directly to influence us in our gospel work. And so it will comprehend the holiness of God, the absolute beauty of His nature and will, His penetrative knowledge (particularly of hearts), His jealousy and justice, which burn as a most bright and vehement flame' (1062-63).

To make the point, John, as he so often does, repeats the concept in the negative to draw out the contrast. 'Light' and 'darkness' speak of moral qualities. John is saying that God is absolute perfection and flawless purity. This concept of light is rooted in the Hebrew Scriptures. Light is frequently a metaphor for the revelation, life, or salvation that God imparts (Pss. 27:1; 104:2). God is the source and essence of holiness, righteousness, goodness, and truth. Being all of this, God is life; He is the life that God's anointed, the Christ, came to reveal (John 1:18). In Him, there is nothing that is unholy or unrighteous, evil or false. Light revealed is the conscious perception of divine holiness, majesty, beauty, and power; God's disclosure is the revelation of His essential character in Christ. It speaks of flawless perfection! To walk with God is to have the standards of perfection that He alone possesses. Some commentators define 'light' as life, which has considerable contextual warrant, but 'darkness' in the letter is defined as sinfulness. The contrast seems, therefore, to be moral in nature and, in effect, unwittingly and through distortion played into the thought of the false teachers by suggesting that those who are not perfectly holy cannot claim to know God. This seems to be the drift of John's argument in rebutting the false teachers. John is saying that we can know God without defining away human sinfulness or without lowering God to merely human standards. John, therefore, states at the inception of his argument that the false teachers err in not understanding or knowing the God that they are claiming to profess. God who is life is also the standard by which the possession of life is to be judged and rightly determined. However, life in God, perfection through Christ, is not such that sin is eradicated when one comes to Christ or matures in Christ. Life, eternal life, and sinfulness are not antithetical realities, says John. The mark of the believer is not so much a perfected state as a struggle with sin, always regrettably and lamentably so, while waiting in hope for the day of redemption (3:2-3).

'Darkness' is the opposite of light; it is the opposite of life (2:11). It has nothing to do with God! John delights in stark, comparative statements! Ten times in the epistle darkness means an unholy lifestyle. While darkness is present in the life of every child of God, it is not engaged in with habitual delight and boasting, but with sorrow and repentance. To be in complete darkness is to be devoid of light, the life of God.

Parenthesis 3: This is worth a sermon
Living in a culture of moral permissiveness, the denouement of absolutes, and the elevation of virtues of toleration, what we have under the guise of liberation from bondage is the portent of disaster. To live in a world without moral limitations is to exist without sure guidance; as history repeatedly has shown, 'freedom' from a restrictive past may be bondage to a tyrannical present and future. What we can learn from this verse is as follows:

First, the criteria of what is right and wrong cannot be found in examination of the creature based on pleasure, plurality, or utility because surety, sensitivity, or positive outcomes may prove disappointing. There must be criteria or standards that are not subject to deception, coercion, or error. Without a God, there can be no criteria of right and wrong simply because there is no objective standard. Without the God revealed by Jesus Christ, there is no remedy for the wrong.

Second, God is the basis of all ethics. To state it bluntly, God defines what is proper and improper, right and wrong, for all of us. The ground of ethics is the Trinitarian God revealed to us through Christ's incarnate ministry of revealing the Father, the purchasing redemption in His own sacrifice, and procuring the gift of the Spirit who is the life of God in us. God the Father is life, Christ the Son is life revealed and purchased, and God the Spirit is life possessed!

Third, while it is common among all of us to think that if we do many things correctly, one thing bad is not so bad after all, that is not the case from the divine perspective. God demands absolute conformity to His will. God does not cut deals when it comes to defining righteousness; it is all or nothing.

Fourth, how can God be absolutely just in His ways, and hence in His demands, and yet the creature find hope? The answer is that Christ has come among us and paid our penalty by dissolving our debt, releasing us from its penalty, and clothing us in His righteousness. This means that we do not have to have false perceptions when it comes to sin. We can face the fact of our failures and yet find solace and safety because God has provided for us a means that, without surrendering His justice and holiness, He can justly forgive us. Do you rejoice in that?

Fifth, do you find the holiness of God frightening or a source of great delight and hope? In this world there is much uncertainty; advice that is creditable is often rare. You and I have an anchor, a surety in a sea of change, and that is that the God we serve is absolutely all the Bible says of Him. In Him there is direction and guidance, peace and repose, life out of darkness!

• • • • •

2. The errors about life in God: Human perversions (1:6–2:2)

If God is holy, and you and I are not, how can we say that we know God? Apparently some taught that the true claimant to eternal life could obtain a state of sinlessness, either by some form of eradication, or by blatant denial of sin's existence, or simply by redefinition of terms (that sin no longer matters). 'Since God is holy, and since we have obtained holiness, we know God,' some suggested. Or, 'since God is holy in every way, and since we know God, we must be holy in every way.' John says that sinless perfection is a delusion, but fellowship with a holy God is not. The way of psychological deception is not the path to life in God, to fellowship. The perfections of our substitute, Jesus Christ, make it possible truly to know God. We are sinners; Christ is righteous; and we are in Him. Sinful people can walk with a holy God if they are in Christ as their righteousness!

The paragraph before us (1:6–2:2) has a distinct structure: three false claims ('if we say' [vv. 6, 8, 10]); three disclaimers ('we lie and do not the truth' [v. 6], 'we deceive ourselves' [v. 8], 'we make him a liar' [v. 10]); and three correctives or antidotes ('but if,' 'if,' and 'and if' [1:7, 9; 2:1-2]). John stresses three errors of the false teachers and the remedy for each: the incongruity of spiritual life and habitual sin (vv. 6-7), the corrective being obedience; the incongruity of spiritual life and guiltless behavior (vv. 8-9), the corrective being confession;

and the incongruity of spiritual life and a perfected state (1:10-2:2), the corrective being the fact we have an advocate who pleads our case. The distinctions in the claims are difficult to differentiate because they overlap. John may be citing claims from various errant teachers, not simply one or a single party. Perhaps the secessionists are not completely agreed among themselves, so John is gathering the gist of several of their approaches. What is common to all three assertions is that they concern the believer and wrongdoing.

(a) The incongruity of spiritual life and the practice of sin (1:6-7). The false claim (v. 6a). The issue that John finds unfathomable is the assertion that sin does not matter, that a person can be characterized by sinful, perpetual practices and still claim to know a holy, life-giving God. Several observations can be made concerning this claim. First, and perhaps foremost, the claim is that of possessing spiritual unity with God (fellowship being a synonym for 'life' or 'eternal life' in the letter). Second, the antecedent of the pronoun 'Him' is God the Father, being connected with the same pronoun in verse 5 (the second 'Him' in the verse) and identified in verse 3 as the Father ('and our fellowship is with the Father'), though the Father and the Son are inseparable in this case. Third, the NASB correctly adds to *and* the word *yet*, thus signifying that the conjunction has a negative overtone.

Fourth, and perhaps most important in the interpretation of the verse, is the term 'walk'. The tense of the verb is present, suggesting ongoing or continuous action. John is speaking of a settled, perpetual type of behavior, a lifestyle, not a momentary lapse. What were the perpetual errors of John's opponents? The answer is threefold:

(1) *doctrinally,* they denied that Jesus was the divinely anointed one, the Christ, sent from heaven to reveal to us the identity of God by identifying with us in His humanity and paying the debt through substitution that only one equal with God could render. In denying His true identity they rejected His atoning work; in so doing, they denied the utter gravity and devastation of sin in human lives.

(2) *ethically*, they failed to exercise divine love by perpetuating falsehood; they failed to truly love those they claimed to help.

(3) *morally*, they destroyed the unity of the believers by leading a schematic movement.

These errors have in common the traits of habitual and calloused action; they are not momentary lapses. The basic claim is that John's opponents claimed to know God, even boasted about it, but possessed only contrary evidence to their claim by their moral deportment! Says Smalley: 'The first error to be treated concerns the belief that sin is unimportant; that it is possible to be in a right relationship with God while behaving unrighteously' (21).

Parenthesis 4: The Christian and sin
Using the forest metaphor, the Christian has a remaining 'forest' in their very nature. In that 'forest' are the entanglements of sin's once universal dominion over all our actions; however, the redemptive mercies of Christ by the Spirit has brought the beginning of what will be a total reclamation when the 'forest' will be completely eliminated. Trees, weeds, and vines remain; yet a remarkable transformation has begun. The spiritual life, in part, involves certain actions, called spiritual disciplines, to reduce the remnants of sinful actions and attitudes, actions that instead promote a healthy growing conformity to Christ and a serious struggle to remove from our lives those things that hinder our growth – our Puritan forefathers called these 'vivification' (actions promoting positive growth) and 'mortification' (the putting to death of the remnants of our 'forests'). While the saint struggles with sin, as does the unbeliever, the turmoil is markedly different in several ways:
First, the presence of sin in a believer's life causes him anguish, knowing that it should not be present in one so graciously granted divine mercy.
Second, though some sins are more difficult to conquer than others, there is in us a sense of duty not to allow a particular sin to predominate (we take evasive action at the least).

Third, we know that the object of our sin is foremost the God that we have been allowed to know; while sin has human ramifications, the realization for us, like David of old, is that we have offended God (Ps. 51:4).

Fourth, the Christian does not excuse the 'forest' that remains in his life, but brings it to God in confession, in agreement with God that he often entertains wrong behaviors and thoughts.

Fifth, Christians do not allow sin to become a defining characteristic of their lives in which they justify its presence by saying, 'we all have our problems' or 'I am not as vicious as my neighbor.'

Sixth, since the criteria of moral choices for Christians is not cultural values, their God being absolutely holy, they should live with a sense of fear that they would trample upon His goodness and grace, and demonstrate by their behavior a lack of appreciation for God's mercy through their loving, atoning Savior.

Seventh, redemption by its very nature is the life of God in the soul expressed by the Spirit's presence and revealed by His character, the fruit(s) of the Spirit which the Bible describes, among other features, as love, and is a dominant theme in this letter.

• • • • •

'Walk in darkness' suggests a habitual, calloused lifestyle of disobedience that would encompass little guilt and even delight in wrongdoing, devoid of any notion of dishonoring the God of absolute holiness, beauty, and grace. The notion of 'darkness' here finds its parallel in the prologue to John's gospel. John tells us there that 'the light shines in the darkness and the darkness did not comprehend it' (John 1:5). In John's commentary, following the Nicodemus story, he wrote, '... the light came into the world but men loved darkness rather than light because their deeds were evil' (John 3:19). In John's world, a sharp dichotomy exists between those who have life and those who do not. Life is found in the Light, the revealed presence of God, and its opposite is found in darkness. While spiritual life, or the absence of it, cannot be physically analyzed, it can be surmised or discerned by the ramifications or expressions of it in a discernible lifestyle. That an effect partakes of the character of its cause seems to be an assumption of John. There are genuine evidences; and there are indicators that the delusion of moral perfection is not one of them.

The disclaimer or condemnation (v. 6b). John is adamant. The claim that sin does not matter is evidence that sin does matter! The specific sin or sins of John's opponents are not stated here (again, we are listening to a one-way conversation), but we can see, in John's judgment, that they are deceived, deceivers, and unbelievers. They do not merely suffer from self-deception; they actively promote error.

Another central concept in John's letters is truth. John defines truth as that which is revealed by the Light, meaning truth is what has been disclosed by Jesus Christ to His apostles and conveyed subsequently to John's readers. It is the revelation of the knowledge of God, including His provisions of access through the Christ. In essence, the phrase 'practice the truth' means that which is worthy of emulation as the basis for living. It is interesting that John says that his adversaries 'do not practice the truth', indicating that truth can be made evident by behavior. Consequences are the product of their source. Error produces lies and self-deception because the source is other than a holy God. Truth produces holy behavior that can be observed because the source, God, is holy! 'Doing the truth' to John is evidence of possessing truth!

The 'we' (vv. 6. 8, 10) is a little perplexing. Is it a hypothetical 'we,' putting words in the mouth of John and his audience; or, is it simply a rhetorical device used of anyone who would make such false claims? It is difficult to be definitive on the issue of the referent. Clearly, the 'we' is not a direct reference to John's opponents, though it is indirectly.

The antidote or corrective (v. 7). There has been considerable discussion concerning the nature of the prescribed antidote. Does confession of sin refer to the initial redemptive miracle or does it refer to an ongoing necessary practice of believers? Is this text a salvation verse or a sanctification insight? Is it a once-for-all-time event or the normal reoccurring pattern? It would seem from the context that the latter is the case for these reasons: first, the present tense of the verb 'walking' suggests an on-going behavior based on the continuous action of divine cleansing; second, if the topic is initial justification and an obedient lifestyle is a prerequisite, it would seem to contradict the Bible's clear witness that salvation is an unmerited, discriminatory, and grace-filled gift; third, the topic of the letter, being addressed to believers, is not justification, but sanctification; it is about a lifestyle as evidence of spiritual existence or life which John's opponents denied.

Fourth, the topic at hand is walking in the 'light', not coming to the 'light'. It is interesting that John instructs us to 'walk in the light', not 'come to the light', since 'coming to the light' would require an attitude that sin is not sinful, the claim of John's opponents (his opponents claim is that they *have already* come to the light and, consequentially, they are no longer bothered by sin – they are not arguing their state before meeting Jesus; what they are teaching is a state *after* coming to the 'light'). The point is that John wants his readers to understand something about sin after experiencing forgiveness. It would seem that the false teachers pointed out what should bother all of us, that sin and a claim to spiritual life are incompatible. This seems to have jolted the believers to whom John is writing. Sin bothers true believers, causing doubts in all of them, or at least it should. John's point is that sin and life are not opposites because we have been given a divine substitute in whom we have been placed. Neither a denial of sin, nor a redefinition of it, is the answer to the problem. We have been given life through another; our holiness, for now, is through and in God's anointed one, Jesus Christ! Though John does not specifically define what 'walking in the light' means, it would seem in the context of the letter that it means embracing the revelation of God through Jesus Christ expressed in fidelity to the apostles' teaching concerning Christ and an active love for other believers. 'Walking in darkness' is the rejection of such teaching; it is a life devoid of the life of God evidenced by hostility to the apostles' doctrine and an unloving demeanor toward believers.

Two statements are made as a consequence of 'walking in the light'. The first is that the change of lifestyle (conduct pre-dicted upon new priorities, new propensities, and new goals) makes it possible to live in harmony in a new community, with those of like values. Because of the difference that redemption occasions, the believer can live in harmony, fellowship, and intimacy with the apostles and with each other grounded in fellowship with God (v. 3). The second is that those who walk in the light do so because of the continuing efficacy of the work of Christ on their behalf. We can have a life characterized by 'walking in the light' because we are seen through the cleansing blood of Christ, a single act with perpetual ramifications (the tense of the verb is present signifying continuous action). The term in reference to Jesus' sacrifice occurs four times in I John (1:7, 5:6 [twice], 5:8) and three times in the Revelation: 'To Him who loves us and released us from our sins by His blood' (1:5); '…Thou wast slain, and didst purchase for God with Thy blood *men*…' (5:9); '…they have washed their robes and made them white in the blood of the Lamb' (7:14). There is no need to deny what is a painful reality; instead, relief is found in the embrace of the wonder of what Christ has provided for us. 'Blood of Jesus Christ,' or His life-giving death, is the ground of walking with God. It is not about saying that sin makes no difference or that the saint is devoid of it since the believer possesses the life of God. The phrase, 'His Son,' tells us that Jesus is God ('Like father, like son'); it also explains why His death cleanses from sin and allows us to have communion with God and each other.

The significance of the verb 'cleanses' is so powerful that one is stunned by the thought. 'Cleanses,' as previously stated, is in the present tense, suggesting continual action. If we know God in Jesus Christ, we are continually being cleansed. The verb suggests more than to forgive or cancel a debt; it means to erase the stain of sin. We are continually being washed! There is something superficially contradictory here. Why does a person walking in the light need cleansing since to know God, to walk in the light, is to have been the recipients of a divine cleansing? While these are questions that were likely voiced by John's opponents, the answer is that those who walk in the light need cleansing, not to obtain life, since it is already possessed, but because regeneration does not eradicate the inherited propensity to sin. Spiritual regeneration and physical death combined does deal with the problem; the former inaugurates a process culminated by the latter.

The phrase 'from all sin' can be troubling because the cleansing, being universal, unwittingly and potentially may suggest that the topic of the cleansing is initial justification. It would seem that the 'all sin' is qualified in several ways. First, the topic in context is the daily confrontation with the 'forest' (see *Parenthesis 4: The Christian and sin* in 1:6-7 [pg. 55]); it is sin in the post-conversion experience. Second, the 'all' seems to be connected to sins that are wrong behaviors on the believer's part after coming to the 'light' or since possessing the life of God. Clearly the suggestion is the appearance of a present reality. Another of John's literary quirks is that he does not always draw a distinction between the use of the singular and the plural in the same immediate context; in this case between sins (v. 9) and sin (v. 7).

The application of this verse can lead to some utterly invaluable insights for the troubled, conscience-burdened believer. First, it tells such that the death of Christ actually and truly addresses the problem of human sin. Second, it reveals to such that the benefit of pardoning grace through Christ is an ongoing truth. His blood not only cleansed the guilty at the bar of justice; it cleanses daily. Third, it indicates that when their consciences trouble them, suggesting that wrong actions and attitudes indicate that perhaps they have never experienced divine cleansing, we have no right to entertain or be troubled. The fact of being troubled when the object of being troubled is that we have offended the person that we intuitively love, is evidence that we know God and as a result should condemn our fallen consciences for such awful imaginings (unbelievers may fear judgment, but the believer fears that their inordinate actions violate and treat far too lightly the fact of our being loved with such great and divine unconditionality!).

3. The incongruity of spiritual life and guiltless behavior (1:8-9)
The initial false assertion was that sin is not such that it affects in any way our fellowship with God, the reality of a salvation claim. Perhaps, it could be argued that sin, though it really matters, does not require any reaction on a believer's part. Disobedient conduct does not require confession and forgiveness because there is no guilt in misconduct for the believer. Calvary handled all issues of guilt for him; Christ's

death not only dealt with the sin of separation from God, it also dealt with all temporal aspects of sin's potential for disharmony with God forever (or, in the case of John's opponents, that subsequent insight into Jesus' teachings had led to a triumphal, experiential plateau over sin in their daily experience). The phrase, 'to have no sin,' is found only here in the letter, but it is found four times in the gospel (9:41; 15:22, 24; 19:11). In each instance in the gospel, it refers to the guilt of sin. Thus, the claim of John's zealous opponents is that, for the believers, for the truly insightful believers, a plateau can be acquired where the moral conduct of those believers no longer matters since it no longer entails or brings the threat of punishment. Their error is threefold: first, they did not understand or grasp the idea that sin remains an offense against a holy God; second, they were blind to the fact that believers remain sinners; and, third, in spite of these two realities, they thought that a person can truly know God and practice moral indifference, that the possession of the life of God has no necessary effect on one's behavioral patterns, motives or priorities.

The false claim (v. 8a). The second errant claim is a little difficult to discern (again we have a one-way conversation without rebuttal or qualification). The literal rendering of the Greek text is 'that sin not we have'. The reference to cleansing (v. 9) means the removal of stain; it is a washing metaphor. Do the believers' misdeeds involve guilt? Can you have misconduct, a holy God, and no consequences? John's opponents seem to be saying that sin does not bring judgment for Christians because Jesus, in some way, took that judgment upon Himself, so that the absolution of eternal punishment excludes any threat of temporal consequences for sin. Brown's point is well taken: 'The author is warning people who have sinned that they cannot claim, "we are free from the guilt of sin"' (206).

Parenthesis 5: Does Revelation 2–3 provide insight that helps us make sense of the claims of John's opponents?
Though speculative, being without specific textual warrant, but based on the assumption that John's audiences in the epistles and the Revelation are generally the same, or at

least overlap somewhat, the comments to the seven churches may help us to understand why a teaching that sin does not matter in a Christian's life would be appealing. Persecution for consistency of Christian witness seems imminent in the churches of Revelation. Some in the churches sought relief from impending physical dangers by moral, social, and religious compromise. The weakness in the church at Pergamum (2:12-17), for example, involved acceptance of pagan cultural practices, principally immorality associated with idolatry. They fell victim to the curse of Balaam and followed the libertine teachings of the Nicolaitans. In that culture, social acceptance, economic advantage, political prestige, and pagan worship combined with the practice and sanction of temple prostitution. Nicolaitans argued that freedom in Christ allowed for such social practices. The warnings to the Thyatira church (2:18-29), for example, are as dire as is their spiritual seriousness. The adoption of cultural mores had become a very large part of coping mechanisms for some in the church. Their socializing (likely dining in pagan temples where the fare was cheaper) had led to the embrace of the favors of false religion (sexual permissiveness). Perhaps the false teachers in John's letter taught that moral compromise was not prohibited and the benefit of such teachings was that one could claim to be a Christian and not need to feel the consequences of social ostracism which had far more negative implications than in the social setting today, at least in the West.

• • • • •

The disclaimer or condemnation (v. 8b). John's reply is a stiff rebuff of his opponents' claim. His judgment is twofold: they are wrong in their assertions and they are devoid of the truth. The nature of the deception can be further elucidated by comments in the letters. For example, this deception has spread through deceivers (2:26), and these false teachers having imbibed the 'spirit of error' rather than the 'spirit of truth' (4:6). To John, inward character and outward conduct are inseparable. The flawed character of the devil is why there is no truth in him (John 8:44).

The antidote or corrective (v. 9). John's point is that sin is a reality for the believer and it is no remedy to suggest, for whatever reason, that it does not produce negative consequences. The true believer in God is not one who says that sin does not exist in his life, because he knows the 'forest' does exist (see comment on *Parenthesis 1: the Christian and sin,* 1:6-7); but he who recognizes the reality of it and turns to God for forgiveness.

'Confess' means to agree with God in His evaluation of our behavior. Interestingly, the word occurs only in John's writings in the New Testament literature (however, there are several equivalents such as 'repent'). The remedy for the sinning believer is not denial; it is confession! The basis of forgiveness in not in the confession of sin itself; rather it is grounded in the character of the promise-keeping God to whom confession is made. Says Yarbrough: 'John's optimism about such confession is based on conviction regarding God's magnanimous character, not a facile theory of self-management' (64). Notice that 'sins' is plural and the tense of the verb 'confess' is present. Our sins are many and agreeing with God about them, having the same attitude that God has about them, is a never-ending practice in this life. Further, 'unrighteousness' is parallel to sin (1:7), with the slight nuance that the latter is a more general term, while the former suggests specific acts (see 5:17 where the term is once more used, 'All unrighteousness is sin' [all specific acts of wrongdoing are sinful acts]).

The 'He' in 'He is faithful…' has occasioned considerable discussion as to the referent of the pronoun. Is it Jesus Christ or the Father? To whom is confession to be made? The answer is the Father; however, the problem is that in most occurrences of 'confess' in John's writings (four in the gospel [1:20 twice; 9:22; 12:42], four in I John [2:23; 4:2, 3, 15], twice in II John 7, and once in Revelation [3:5]) the object is Jesus Christ. The justification for the conclusion that 'He' here refers to the Father is the context of the occurrences. The topic in each of the above cases is that of coming to Christ, not action after having come to Christ. The person revealed to us as the way to life, the forgiveness of our sins, is Jesus Christ. Christ is the intermediary of our forgiveness always. The person that we have been brought to by Christ is the one who grants us forgiveness daily, the Father (Jesus' role is not the granting of judicial forgiveness; it is as our advocate, the one who pleads the veracity of Himself and His work as our atoning sacrifice). In the first instance, it is about entering into a family; in the second instance it is about living in the family. In John's mind, the recipients of the letter are believers already (3:2).

Parenthesis 6: Sin and the experience of it.
That confession of sin as an ongoing reality for the child of God, not a one-time regenerative event, is evident for several reasons.

First, the focus of conversion is the wonder of God's revelation to us of the beauty of Christ as our redeeming sacrifice. Though knowledge of our great need is certainly a part of God's wooing mercies, it is Christ who is the object of our relief.

Second, in the miracle of God's redeeming, revelatory mercies through Christ, it does not seem possible that we are capable of confessing all our sins. It seems that John's topic comprises a horizontal, parental, and linear relationship, not an instantaneously vertical one (sanctification, not regeneration and conversion).

Third, we have all learned that conquering a 'forest ridge' frequently leads to the perception that there are further ridges in the distance that we did not know existed. When an occasion does not exist, sin does not; yet this does not mean that we are without it latently, only that we are without occasion to manifest it. A beautiful apple in appearance may be rotten on the inside without any evidence outwardly because the decay emanates from its seed, and not necessarily from external circumstances such as heat or insects. The fact of our corruption is simply hidden in the recesses of our hearts requiring an occasion to manifest itself. The absence of sin does not mean that we become immune to corruption! Unbelief has many venues; many we discover only with the passing of decades. The walk to glory is not a step; it involves many steps. It is a journey! Have we not all read *Pilgrim's Progress*, John Bunyan's great allegory of the spiritual life (the walk to the celestial city that included the slough of despond and the alluring call of Vanity Fair)? Christian experienced the reality of the celestial city from afar, but his burden (sin) was not entirely lifted until he entered it.

Fourth, John is writing to believers so that the action he is commending is that of those who have experienced the grace of God. This is something that those who are Christians continually do, even as God's continual forgiveness is the constant remedy.

• • • • •

The promise that God will forgive and cleanse us of our sins is simply magnificent. The repetition of the word 'cleanse' from verse 7 indicates that this verse expands the thought. Forgiveness is the response of God to our errant conduct; cleansing or purification has to do with the stain, the blight of it. A parallel statement to this is that by the writer of the Letter to the Hebrews where he repeats the superior promises of the New Covenant to the former one: 'I will be merciful to their iniquities and their sins I will remember no more' (8:12). God is faithful to forgive us because of His promises to His Son; He is just or righteous in forgiving us because His Son died for our sins. God can rightly forgive us because Jesus paid the debt we owed to God.

Before continuing the commentary, there is worth in meditating upon the description of the character of God the Father in this verse; He is described as faithful and just. The former term indicates reliability; God is to be trusted when it comes to the extension of His promises (He is honest, right, righteous, and just in doing so). He is just in being faithful or reliable in His actions toward us because of the actions of Jesus, His Son, in becoming our atoning sacrifice. As John writes later: 'He loved us and sent His Son to be the propitiation for our sins' (4:10). Jesus' satisfying, substitutionary, and atoning sacrifice is the ground of the manifestation of divine justice in forgiving us! Paul's grand statement is that God is 'just and the justifier of the one who has faith in Jesus' (Rom. 3:26). Imagine, we have been forgiven because of the atoning sacrifice of Christ! Because of what Jesus Christ did for us in taking our place, in enduring the infinite penalty for all our transgressions, God, who by nature cannot set aside the punishment for any act contrary to His character, has justly forgiven us.

4. *The incongruity of spiritual life and a perfected state* (1:10–2:2)

(a) The false claim (v. 10a)
Though it is clear that perpetual sinfulness and the claim that we know God is as false as the claim that sin does not matter, since it is not a stain that causes a severance from the 'light', it might be argued that although we have sinned we subsequently can reach a place where we cease to sin; this is the teaching of perfectionism, sometimes called eradicationism. Here, it seems that John is claiming that his opponents are teaching there is a plateau that can be reached, a special anointing perhaps, which has brought them into a sinless existence. Sin may have existed in the inceptive stage of their instruction from Jesus, but in subsequently assimilating Jesus' instruction completely, they have reached the elevated and enviable stage, the rarity of a sinless life.

(b) The disclaimer or condemnation (v. 10b)
'If we say we have no sin' can suggest two interpretive possibilities: first, that in the experience of conversion to Christ sin has been eradicated from our account in every sense (and therefore since becoming Christians they have not sinned); or, second, that a post-conversion state has been achieved in which sin does not exist. It seems hard to make an exact judgment between the two options. However, the perfect tense of the verb would carry the weight of suggesting that there was a time when they sinned (the tense suggests past ongoing action with continuance), but at some point in the past that changed. The same phrase occurs in the gospel four times (John 9:41; 15:22, 24; 19:11) and in each case the prior state of sinfulness is acknowledged or made apparent by a subsequent, revelatory action. 'If I had not come and spoken to them, they would have no sin, but now they have no excuse for their sin' (15:22). The point is that no one can claim to be without sin since Christ has come to reveal it. It is a lie and is evidence that such claimants do not know God,

writes John. Those who deny the presence of sin in their lives fall into the serious error of making God out to be a liar, of casting dispersion on the character of God who is Light (1:5)! Further, as in the four previous verses, so here is an argument from the context concerning the topic of dealing with post-conversion sins: how to live out one's life having experienced the light. '... to deny the fact of sin in one's life is to deny the holy and forgiving nature of God; it is to impute falsehood to him, and to challenge his own verdict on man's guilt as a sinner...' says Smalley (32).

The rather strong phrases concerning John's opponents throughout this section ('walk in darkness and do not practice the truth' [v. 6], 'we lie and the truth is not in us [v. 8], 'we make Him a liar and His word is not in us' [v. 10], as well as denominating them as 'antichrist' (4:3), makes it evident that John does not see them as believers caught in error and perpetuating it in ignorance; they are not Christians. These are those who are religious (perhaps quite winsome, kind, and even moral), but are not walking in the light, without true life, and not in true fellowship with God, the apostles, or the assembly of true saints.

(c) The antidote or corrective (2:1-2)
John begins with declaring that his recipients are 'my little children', a term used six additional times in the letter (2:12, 28; 3:7, 18; 4:4; 5:21) indicating endearment (to bring out the nuance of the term some translations add 'little'). Actually, John uses two additional terms. 'Child' is found nine times in the letters. In eight of the occurrences it refers to the children or family of God, the church or churches (I John 3:1, 2, 10, and 5:2; II John 1, 4, 13; III John 4); once it is used of the devil's offspring (I John 3:10). A second term for child is found in I John 2:14, 18; however, the terms are equivalents (see 2:12, 14). These terms always are found in the plural, and so suggestive of a group. The brief excursus contains a personal appeal, the first in the letter, and a personal reference ('I am writing') for the first time, suggesting John's passionate interest in the subject of discussion.

There is discussion among scholars as to the referent of 'these things'. There are two interpretative options: it can refer to the entire letter as 'these things' does in 1:4 or to the immediate context (1:8-10). The latter seems preferable since the topic in 2:1 continues the theme of 1:8-10, the reality of sin in the Christian's experience.

While the saint is not sinless, John makes the point that his teaching should not be interpreted as promoting sin. He does not wish to give his readers the idea that sin may be regarded as normal (thus not treating sin in a serious manner), and hence an excusable phenomenon in the Christian life. Further, he does not desire his readers to surmise that there is no forgiveness for the believer's errant way. 'If we do sin' there is an answer, not through denial, but by turning to Christ and His provision for us.

The gravity of the claim that sin does not inflict a moral stain caused John to pause and interrupt the flow of his argument with a personal comment. This is indicated by shift from the collective 'we', the witness of the apostles', to the first person singular ('I'), confirming the suggestion that the 'we' in 1:1-4 is not rhetorical, since here he uses a personal, specific pronoun and addresses his readers with a familial title, 'My little children.' Either his readers are the fruit of his work or he has so identified with them in the pastoral-shepherd-elder role that he counts them as part of his spiritual family (1:4).

The tense of the verb, 'may not sin,' since it indicates indefinite action, has caused some discussion. Does the sin involve something that is ongoing, a habitual practice, or simply any sin in particular? The weight of the letter suggests that the issue addressed here is particular sins, because sin is clearly present in our lives, and not a habitual practice of sin since such is evidence that we are without the life of God (a clue in favor of this interpretation may be John's comment in 5:16 if it is interpreted as a non-habitual principle in one's conduct). This may be illustrated with a blank sheet of typing paper, a pencil, and dot marks on the page. If our sins are disconnected dots on the paper, the remedy is confession of them. If the dots are so interconnected by reoccurring repetition accompanied with a lack of repentance over a considerable period of time so as to become a line, it is indicative of an abiding principle. If such a state exists, John would raise the possibility that we are devoid of the life of God.

Parenthesis 7: Sin and choice
If the readers accept the claims of the false teachers, in John's opinion they will fall into sin and thereby incur its accompanying liability (corruption or guilt), the 'these things' referring to 1:8-10. How is sin a choice when we possess a corrupted, blighted nature from birth, a fact that regeneration does not cure? The answer seems to be established by the willingness of all of us to accept a corrupt choice as a valid one. Inability to resist sin at times does not cancel liability for its consequences because the motive that precipitates our choice is a voluntary one; we wanted to do it. The issue is that when we sin we intuitively believe that the action is to our advantage somehow. External circumstances may solicit a negative response, but the choice of response belongs to the individual. Our problem is that sin has not been conquered completely, but the remnants of sin, the remaining trees in the 'forest' awaiting our final redemption, are very much a part of us.

• • • • •

The answer (2:1b). John's answer brings us to one of the most comforting concepts in the Bible; we have one who pleads our case for us in heaven, a unique person in character, accomplishments and position. The resurrected, living Savior now stands in heaven for us as our defense attorney, our advocate, and our comforter (the latter term is unique to John). The judge, who has been judged for us, stands before the Judge for us, claiming the efficacy of His self-imposed judgment as the remedy for all our transgressions. It is interesting that this is the only time in the Bible that Jesus is called our advocate or go-between (in the gospel, John tells us that the advocate is the Holy Spirit, though Jesus is presented by Paul in that capacity ['who also intercedes for us,' Rom. 8:34] and by the writer of the Letter to the Hebrews ['He always lives to make intercession for them,' 7:25]). Since the Spirit is the benefit Christ purchased for us (Eph. 1:13), and he applies those benefits to the believer, the ministry of

Christ and the Spirit overlap (John 14:26; 16:7). Isaac Watts captured the thought poetically in his 'Jesus, My Great High Priest' (1709).

Jesus, my great High Priest,
Offered His blood and died;
My guilty conscience seeks no sacrifice beside.
His pow'rful blood did once atone,
And now it pleads before the throne.

To Christ, my substitute,
Will I commit my cause;
He answers and fulfills His Father's broken
    laws.
Behold my soul at freedom set –
My Jesus paid the dreadful debt!

My advocate appears,
For my defense on high;
A gracious Father hears and lays His thunder by.
Not all that hell or sin can say
shall turn His heart, His love, away.

Should all the hosts of death
and pow'rs of hell unknown
Put their most dreadful forms of rage and
    mischief on,
I shall be safe, for Christ displays
superior pow'r and guardian grace.

Jesus can be our advocate, the one who pleads our case, because He is righteous. That is, He alone can appear before a holy God because He meets God's righteous standard of justice and holiness (1:5). He can, as it were, plead His own righteousness before God and ask that sinners be forgiven on the basis of His righteous action. Jesus is our Lord's earthly generic name, meaning deliverer (the Old Testament equivalent being Joshua); Christ, the promised one, the Messiah, speaks more clearly of His work as well as His person, the anointed one. He is 'Jesus Christ, the Righteous

One.' Says Henry, 'He who was our Judge in the legal court (the court of violated law) is our Father in the gospel court, the court of heaven and of grace' (1065).

An expansion (2:2). One should tremble when approaching these magnificent words; what we have here is a succinct statement of the wonder of Christ's atoning sacrifice. The coupling of two pronouns ('He Himself') is for emphasis ('He Himself alone and no one else' is my attempt to capture the nuance here!).

Not only is Jesus righteous in character, and thus can appear before God, the Father only accepting that which is in perfect congruity with Himself as the ground of all His mercy, but the essence of the accomplishment of Jesus' work is stated. The reason that Jesus can plead the sinner's case is that He is 'the propitiation for our sins', or the atoning sacrifice for our sins. The word 'propitiation' means to satisfy or placate an offended party. The atoning sacrifice is, of course, in the death of Jesus. This is clear from the fact that in the parallel statement in 1:7, it is the blood of Jesus that cleanses us from sin, blood being a metaphor for His sacrificial death. John uses this term only one other time in the letter (4:10), there stating that it was God's love for us that was the ground of Christ's earthly ministry that culminated in His redeeming death.

Parenthesis 8: The meaning of propitiation
In reading John's letter the concepts of satisfaction or the removal of wrath (propitiation), cleansing, and blood are profoundly interconnected. Twice Jesus Christ is identified as the one through whom satisfaction for sin is rendered. In 4:10 He is the one sent from the Father to do so and in 2:2 it is based upon His qualifying character. What Jesus affected by His satisfying work is cleansing (1:7, 9) and forgiveness (1:9), both predicated upon His personhood (1:9). The equivalent Hebrew term means 'to cover'. The issue of sin was handled in the Old Testament by the offering of an animal in suffering death, the spilling forth of its life as life was in its blood, offered by an intermediary for the repentant. Christ offered himself as the covering for our sins. What is anticipated in the Hebrew Scriptures is thus unfolded in the Greek Scriptures. Says Law: '...Jesus Christ the Righteous – who is the propitiation....

John does not speak of Christ as "making propitiation". He Himself, in virtue of all that He is, He who has lived the Life of God in man, in whom that Life has triumphed over the world and reached its last fulfillment in the self-surrender of death – He is the propitiation' (171). Christ's act of self-sacrifice in the place of sinners does not render us innocent of the crimes for which Christ died, the term being much richer in nuance. It is that our sins have been pardoned, the debt of death having been paid, rendering the divine judge satisfied and the guilty acquitted. It is not that we are no longer sinful; it is that God sees us through the sacrifice of His Son! In the New Covenant the writer to the Hebrews expressed it this way: 'I will remember (not "forget", but no longer credit or charge) their sins no more' (8:12b), quoting Jeremiah 31:34.

• • • • •

John extends the parenthesis by arguing that Christ's atonement encompasses not only His believing audience, but the 'whole world' (see also 4:14, 'Savior of the world'). These words have been the occasion for considerable fracturing within the Christian community, the focal point at times dividing the great Protestant traditions. If 'world' is to be taken literally for all and every person, and is connected to 'satisfaction', it is impossible to avoid the universal redemption of all and every person (a view defended by some Evangelicals of recent vintage, but clearly not supported by the overall witness of Holy Scripture exegetically or theologically, nor by John in the letter [5:11-13, to be without the Son is to be without life]).

If both terms, propitiation and world, are taken as universals, as in the approach above, it can be salvaged somewhat by reducing the force of 'propitiation' by making it hypothetical or contingent upon individual acquiescence or confession of that provision in Christ. This approach has the advantage of interpreting 'world' somewhat literally, but seemingly at the cost of limiting the meaning of propitiation in relationship to it. It would also suggest that humanity possesses the power to limit the actions of God, or even cause or generate them, a view that is also unwarranted by Scripture. Says Calvin: 'People seeking to avoid this absurdity have said that Christ suffered sufficiently for the whole world, but efficiently only for the chosen. This solution has commonly prevailed among theologians' (30). What can be said is that the Bible places responsibility for redemptive outcomes in human dereliction, not deficiency of divine grace ('He came to His own, and those who were His own received Him not. But as many as received Him, to them He gave the right to become children of God, even to them that believe in His name,' John 1:11-12). However, as stated above, choice is in the power of all of us, but not the perception of the beauty of a transcendent object. Condemnation is based on heart-callousness toward whatever revelation God has allowed to shine forth of His person. Clearly, the extent of divine election, predestination, and Christ's priestly advocacy cannot be anything less than the determination of God which was pre-temporal and not contingent upon the knowledge of God relative to future events, such as who or who would not embrace the provision of Christ. That would make God's action dependent on the creature!

It would seem that two approaches to the conundrum are possible. First, since John uses the word 'world' in the gospel in a universal sense (3:16-17, 12:46-47), we might have entered into the sanctuary of the unrevealed mysteries of God and should leave the explanation there. Or, second, we can think about the term 'world' as referring to groups of people, rather than a world composed of all people (for additional comments, see the comments on I John 4:13). In this manner of thinking, the 'world' would be interpreted as Jews and Gentiles; Christ's death, entailing satisfaction, embraced all groups of people, though not everyone. This approach would do justice to the complete efficacy of Jesus' atoning sacrifice. If Christ's ministry as our great high priest is limited in scope and intent ('… I do not ask on behalf of the world, but those whom you have given me,' John 17:9), it would seem in the context of the letter that 'world' means the community of the faithful. Possible support for this approach can be gleaned from 'not *ours* only' (2:2). John would be saying that the atonement was not for himself and the community of believers to whom he is writing only, but to other believers as well. In favor of this reading is the non-universal scope of redemption reflected in Jesus' comments throughout John's gospel (5:21; 6:70; 8:47; 10:26; 12:32; 13:18; 16:19).

Parenthesis 9: How do you make decisions when creditable answers conflict, each offering their own difficulties as well as helpful insights?
The first step is to realize that prejudice and presuppositions play a large role in all of our choices. It is important in evaluating options to know how we are conceiving the context of the answer. For example, some see the controlling issue as being the integrity of the gospel witness (can we assert the willingness of God to save if a provision has not been made?). Others see such a view as diminishing the meaning of 'satisfaction' by introducing human contingency as having prominence over divine provision. One view is said to reduce God to the stipulations of a cause outside Himself, reducing sovereignty to wishful desiring, while the opposing view appears to weaken the integrity of the universal, divine imperatives that seem to place the decision of faith squarely on human choice. The initial approach to a conundrum or question should be an evaluation of the benefits and detriments that options occasion when compared to Holy Scripture.

The second step should entail a study of the origins of the disputed issue in its historic content to see what the initial questions were that caused a division of answers. Perhaps, the issues have changed with the emergence of changing contexts so that the repetition of previous arguments may not have merit. Knowing that questions may have changed might avoid empty wrangling.

The third step is to grapple with the reality that Scripture is the product of an infinite mind while the finite mind is limited in options and is, therefore, blind to some degree. No one has the perfect answer; if we did, the issue would be resolved. The approach to a question and the manner of weighing what are the most important arguments, are keys to resolution.

The fourth step is to realize that options have validity and truths denied are truths denied, a precarious position for any party in a dispute. This should deliver proponents of any view from harsh, unwarranted accusations of others. Sadly, many discussions, like this one, often lead to questions of character, competence, and error by the way they are handled. Often in these instances sociology trumps theology!

The fifth step is to weigh the options by the content of Holy Scripture and, in determining what is permissible, arrive at a choice based upon a twofold criteria: first, which view in your judgment answers more questions than the problems it creates and, second, which view in your judgment creates fewer questions than the problems it causes?

It would seem to me that the method of resolving controversy can be summarized in a fourfold recognition of needs: first, the need for understanding what the other person is actually saying; second, the need for understanding why the other person feels compelled to say what he is saying (this entails a depth of knowing the other view to the extent that it engenders compassion); third, the need for pointing out the weaknesses and traps of the option; and, fourth, the need to positively state the reasons for your conclusions on the matter. The benefit of this approach would be the avoidance of weak, needless arguments both of those opposed to your view and your own, a dialogue that is characterized by godly concerns and does not degenerate into false accusations, and a witness that disagreement within the family of God possesses boundaries of mutuality of care that does not allow the perception of 'truth' to take precedence over the limits of acceptable conduct.

• • • • •

In conclusion, what can be deduced from the three false claims by John's opponents are that the errors collectively concern a failure properly to understand the human condition and the remedial benefits procured through the atoning work of Jesus Christ. In the presentation of each corrective, and in response to each of the errors, the focus is upon the death of Christ. This lends credence to the suggestion that the error of the secessionists is the failure to understand that sin is resolved in the redeeming event at Calvary. Thus, John's opponents did not deny the reality of Jesus; they denied that Jesus was the Christ, the one sent from God to obtain life in God for us through His atoning sacrifice.

Applying the section: What can we say this paragraph teaches?
(1) It tells us that truly to know God is to possess the righteousness of God (v. 5). Being a Christian is not caused by the adoption of a specific lifestyle that is the mere consequence of a change in priorities and values that redemption occasions; an alteration in priorities and values is the effect of redemption, not the cause. Further, it is impossible for any creature to cause a divine effect. How can a mortal, finite being ascend to the criteria of infinity? We clearly need someone to stand before God for us. However, that standard only can be met for us, not by us. But, who could that be? Who could qualify, having met that standard? We need a legal advocate who is righteous and willing to plead our case. Jesus Christ qualifies to be our advocate because He is righteous (1:9; 2:1). Being God, He alone can stand for us before God to plead our case. Being faithful or reliable, He will not disappoint.

(2) It tells us that because of the magnificent person of Jesus Christ and the grandeur of His accomplishments, we do not have to redefine sin. We do not have to deny the presence of sin in our lives, perpetuating a life of self-deception requiring us to pretend that defects are not defects. Nor do we have to pretend that we have arrived at some celestial stage of living that has caused us to rise above the sins that demarcate our behavior. We have an ever-present Savior whose atoning benefits cleanse us continually. We do not have to live in the surreal myth that our sin nature has been liquidated. Jesus brought us righteousness through His death and He is our righteousness in life. Jesus does not plead our righteousness, but His own as our heavenly advocate!

(3) It tells us that humility should characterize our lives; that the self-esteem movement, the cultural assumption that we must think well of ourselves to be healthy, productive people, is a lie. In fact, you and I are flawed and the recognition of the blight is the first step to recovery. We will find little solace in the labyrinth of our coping mechanisms, looking within; we will find little peace by the wise counsel of friends, looking outward; but we will find all of that and more by looking up, up to the cross and the atoning Savior, up to heaven and a pleading advocate.

(4) It tells us that sinners can have assurance of salvation. It reminds us of one of the great truths of the Christian faith recovered by the sixteenth century reformers and faithfully communicated to us by generations of faithful men and women: that one is simultaneously righteous and unrighteous and that our unrighteousness is not a barrier to the possession of righteousness because the righteousness of God is a gift, an alien gift, made possible by our divine substitute. He alone is our only boast of righteousness. One does not have to be perfect to possess the life of God, which is impossible at any rate; Christ is our perfection and we have been placed in Him. When God, the Righteous One, sees us, He sees us through the lens of His altogether righteous Son! The poet Charles Wesley said it well in 'Arise, My Soul, Arise' (1742):

> Arise, my soul, arise
> Shake off thy guilty fears;
> The bleeding sacrifice
> In my behalf appears.
> Before the throne my surety stands...
> My name is written on his hands
>
> He ever lives above,
> For me to intercede,
> His all-redeeming love,
> His precious blood, to plead;
> His blood atoned for all our race...
> And sprinkles now the throne of grace.
>
> Five bleeding wounds He bears,
> Received on Calvary;
> They pour effectual prayers'
> They strongly speak for me;
> Forgive him, O forgive! They cry...
> Nor let that ransomed sinner die!
>
> My God is reconciled.
> His pardoning voice I hear;
> He owns me for His child,
> I can no longer fear;
> With confidence I now draw nigh...
> And 'Father Abba Father!' cry.

(5) This is the message that the apostles announced (1:3); they received it from their Lord and were commanded to proclaim it as well. They did so. They passed the torch, the Spirit-inspired ancient message, the light, the revelation of God, and the evidence is the first chapter of John's letter. However, the duty did not stop with them for the simple reason that they have passed it on to us; the task is, as yet, incomplete. In the phraseology of Paul it would be this: 'And the things that you have heard from me in the presence of many witness; these entrust to faithful men, who will be able to teach others also' (I Tim. 2:2). Here is such a wonderful truth that must be announced: sinners can stand before a holy God without facing a wrathful judge because Jesus Christ's atoning death cleansed and cleanses His children from all sin. It is our duty to allow the whole world to hear his story!

Matthew Henry draws a wonderful application from this paragraph concerning Christianity that is worth our meditation: 'The Christian religion is the religion of sinners, of such as have sinned, and in whom sin in some measure still dwells. The Christian life is a life of continued repentance, humiliation for and mortification of sin, of continual faith in, thankful for, and love to the Redeemer, and hopeful joyful expectation of a day of glorious redemption in which the believer shall be fully and finally acquitted, and sin abolished forever' (1063). It is amazing that Christianity is for sinners who to some degree remain so, but who long for the day when it won't be so! Jesus made the point that He did not come for the healthy but for the sick and infirmed.

2

The Reality of Life in God Tested
(I John 2:3–5:18)

The apostle now turns to tests or evidences that we do have life in God, that we do know Christ, though sin is present in all our lives. John's point is that the miracle of regeneration through the mercies of God is a life-changing, renovating experience. The effects of knowing God, as well as being known by Him as His child, are grounds of assurance. Our experience with God and our works are grounds of assurance for us. Profession must match practice, not perfection! John lists five evidences of a gracious work of God in our lives. As argued in 1:6–2:2, the issue is not perfection or denial of sin in the life of a believer; it is that sin no longer has a universal grip on our lives with the result that, in many instances, attitudes, priorities and affections have been reoriented. Redemption does not eradicate our natures or our human characteristics; the presence of the Spirit (3:24, 4:13, 5:6-7) provides, actually *is*, a new set of characteristics that simultaneously exists in us, the fruits of Galatians 5:23-24 as opposed to the once singularly prevailing deeds of the flesh (Gal. 5:19-21). The reign of Christ as sovereign monarch over His creation was inaugurated in His resurrection and ascension and His reign is increasing daily. However, it will not reach its fullest manifestation until the eternal state when His enemies are made a footstool under His feet and the extension of His redemptive mercies are complete. As there are 'now and not yet' aspects of Christ's reign, so there is in the human emancipation from the grasp of sin. The profession that we possess the invisible life of God is evidenced by the visible consequences or affects that it effects. As the creation awaits redemption from the effects of the fall, groaning and yet magnificent at times (Rom. 8:19-21), so the saint of God (3:2).

Parenthesis 10: The sinning saint and assurance
Two of John's points in the letter are that the child of God is not without the ravages of the terrorizing consequences of sin and that, in spite of its presence, a believer can have assurance of God's redeeming grace. The grounds of a believer's assurance are twofold: first, and foremost, the miracle of the regenerative intrusion of God through the indwelling presence of the Spirit, who is the life that Christ purchased in His blood and whom God the Father bestows justly and freely because the debt has been paid. His presence, however, is not empirically demonstrable in itself because the Spirit is invisible and the experience of Him is subjective. However, the presence of the Spirit, being God, necessarily brings with it manifesting qualities. Just as the Trinitarian attributes of God inherently demand expression, such as glory, justice, mercy, and love, so God's handiwork in creation reveals His character – His handiwork in all creatures through common grace, and His handiwork in His children more so through special grace. The Spirit's evidential work in conforming us to Christ is the objective ground of assurance; it is rooted only in the primary, howbeit, subjective ground of the divine rebirth.

Some have argued that to preserve the integrity of the absolutely free, unmerited, uncaused grace of God any intrusion of works or any consequential emphasis on behavior modification must be left out of any discussion of the miracle of redemption lest the role of grace and works be muddled, the classic confusion inherent with Roman Catholicism, the point being that in the wonder of redemption justification and sanctification must be separated. However, justification and sanctification appear in the Bible to be a seamless, single garment (distinct, yet inseparable). The one is a fact of divine grace, the other a consequence of it, but the two are inseparable unless a justified person can be also an unsanctified person.

An insight that might resolve the contrast of opinions, often expressed in unsanctified accusations by each side of the divide, is to think of how each side is using the concept of salvation. If salvation is conceived within the framework of the miracle of regeneration, the instance of rebirth, the singular intrusive vision of a beautiful Savior, the perception of the moment of sins forgiven, then it seems that the ravishing encounter with God in Christ by the Spirit does not entail in that instance any implications. Implications, however, are a logical and necessitated consequence because of the renovating nature of the insight. One cannot have life from above and remain unchanged by it below. The content of regenerative mercies is the perception of the love of God for a broken creature, and the life of God infused into us is the life of the Holy Spirit, who is love possessed and expressed. Therefore, a profession of life without it is empty. If salvation is conceived in a broader framework, and not in the narrow confines of the regenerative experience, of all the mercies of God from eternity past to our final redemption at the Last Judgment, then sanctification is necessitated. Remember, God's commands are an expression of His will for the believer more than an expression of the capacities of the believer, His will being expressed in the imperative mood (II Thess. 4:3, for example). The point being that sanctification is a part of salvation, and without it there is no ground that the cause, the divine pronouncement of acquittal, has happened!

Is it appropriate to speak of grounds or tests of assurance? If the penultimate ground of assurance is faith in God's acceptance of the provision rendered by the Son He sent to be our atoning sacrifice, is it appropriate to seek assurance in lesser things? If lesser grounds of assurance are inferior to the primary ground, is there value in them? The difficulty with lesser grounds of assurance is the imperfection that all Christians encounter. If we are not always obedient, and no one is, how much obedience is the ground of peace? John makes this point in 3:19-20: when our consciences trouble us we should turn for solace to the God who is greater than us and knows all things. Evidence does not prove that something is true (who possesses all the data that is available? we are all data insufficient; we all possess inherent contrary evidence to the fact). Instead evidence points to the reasonableness that it is so and justifies the propriety of an action. Generally, when persons say that something is true, what they are saying is that it is more reasonable to believe it is so than it is not. Reasonableness is that which is in congruity with one's assumptions, but an assumption by its nature may not be warranted. Does it not come to faith? Is there ever enough evidence to make choices without faith? Do we ever have all the information or simply enough to make a choice (for example: a university or college degree program, career choice, a mate, or a job)?

If faith is the certain criteria of redemption, how do lesser criteria prove helpful?

First, love, truth, and obedience are intertwined in John's mind as is evident from 5:1-5. To John this triumvirate is so interlaced that it forms a single reality. If any one of them is missing, the reality is nonexistent!

Second, the tests are to help believers discern between who is in the family of faith and who is not ('By this we know that we have come to know Him...'). John's opponents are not in the family and the evidence is that they have left the community ('they went out from us but they were not of us...,' 2:19). The tests are in a sense arguments of warning to be aware of and identify any who would destroy the flock of God.

Third, the tests further function to encourage believers that in not following the false teachers they are indeed wise. The tests verify the validity of previous action.

Fourth, the tests presented in the remainder of the letter function to encourage believers to pursue the proper course of action; they are encouragements for continuance in the faith.

To find that one indeed meets these tests of authenticity, the issue being not the degree of conformity but the fact of conformity, would be a great encouragement in times of disappointment and discouragement. Imperfection, pain, and discouragement are occasions for all of us to determine what is valued by how we react and, most importantly, to whom we turn for solace.

• • • • •

As stated previously, scholars have not been able to arrive at a consensus of the structure of I John. The observations of Robert Law, an early twentieth-century Scottish minister in Edinburgh, if judged by his influence upon subsequent writers, have been formative and, therefore, worthy of recognition. Law argued that John's thought in the first letter centered around three basic tests that are repeated in an upward spiral. He saw three cycles (1:5–2:25; 2:26–4:6; 4:7–5:21) with three subsections in each cycle. Each cycle consists of the same three topics: righteousness, the moral test; love, the social test; and truth or belief, the doctrinal test. While the work of Law, repeated by Boice and Stott among others, is important, the outline of the letter is uncertain. Therefore, I have ventured out in a slightly different direction, though not an antithetical one, recognizing the same three central themes of righteousness, love, and truth. However, I perceive these themes intertwined with five evidences of the assurance of life in God: obedience (2:3-17), fidelity to the apostles' teaching (2:18-27), moral purity (2:28-4:6), love (4:7-21), and faith (5:1-12).

A. The test of obedience (2:3-17)

Because consequences must have a cause, being an effect, they cannot be themselves the cause. Hence, works play no causative or causative-cooperative part in the acquisition of redemption, the revelation of God's utter beauty in Christ in the innermost being of the soul, the affections, for those who have experienced the touch of the divine presence. Regeneration is felt as a transforming vision of light cast upon the soul, instantaneously welcomed with delight and warm embrace. This is not to denigrate the importance of faith, but it is to embrace the truth that faith is a response to God, not a cause of God's action. Salvation is a gift, not a bilateral contract. Faith is expressed toward an object; it does not create the object that it embraces. The echo that one hears here emanates from the Upper Room Discourse: 'If you love me, you will keep my commandments' (John 14:15).

Parenthesis 11: The mechanics of choice making
Human beings have the ability to make choices; they do not have the ability to create the choices they make. All decisions are made in an existing context, in a swirl of contingencies or circumstances. The criteria of our choices, the function of our decision-making or willful action, is simply the attempt to maximize what we deem as pleasurable at the moment, or with reflection subsequently, and at the same time minimize pain or negative consequences of any particular action when confronted with options. Our wills are not a creative mechanism or force; they are a selecting force based upon criteria. We simply chose what is most pleasurable. Unbelievers use the same method in making choices as the saints, but the difference is the object of what is considered delightful and profitable. Unbelievers and believers choose willfully, thus the ground of praise and blame is established, but we all choose out of the fund of preconceived options. In the miracle of redemption, we receive sight of the most beautiful of options, the light and glory of God in the person of Jesus Christ, and we choose freely, not because of a lack of context, but because of the object of pleasure set before our eyes. An effect must have a cause; an effect partakes of the nature of the cause. 'By their fruits, you shall know them,' and not by their flowery rhetoric, dashing persona, or bountiful giftedness, nor by the 'numerous leaves of the tree', but by their fruit (fruit being character revealed in conduct).

● ● ● ● ●

1. The standard stated: the commandments (2:3-6)
The conjunction 'and' that commences this section takes us back to the same word that appears in 1:5. It would seem that after discussing the three false claims of his opponents and refuting them, John returns to the topic of the character of the divine. In this instance, it is not to refute his opponents, but to expand the implication of divine holiness for the believers' ground of assurance (a topic also approached in 1:6–2:2). The fact of a new section seems to be indicated by the phrase, 'by this we know, that we have come to know…'

(a) Stated (v. 3)

The referent of 'by this' is likely to be what follows in the verse ('that we know Him') as it does in several other instances (2:5; 3:16, 24; 4:9, 10, 13; 5:2). When 'by this' is followed by a subordinate clause introduced by the word 'that', the referent is to what follows (generally when a subordinate clause does not follow, the 'by this' refers to what preceded – though not always and in such cases the context is the clue). It seems to be a wordy way to say something that is succinct, perhaps so for emphasis. Further, the subject of knowing fits the content of what follows, not what preceded.

The pronoun 'Him' has occasioned some discussion as to its antecedent. Is it God the Father or Jesus Christ? It would seem that the referent is to the Father since the 'and' that begins the verse is connected to 1:5 ('God is light'). The issue that John is grappling with is that of knowing God, not Jesus (his opponents claim to know God, but because they have misinterpreted the function of Jesus in knowing Him, John's verdict is that they do not know God. God is only known as He is revealed in Jesus, the Jesus of apostolic witness).

It is also difficult to discern the significance, if any, of the verb tense change of 'know' from a present to a perfect. If there is more than evidence of literary style, it may be that John is comparing a present reality, 'we know,' based upon an event in the past ('that we have'). Contextually, this seems appropriate since John's opponents claimed that his readers were deficient from their perspective. The question in the letter seems to be about how we know that the readers presently retain that reality in the context of the teachings of John's opponents, who instructed contrary to the apostles' teachings, and yet were persuasive.

The verb meaning 'to know' occurs over forty times in this brief letter; it is a focal point of the author's interests, as well as the central theme (5:13). It does not appear as a noun in the letter, but in a variety of verbal tenses. The idea expressed by its usage is more than cognition or awareness; it indicates spiritual, emotional insight or perception.

The 'if' is interesting because it can be somewhat mis-leading. Does the term indicate some contingency? I think that it does, otherwise John would have more likely used 'that'. Obedience is not an absolute proof of the possession of the life of God; it is an indication or evidence that such is the case since no one's obedience is unblemished by failure (at best it is an important secondary evidence within the context of the primary – the indwelling of the Spirit and clinging faith). The mark of true faith in Christ is rooted in the perception of Christ as altogether beautiful, which leads to striving after Christ, though no one does it with constancy or perfection. Christ is not only our perfection; He is our desire!

Parenthesis 12: What makes action evidence?
An action in itself does not indicate its cause since an act is the result of an internal choice caused by personal motivation (attraction due to perceived benefit or disaffection caused by perception of harm). What causes an act to be proper or improper is not the act itself, but the motive behind the act. Motives are not discernible except as they are expressed in subsequent behavior. The act of helping a needy person may or may not be a benevolent or virtuous act. If it is done without ulterior motives of personal aggrandizement it may be, but if it is done to isolate a person so as to steal from them it is not. Thus, consequences suggest motive. Consistency of consequences indicates consistency of cause, not momentary, isolated action one way or the other.

• • • • •

The phrase 'his commandments' occurs seven times in the letter (2:3, 4; 3:22, 24; 5:2, 3 [twice]) and 'this commandment from him' once (4:21). In the context of the letter, it would appear to be related to the instructions that the apostles received from Christ (1:1-4) and John is delineating them. There is no explicit indication that John has the Mosaic Code in mind (there are no citations and, at best, one allusion [the Cain-Abel incident, Gen. 4] to a specific Old Testament event), so it seems best to understand the commandments as general moral instructions without specification. Redemption places a new vital principle within, the life of God in the person of the Spirit of God, which creates within the believer a deep longing to conform to the object of highest affection.

(b) Compared (vv. 4-5)
Negatively (v. 4). The phrase, 'the one who says,' should remind the reader that John is introducing a false-claims formula as he did in 1:6, 8, and 10. There is a difference in the formulas ('if we say' to 'the one who says'), but it is difficult to isolate a specific necessitation for it unless the 'we' has specific reference to the false teachings and the 'one' is a generic and consequential statement about them. The pronoun 'Him', as in the previous verse, is a reference to the Father, the one Jesus came to reveal. Further, the phrase ('the one who says') occurs three times in this section (vv. 4, 6, 9) as 'if we say' did in 1:6–2:2. (I have come to the conclusion that variance of parallel wordings and even tense changes may be more stylistic than substantive frequently in John.)

John's estimation of the perpetually disobedient is succinct; they are deceived in thinking they know God and are devoid of the truth. Clearly, John is saying that the disturbers of the church, the secessionist party, are not in the light, but in darkness. They claim to know God, but they do not because they do not know Him as He was revealed in Jesus Christ and described by the apostles (1:1-4).

Positively (v. 5). The adversative 'but' alerts the reader to a contrastive claim. Obedience indicates life in God; disobedience to God does not. This is because the nature of redemption is revolutionary; it brings to us new horizons, priorities, delights, and, most of all, a person who has captured our affections. Simply stated, to love is to obey. To enter a marriage covenant, assenting to marital purity and fidelity, yet determined to keep the promise only the majority of the time, is not obedience to the promise one has made!

The phrases 'His word' and 'My commandments' are synonyms; the pronouns in each case refer to the Father. The reference to God's love may be a clue to the nature of the commandment-statement in the previous verse; that is, we are to love God and to love one another. The phrase 'of God' can mean either our love for God or God's love for us. Since the phrase is repeated in 5:3, and there it clearly is to be interpreted as our love for God, the evidence would suggest that it should be understood in the same way here.

This is the first appearance of the word 'love' in the letter, a prominent term that is found forty-nine times in I John. Brown has observed that 20% of the occurrences of the word in the entire New Testament is in John's letters (254). Clearly, love is connected to knowing!

Perhaps the most difficult word to interpret in the verse is the verb 'has been perfected'. The nuance of the verb does not indicate perfection, making it somewhat confusing to the English reader. The verb is found four times in the letter (2:5; 4:12, 17, 18). Clearly it is a claim of the false teachers and John's rejoinder is that saints are not perfect people, but their identity is in Christ who is their standing before God. The word 'perfect' has been translated in various ways: to bring to maturity, to bring to a goal, to finish, or to accomplish (perfect does not mean perfection!). Perhaps the best way to envision the meaning of the idea behind the word is that when we express love, the love given to us because indwelt by God who is love in essence, we fulfill the purpose of the gift of love, which is to reveal the divine character through ours. When the divine character is seen through our actions, the purpose for the gift of love, the indwelling presence of God, has been fulfilled. I would add as a corollary that here is a clue to what it means to glorify God, which is the most fundamental of duties and the purpose of our creation; it is to reflect through our lives the character of God. When the love of God, the love that God possesses in Himself, is expressed in our attitudes and demeanor towards others, God is not only glorified, His purpose being the revelation of Himself through us to the observing world, it thereby has obtained its purpose or goal.

We again encounter the phrase 'by this', which can refer to what has been previously stated or to what follows. Because the phrase is not followed by a subordinate clause, meaning it can refer either to what has preceded or to what follows, it must be decided by other than grammatical clues. Hence, it must be decided contextually. Some suggest that it refers to what follows since in this verse John refers to 'in Him' and in the next verse to 'abiding in Him'. Yet it seems more probable that it looks back to what has been stated previously. Our unity with God the Father means that we possess through the Spirit, the life of God, our creaturely identity with the character of God. Because God is characterized as a loving being (4:7, 16), we possess the same characteristic. To know God is to experience His love and share His love with others. Love possessed is redemption; love expressed is the consequence.

(c) Concluded (v. 6)

This verse draws together and summarizes the apostle's thought to this point. It begins with a claim ('the one who says' or 'whoever says'), but it does not have a counter claim; instead, there is a statement of duty. The duty is to emulate Jesus as revealed through His earthly ministry. The term 'walk' is a metaphor; it suggests a lifestyle of obedience, specifically the command to love.

It is interesting that we encounter the term 'abide' at this juncture and for the first time in the letter, though it appears some twenty-four times. The word essentially means 'to remain' or 'to stay'. Unfortunately, two misperceptions have surrounded the term: first, it has given an allusion to some that abiding or remaining is a temporal state that a person can discontinue and later reestablish. While John speaks of 'abiding in', the equivalent Pauline concept is 'in Christ'; it denotes a never-ending reciprocal relationship of mutual cohabitation, the believer in Christ and Christ in the believer. Many permanent realities in the Scriptures have exhortations attached to them, not so much to indicate contingency as it does importance. Fourteen of the twenty-four occurrences of the term describe the bond between the believer and God (3:24 [twice]; 4:12, 13 [twice], 15 [twice], 16 [twice], and in the text before us). It is clear, for example, that the state of abiding and the possession of the indwelling of the Holy Spirit is the same (3:24; 4:12). Three times the word is used of Christ and the believer reciprocally (2:27, 28; 3:6). One scholar has made the point succinctly: 'It is the new and very real spiritual existence that believers enjoy, and which is effected through the agency of the Spirit, who bears witness to the truth' (Kruse, 81).

Parenthesis 13: Redemption, abiding, and obedience

At first glance it seems that 'abiding' is a temporal state. Why would the apostle command what is a certainty? If a state is certain, unalterable by human contingency, why are we commanded to take that action? John does not know of two classes of Christians: those who walk in obedience and, therefore, flourish in the benefits of abiding, and those who temporarily walk in disobedience, and are not abiding. While these two circumstances do prevail in the experience of all of us, they are each non-permanent, temporal conditions (sadly or thankfully depending on which temporality). Because 'abiding' is a synonym for the presence of God in one's life, that life being the gift of the Holy Spirit, why does the apostle instruct us to do what we cannot otherwise do?

Simply put, there are at least two answers. First, the great covenants of the Bible (i.e., Adamic, Noahic, Abrahamic, and New) are unilateral, expressing solely the work of God without contingency, yet they came with covenant obligations. The obligations came after the promise and they were given, not to maintain the promise, but to show respect and appreciation for the promise. The New Testament repeats many of the commands that are given in the Hebrew Scriptures and cites additional ones; unconditional grace and security is not opposed to obligation and instruction.

Second, in light of the sluggishness of all of our hearts to maintain a proper respect for the mercies of God, he has graciously revealed a willingness to remind us that privilege brings with it the consequence of duty. In other words, those who see two strata of Christians, abiding and non-abiding, are confused; instead, we should see, as does John, only two classes of people, saved and lost, but, unfortunately, there are times when believers act out of character. It is a temporal condition followed with remorse and repentance. The line of an of old hymn captures the thought: 'Prone to wander, Lord, I feel it, Prone to leave the God I love.'

• • • • •

As stated above, some have used these types of verses to discern two classes of believers: those who walk in obedience, a temporal condition for everyone, and those who walk in disobedience (sometimes called the carnal state). However, the notion of abiding is the same as that of fellowship. The issue is not two types of Christians; however, there are two types of people known to John, the redeemed and the unredeemed, those who know God and those who do not, those who walk in the light and those who have never seen the light and walk in darkness. It is clear that the false teachers simply never encountered the risen Lord. 'They went out from us, but they were not of us; for if they had been of us, they would have *remained* with us...' (2:19). The false teachers never were more than deceived and their behavior eventually verified it.

Parenthesis 14: Sin and the saint
When God redeems His people, He reorients the 'forest' of their lives. Remarkable changes result, but the presence of sin remains, though no longer universal in its grip upon them. When a person claims victory over a particular sin, for example greed, it is actually victory over the sin in a particular circumstance. This is evidenced in that the sin often simply reappears in a new guise under a different set of circumstances. There is growth in the Christian life, as the Bible fully attests; however, the Christian life is also the discovery, as new circumstances arise, that there are areas in their lives, applied to specific circumstances, where the light of the gospel has not shown. The living saints are always victorious and defeated; they bask in the light of heaven, but not fully as yet. Carnality is not a state for the saints; it is a temporal realization that they all have areas that need the light of the gospel (and we discover the immensity of them as the decades pass).

The spiritual life is not about conquering the big sins and learning to hide the little ones. It is about falling in love with the altogether lovely one and bringing every need we have to the foot of the cross, finding our refuge in our ever-present comforter, Jesus Christ. Carnality is the state for the unredeemed, not because sin is present but because sin is present with habituality and delight, evidencing the reality that the Spirit of God is absent. The evidence of being a saint is not that we are doing well; it is what we do when we are not doing well! Why? It is because the light of the gospel has been revealed to us by the Spirit of God and, consequently, that we are in the process of being transformed by it. Spirituality is not a mere psychological state; it is the reality of the life of God evidenced by obedience.

• • • • •

The referent to 'He' in this verse is clearly to Jesus Christ as verified by his incarnate ministry ('as He walked'). The one who knows God has the moral obligation to pursue a life of living in conformity to Him. While obedience is a sign of knowing God and disobedience of ignorance of God, how absolute are these ideas? Obedience is not about perfection or sinlessness as indicated in 1:6–2:2. Love can reach its perfection in us without our becoming perfect simply because 'perfect' entails the notion of the accomplishment of something in us and not the perfection of that something in us (perfection awaits the coming of Jesus a second time, 3:2). I think the issue is the general tendency and desires we have, not 'perfection', but attraction and priority. To reveal love in our choices fulfills God's purpose in loving us; we love because He first loved us (4:19). It shows that God is love! We are to love because in loving we reveal the character of God, and that is God's penultimate purpose for redeeming us. The love of God expressed through us is love that has reached the purpose of its giving.

2. The standard elaborated (2:7-17)
The circuitous nature of John's literary style is evident in this paragraph. The shifting from one topic to another and the addressing and re-addressing his readers is befuddling, though the essential points that he makes are not. Believers are those who manifest love in their social relationships because of the love of God; unbelievers cannot do so because the love of God has never become an infused principle in their souls. Christians are those who distance themselves from the world of darkness in their lifestyles: their priorities, passions, and goals being different; unbelievers do not.

(a) The instruction: the command to love (vv. 7-11)
The command is stated in verses 7-8. 'Beloved' occurs here for the first time, but is found five additional times throughout the letter (3:2, 21; 4:1, 7, 11). Obviously, it is a term of endearment

and affection. Using the term, John is suggesting that they are to love as God loves them; it is a commandment for all.

The shift from the plural ('commandments,' v. 3) to the singular ('commandment,' v. 7) is likely because John sees all the commands fulfilled in one commandment, to love. The sense that the commandment is not new is most likely linked to the phrase 'which you had from the beginning', that is, from the inception of Jesus' ministry (1:1); it was a message that the apostles learned from him. This assertion would be important because John's claim, in part, is that his opponents were inventors of novelty and heresy. His message was what the apostles had learned from Jesus' teachings (John 13:34).

John seems to reverse himself in verse 8 by saying that in some sense the old commandment (v. 7) is a new commandment. It is old having been previously stated in the Hebrew Scriptures (Lev. 19:18; Deut. 6:5). In what sense is the old commandment the same as the new, assuming that the subject has not changed? It would seem that it is new in the heightened clarity of the command through the ministry of Christ, defining it by Himself, because the kingdom has arrived in His resurrection and ascension ('the darkness is passing away and the true light is shining'), and the ministry of the indwelling, abiding Spirit (3:24; 4:13; 5:7). I am assuming 'that' is to be interpreted causally; the reason that the commandment is new, yet old, is that the kingdom has come to earth in our Lord's church.

The word 'true' is a little difficult to grasp precisely in translation. The point seems not to be that the new commandment is valid in itself. This is certainly correct, but that it is exampled and expressed in Jesus and in John's readers is new. John is expressing his confidence that his readers join with him in the truest of Christian fellowship (1:3), life through Jesus Christ.

Parenthesis 15: The word 'true'
The word 'true' is quite intriguing. It seems that there is a connection with the comment in 1:5 that 'God is light' and the prologue to the gospel where Jesus is described as the 'true light' (1:9). In the gospel, when the word is used in reference to Jesus, it functions in a comparative sense with the ancient

people of God, a particular ethnicity, Israel. For example, in John 15:1 and 7, Jesus refers to himself as the 'true vine', an image of Israel in the Hebrew Scriptures (Isa. 5). Israel was to be the 'vine', the giver of the life of God to the world, the bearer of spiritual fruit, but they failed. Jesus is the 'true vine' – He is all that Israel failed to be. In John 8:12 and 9:5, Jesus claimed to be the 'light of the world', again something Israel failed in becoming. It would seem that John's readers would have made the connection between the comment in the letter and the comments in the gospel. Jesus is the 'true light' that is shining!

• • • • •

The phrase, 'the darkness is passing,' suggests that the false teachers have taken a wrong path ('walk[ing] in the darkness' [2:11]), which is not a journey into the light. It is interesting that the verb is present in tense and passive in mood, meaning that the not-yet aspects of the kingdom are diminishing through the actions of God. This must have been a wonderful encouragement to the believers, so troubled by the secessionists – believers are in the middle of an unseen march of divine progress that will end in the triumph and glorious reign of God with His children over all evil! This seems to be the essence of John's message in the Revelation.

The essence of the darkness is evident – worldly behavior (2:17). The 'shining light' is John's description of the progress of truth through the person of Jesus Christ. Just as God is the light intrinsically (1:5), meaning the disclosure of moral purity, Jesus is that light revealed. Believers are to conform their lifestyles to that light (2:6). In fact, the false teachers are later described as 'antichrists' (2:18), suggestive of eschato-logical portents, shadows that point to a greater fulfillment in a later time.

The contrast of the commandment is applied in verse 9. We encounter in this verse another of 'the one who says' clauses (see vv. 4, 6). The point of the verse is that John's opponents have made a false claim – the second in this section (v. 4). I see the 'one who says' in verse 6 as not advancing John's argument, but concluding a section; verse 4 and verse 6 begin a unit and the repeated phrase serves to frame the unit of thought as bookends. The phrase in verse 6 is not a false claim, but is a moral directive. While the secessionists may claim to be in the light, walking in conformity with Jesus, they are not. To walk in the 'light' (to know God, to fellowship with God, to abide in God) is evidenced by a walk in love (1:6). Their actions betray the falsity of their claim.

It is interesting that John has, to this point, argued that the essence of a believing heart manifests itself in love for God expressed in moral obedience (vv. 3-6). Here, however, there is a shift from loving God to acting appropriately toward others. In the mind of the apostle, love of God and love for others form an inseparable bond. Love as defined and expressed by the mandate of God will never prove to be a detriment to proper behavior.

The stark, even abrupt, antitheses of the apostle are nowhere more evident than here (light/darkness, love/hate). There is simply no revisionist grey in the apostle, either in this letter or in the gospel (1:5, 8:12, 12:35-36). Remember, this is the man who once tried to call fire down upon the Samaritans (Luke 9:51-55)! F. F. Bruce has made this point succinctly: 'John characteristically sees life in terms of black and white; intermediate greys have no existence to him. So there is no middle between love and hate, and by hate he does not mean mere animosity but mere lack of love' (56). To John 'darkness' is spiritual in nature; it is the opposite of light. It is the realm of death, not life. These false teachers are deceived, and they are deceivers having no spiritual light in them. John perceives a stark and radical dualism when it comes to spiritual matters; there is no middle ground. Smalley's summary is helpful: 'To claim existence "in the light" of God is one matter; but to do so while practicing hatred, rather than love, is a contradiction. Indeed, disobeying the law of love makes a right relationship with God impossible; for abiding in him means living as Jesus lived [vv. 4, 6]' (60). John's dualism is not immaterial/material (spiritual/fleshly); it is moral (right/wrong, love/hate).

John then gives a general principle deduced in verses 10 and 11. It is stated positively in verse 10. Love is an evidence of life and, thereby, is a ground of assurance. There are two kinds of love, not as evident in the manner of expression as in the motive for expression. One we are born with; it is natural, instinctual, and generic to the race. The other is a divine gift that transforms the recipients in the inner core of their priorities and values. The scandalous behavior, the evidence of a lack of love, and, therefore, the proof that the secessionists are dangerous unbelievers, is that they departed from the apostles' teachings concerning the person and accomplishments of Christ and severed the unity of the gathering of the church (2:19; II John 9). The one who walks in the light, here a metaphor for seeing and knowing where they are going, will not lead others astray (we derive the term 'scandal' or 'scandalous' from the word. It means behavior that lacks moral integrity). Such a person, unlike the false teacher, will not fall into darkness, a metaphor suggesting spiritual emptiness and judgment.

Parenthesis 16: Unbelievers and love
The issue of the moral quality of an act is not in the act itself. It is the origin, nature, and object of the action that determines validity. If the origin of an act is a blighted, corrupted character, the consequential action will necessarily partake of its cause. If the motive behind an act is selfish, the act is also. Unbelievers, through common grace, God's provision for civil society, can do acts that are surely commendable in general life, even surpassing believers at times in civil causes. However, if God's criteria of acceptance is Himself, if God determines the nature of virtue by Himself, people devoid of the life-giving character of God the Spirit have no claim to righteousness before God, however commendable, beneficial, or profitable their actions.

• • • • •

In this verse we have the appearance of the word 'brother' for the first time and it is found sixteen times in the letters. Of these occurrences six are connected to love, four to hate, and one to sacrificial living (3:16). Further, it is generally agreed that 'brother' suggests one's spiritual siblings and thus encompasses females and males.

John then states the general principle negatively in verse 11. In contrast with the 'one who loves' (v. 10), 'the one who hates' is lost, devoid of light. John uses light and darkness metaphorically of life and lostness, but illustrates it using the same words literally. Hate, lack of preference for another or due regard for the well-being of others, is an evidence of a lack of life. The 'one who hates' (2:4, 9) is the same as 'if we say' (1:6, 8, 10), though the latter is expressed as participial phrases and the former by conditional clauses. A failure to recognize and deal with sin in one's life leads to hatred, not love, in actions toward others!

The fruit of 'darkness', the third appearance of the term in this verse, is the inability to perceive reality. John in his gospel records Jesus as teaching that those in darkness simply do not know where they are going – they are hopeless without knowing it (John 12:35). John, quoting Isaiah 6, credits their blindness to a judicial darkening of perception (John 12:40), though in the letter it is an act of the 'evil one' (2:14) and later he credits it to 'many antichrists' (2:18). To accomplish a divine purpose, God uses intermediates, both evil and saintly ones. In this instance, He uses the devil or the devil's minions (here meaning John's opponents).

Parenthesis 17: Blindness and salvation
If people are truly blind and deaf spiritually, is there any hope? Is there anything that we can do to help our fellow citizens of this world? Do you and I have the ability to turn haters into lovers? The answer is a resounding 'yes'. When God ordains an end he employs means suitable for the accomplishment of it. The means is what Paul calls the 'foolishness of the gospel', and it is foolish for several reasons: it does not make sense that so much could be gained by embracing so little; it does not make sense that finite words can account for infinite ends; and it is contrary to the way that things work naturally. Why are we told to tell people endlessly of the claims of Jesus? The answer is that people cannot choose what they do not know, what is completely foreign to their experience. Telling the story of Jesus does not bring life to a person, but, in our telling of the story, God opens the eyes and the ears of people. Faith must have an object and telling the story of Jesus is giving a person an object, hitherto unknown and unknowable, should God reveal Himself through our words. You simply cannot choose an object you do not know. It is not that anyone lacks

the ability to make choices; it is that some have no beautiful choice to make because unbelievers do not and cannot know that such exists unless someone tells them, and God wills to use our humble, imperfect attempts in doing so to open their eyes. Faith is not so much a gift as the object of faith, resulting in salvation as a gift (Eph. 2:8). Our duty is to be a vessel for the transmission of the old, old story! Paul said it this way: 'And how will they believe upon Him whom they have not heard? And how shall they hear without a preacher? And how shall they preach unless they are sent?' (Rom. 10:14b-15a).

How can we apply the truth of this section?
(1) When God redeems a person He changes that person from the inside, the heart or affections, and the outside, providing new objects and orientations. While we might need instruction in the application of new attitudes, and while the reorientation is a process, it is instantaneously intuitive. When God encounters us in the miracle of redeeming grace, we see Him for the first time and this new perception of a hither-to-fore unperceived reality is stunning.

(2) The essence of divine forgiveness is the instantaneous infusion of new life, the very life of God. Salvation from a divine perspective is the revelation of the character of God through the gift of God, who is the Spirit of God, into our very core being. It is radical and transforming, introducing us to a realm of reality altogether beautiful, a world that is transforming by the sight of it.

(3) A consistent pattern of self-absorption should cause us to pause and ask: are we the children of a loving Father? We all have our too-many moments, but that is not a ground of a lack of assurance because those moments are not general, habitually reoccurring, delighted-in patterns. The saints of God confess, not condone, their faults to God, pleading forgiveness because of who Christ is (righteous) and what He did in the shedding of His own blood (His sacrificial death) for them, which secured the appeasement of God on their behalf.

(4) The character of God will be displayed in those who abide in Him, those who know Him, those who fellowship in Him. No one should be allowed to imagine that he/she can get away with a claim to be a lover of God on the ground that

salvation is an inward attitude, invisible to others. Neither is it valid that a past childhood experience is substantive when subsequent years are expressive of constant callousness toward God and a repudiation of His commandments.

(5) All the commands of God are summarized in one word – love (Matt. 22:37-39). The multi-faceted character of God, the interrelatedness of the triune God, is overshadowed and dominated by an effusion of the mutuality of love. Hence, all of God's acts, being an extension of His person, are characterized by love – love for His creation, love for His creatures, and love for His people. Therefore, it is no wonder that the first test of the surety of God's redemption is love. God is characterized by love, and His love for Himself caused the effusion of His love. His love is, therefore, the first manifestation of God's character in our lives ('the fruit of the Spirit is love'). Paul tells us in I Corinthians 13 that without love we are false people in our claim to know God. Charles Wesley's great poem from 1747, 'Love Divine All Love Excelling,' captures the thought of God's love infused into the soul.

> Love Divine, all love excelling,
> Joy of heav'n, to earth come down;
> Fix in us Thy humble dwelling,
> All Thy faithful mercies crown.
> Jesus, Thou art all compassion;
> Pure, unbounded love Thou art;
> Visit us with Thy salvation,
> Enter every trembling heart.
>
> Finish, then, Thy new creation;
> Pure and spotless let us be;
> Let us see Thy great salvation
> Perfectly restored in Thee;
> Changed from glory into glory
> Till with Thee we take our place,
> Till we cast our crowns before Thee,
> Lost in wonder, love and praise.

(b) The assurance: salvation possessed (vv. 12-17)
The addressees of the commandment are described in verses 12-14. John's purpose in addressing his readers is to assure

them of their Christian status. Scholars are puzzled to explain the duplication of the threefold encouragement that prefaces this section. In the first statement of age groups, the present tense is used; in the second, the past tense is used. Is this significant? Also, different Greek words are used for children even though the sequence of age categories is the same in each repetition. Also, should we translate the introductory word as 'because' or 'that'? Is John stating a reason for a fact or is he making a declaration of a fact? I think the former is preferable if the reason for writing is, as stated above, one of assurance.

As to the tense changes in the repetition of the trilogies, the best solution seems to be that it is simply a rhetorical device that is unique to John. It is interesting that when John uses the verb 'writes', it is in the present tense. Hereafter in the letter, it is the past tense. I would also say the same for the two different words for children (vv. 12, 13). These are simply literary devices unique to John.

Likely the most discussed issue is how to take the words 'little children,' 'children,' 'fathers,' and 'young men.' Should we interpret them literally as age categories or figuratively of spiritual stages of development? Also, should we divide the trilogies in some manner? If non-literally interpreted, does it refer to three groups or one group described three ways? I take it that John is using a rhetorical device, that of metaphors. He is expressing general spiritual truths that ought to apply to all his readers. As Marshall notes: 'All Christians should have the innocence of childhood, the strength of youth, and the mature knowledge of age' (138).

A hint that we should not take these designations literally is how John addresses his readers ('my little children' [2:1, 12; 2:18; 3:18; 4:4; 5:21], 'my children' [2:13], and 'children' [2:18]). Since 'children' throughout the letter is a metaphor for John's readers, it makes little sense to read it literally here. There is a change of term for children between verse 12 and verse 13; the second is a term that scholars suggest is not diminutive of age and, therefore, 'little' is dropped in some translations (I attribute this to John's literary style and is not therefore significant).

The order of age groups seems to imply a metaphorical reading also (you would expect an age listing from the most aged). If the differentiation is based on levels of spiritual maturity, it would seem unwarranted for four reasons. First, the accomplishments of the groups are wonderfully remarkable and worthy of commendation. Second, the content of the letter, being about the unshakable knowledge of salvation in Christ, would cancel any expectation of degrees of spiritual accomplishment as stages of development. Third, John has made it clear that there are not classifications of believers, spiritual and carnal; all of God's children simultaneously manifest both traits. The temporal dominance of one trait does not imply the absence of another trait, simply preoccupation at the moment. Fourth, from this juncture on in the letter John refers to the community or collectivity of his readership as 'children', not as 'fathers' or as 'young men' (for example, John refers to 'children' in 2:18 and 4:7, which are clearly references to the church as a whole). Though he does not use this threefold designation elsewhere in the letter, he is clearly speaking to the same group of people.

It is ancillary, but interesting, being an argument from silence, that John makes no reference to women in the gathering, suggestive of the fact that first-century churches may have been influenced by the Jewish tradition that men predominated in the life of the assemblies (the first century was not a woman-centered world, though the Christian faith brought significant changes in their status).

An interesting alternative in understanding this duplicated trilogy is to read 'children' metaphorically for John's readers, since it is consistently used that way throughout the letter, but to take 'fathers' and 'young men' literally reflecting the priority of age in the sequence. Says Brown: 'It makes best sense of the order of the titles: first, a general address to all of the author's children; and then seniority within the subdivisions of "Fathers" being addressed before "Young People"' (298). Support for interpreting 'fathers' and 'young men' literally is that nowhere in New Testament literature do these terms refer to Christians as a whole; they only refer to individuals. The counter to this observation is that John is using these two age categories as what might be designated as bookends, meaning he cites the old and young to indicate the entirety of his audience (in literary parlance it is called a merism).

While a definite possibility, as well as an approach that has been embraced by significant scholars, it seems unexpected and unwarranted. If the age distinctions are a literary device suggestive of a whole group, how would this differ from the suggestion that 'children' means the whole group? Would we not be saying that all three categories refer to a totality, all of John's readers? Smalley offers a perspective that is worth the thought when he writes, '… it is quite possible at this point that our author is being deliberately ambivalent' (70).

There has been some discussion as how to translate the Greek term rendered 'that'. Some translations render it as 'because', so indicating the reason for writing or having written. A minority of scholars would render it as 'that', so indicating that what follows declares the content of what is written. Still others take a middle-of-the-road position saying that there is not enough data to make a firm decision. It seems that John is stating a reason or reasons for their right to assurance that fit more cogently the theme of the letter ('knowing'), though this is clearly a subjective judgment based on the broader content of the letter.

While there are six statements for the writing by John in these verses, are there multiple reasons or is this a single reason approached from different angles? Can you have any of them without possessing all of them? From the discussion below, I would argue that we have multiple descriptions of the same reality. What we have are different facets of a many-faceted diamond called 'the redemption that is in Christ Jesus'. To be forgiven, to know God, to conquer, to be strong, and to possess the abiding message are synonyms and the employment of several terms to express the same idea can be accredited to John's literary style.

'Little children' (v. 12). This is a remarkably pointed state-ment of fact; the verbal tense 'is' indicates a completed event in the past and the mood of the verb, being passive, suggests that the benefit of forgiveness is something that is not earned (indicated by the passive voice); it is something given. The ground of forgiveness is because of Jesus' atoning death as the divinely appointed Christ or Messiah.

The ground of divine forgiveness is made clear by the apostle: we are reconciled to God because of what His Son accomplished for us upon the cross. 'His name's sake' is clearly a reference to our Lord's person and atoning work. The quality of Jesus' character, being equal in every respect to that of the Father, evidenced by His flawless life, was the ground for His ability to pay the debt of our sin. He is the only worthy substitute for us because He alone kept the moral law of God, the first 'Adam' having failed to maintain his integrity, plunging the race into spiritual darkness. Jesus, the second Adam (Rom. 5:12-21; I Cor. 15:21-22, 45), alone is all that God is. Being truly human He could stand in our place; being truly sinless He could successfully stand for us in our place; being truly God He could stand before God for us; being truly the God/man He could successfully stand for us before God. Because Jesus was all these things (purity, holy, blameless, deity, and substitute), God the Father could remain just and yet not punish us, and holy and yet forgive us (Rom. 3:26), because of what His Son was and what He accomplished for us ('for His name's sake'). We are forgiven because of Jesus! Brown has captured the thought: 'Thus the idea is not so much that sins are forgiven through or by means of Jesus' name, but are forgiven by God because of Jesus' name' (302).

'Fathers' (v. 13a). The pronoun 'Him' is mostly likely a reference to Jesus Christ, as the pronoun in the previous verse, connecting it in reference to 1:1. Though in a lineal sense, 'from the beginning' here is different from the repetition of the phrase in 1:1 (the reference there being to the apostles), I would take it to mean, 'from the first time we met Him.' The false teachers were claiming that the believers were deceived in professing to know Him because only they knew the facts correctly; that what they might have understood in hearing the gospel initially was in error. John would simply be saying that the believers actually got it right the first time!

'Young men' (v. 13b). The believers have also gained the victory over the 'evil one', clearly a reference to the devil or Satan (2:14; 3:12; 5:18, 19). What is it that has caused them to conquer? It is faith in the person and completed work of Jesus Christ in His atoning procurement of our redemption. 'And who is the one who overcomes the world, but he who believes that Jesus is the Son of God?' (5:5).

'*Children*' (*v. 13c*). What an assurance from the apostle himself that these troubled believers, who are unwilling to follow the false teachers in their midst, do know the Father. The apostles' message is the only true redeeming word. Stott (96-97) makes the observation that the term used here for 'children' emphasizes subordination rather than kinship (as in verse 12); however, the differences may be accounted for by John's literary mannerisms.

'*Fathers*' (*v. 14a*). The second comment about the 'fathers' is an exact repetition of the first, likely for emphasis.

'*Young men*' (*v. 14b*). In returning to 'young men' John, unlike the comment about the 'fathers', adds that they are strong and that God's word abides in them, while he repeats the fact that they are conquerors. It seems that their strong faith accounts for the fact that they were unwilling to follow the false teachers. The meaning of 'the word' abiding in them has been connected by many to three previous references. If the referent takes us back to 1:1, it would be the message of the apostles concerning Jesus as the life-giver and, thus, it would be a positive statement. If the reference is to 1:10, it would be drafted from a negative rebuttal, but referring to the same thing, the message that God gave to His Son. Another option is to see a connection to 2:5 as a particular reference to the command to love one another. There is little gained between options one and three, except for specificity, because the message given to the apostles concerns love. However, though stated negatively here, love is the subject of the immediately preceding verse.

There is an application of the commandment in verses 15-17. Scholars have pointed out that these verses contain three contrastive statements about love: the love of the world and the love of God. In verse 15 the two are mutually exclusive, in verse 16 the two are antithetical, and in verse 17 only one lasts forever. It is interesting from a literary perspective that John employs trilogies frequently (see verses 12-14, for example).

John admits to no middle ground; his rhetorical style is to state stark dichotomies. There are two realities (the eternal and temporal), two objects to love (the unseen and the seen, God and the world system), and two destinies (heaven and hell). What he is saying is that the false teachers live in the wrong world!

In verse 15a, we have *the nature of the appeal*. John begins by stating the command to love in the negative; he tells us what not to love! Love is assumed for all of us; the issue is what has primary hold over our affections, the motivating cause behind the expression of love. The command not to love the world's values is clear, but the question is: if God loved the world (John 3:16), why should we not love it? The word 'world' has a wide range of meanings. As used here, it means the system arrayed against God ('... and the whole world lies in the power of the evil one', 5:19). Thompson's comment is helpful: 'In this passage, *world and everything in the world,* designates a complex web of values, decisions and directions chosen in life without consideration for knowing or doing the will of God' (68). The world, as a composite people, we are to love; the world, as a system of values opposed to God and under the control of the devil, we are to shun. Worldliness does not reside in things, but it does reside in our inappropriate concentration and conformity to things.

Parenthesis 18: The world and things
Without doubt there are many commendable and lovely things to observe and experience in our world. However, as with us, so the environment in which we live has tumbled from its greatness into a grotesque and perverted shell of a pristine world that once existed. There are two ways to be worldly: first, to indulge in its values and priorities (postmodern individualism and tolerance accompanied by an unflinching denial of objective truth or of a world of reality that far exceeds the world of the material senses). Another way to be worldly is to take pride in the spirituality of isolation from it as a badge of Christian accomplishment. We are citizens of this world, dual citizens, yes, yet God has called us here to participate in it without joining it completely. In living out the principles of the kingdom in microcosm within our own spheres of influence, we can point others to a greater, more real, kingdom, yet to be actualized in its fullness. Laboring to succeed in our earthly callings is not to forsake our heavenly calling in the process; the world is not our playground so

much as it is our stage whereupon we are to display and act out our convictions for the glory of God.

• • • • •

Then in verses 15b-17, we have the reasons for the appeal. The first is the incompatibility of two loves, reasoned (vv. 15b-16). Many centuries ago, Augustine, the bishop of Hippo in North Africa, wrote a book called *The City of God*. While seeking to explain why Christian Rome was in a state of decline whereas under pagan influence it had reached heights of accomplishments with impressive roads, aqueducts, coliseums, and temples still visible today, he described the structure of the world. He argued that the world consists of two loves focused on two objects; there are those who love God and those who love the temporal. These two 'kingdoms' exist simultaneously until the end of time when God will return to separate the two, one to everlasting comfort in His presence and the other to judgment with no hope of grace. Augustine argued in a lengthy discourse what John has stated in a single verse!

We are told why we are not to love the world; it is *incompatible* with love either 'of' or 'for' the Father. The Greek preposition can either indicate the love that we should have for the Father or the love that the Father has for us. Scholars debate this. However, the context is about the believer's conduct in a blighted world, possessing a corruptible system of values and blighted behaviors. Further, the broader context of this comment concerns personal tests of the reality of redemption. The false teachers do not have this characteristic (love) and that is one of the reasons they can be recognized as errant; the object of their love is other than God, their interests are twisted!

The second reason for this incompatibility is that the two objects of love, God the Father and the world, are *mutually exclusive* (v. 16). In the world is what has been called the devil's triumvirate of characteristics: inordinate attractions, blighted values, and self-preoccupations.

The first of these are lusts that find their origin in what John denotes as 'flesh', meaning the totality of human nature or sum of human nature as located in the earthly realm alone; it means our base inner attitudes and longings. In the sphere of a fallen world and human existence in it, they are corrupt, having been corrupted. The phrase suggests more than the promptings of sexual promiscuity; allurement is many-faceted in type, style, and origin; it occupies many rooms in the houses where we live. It means to make one's decisions based on merely human standards alone.

If 'lust of the flesh' focuses on the inward origins of solicitation, 'lust of the eyes' relates to outward excitements to inordinate conduct. Some have wondered if there is not in John's mind a veiled allusion to the Fall account of allurement through visual observation (Gen. 3:6). Brown argues that the phrase means to be captivated by mere appearances, without any consideration of deeper significances: 'Twelve times John uses "eyes" in relation to the blind man of ch. 9 where the real significance is not that Jesus opened the man's eyes to physical sight but to the spiritual sight of Jesus as the one sent by God, to which the Pharisees were blind [though they could see physically]' (311).

The meaning of 'pride of life' has occasioned discussion as scholars are divided over how to read it. Should it be read as the previous parallel phrases, the prepositional phrase being the external stimulus designated by the prepositional phrase that follows it? Or, does our inward selfishness cause confidence in material gain? Does security through the accumulation of material possessions cause pride or arrogance? Or, does the inward bent on self-reliance find expression in the pendent to find significance and safety through material acquisition? It would seem that the context would weigh in favor of the second reading (that is, interpreting the three causes in the same way); the false potential of material accumulation causes people in the worldly sphere to put their trust in possessions and so producing self-dependence and boasting. In all three cases, the subject is something deformed, producing something complementary to its source.

In verse 17, we see the impermanence of the world contrasted to the eternality of the one who loves God. John's point seems to be that the 'world', consisting of the trilogy of verse 16, is transitory. It is interesting that John states that these things are in the process of diminution. While the final realization awaits the Day of the Lord, the final judgment, and the advent of the kingdom in its fullest sense, it is occurring now, the 'now-and-not-yet' of reality. The new age has arrived in Christ (2:8) and this world is passing away. The values of this world are temporal. The kingdom of God has intruded in the kingdom of this world, but the final victory of the former awaits us (John tells us of that final consummation in *The Revelation*).

The 'will of God' in this context is moral conformity to the revelation of God revealed through Christ's earthly life (2:16) and communicated through the apostles (particularly, and most immediately, through John's letter). This tells us two things. First, John is asserting that his opponents are not to be followed because their conduct is rooted in fallen motives drafted from fallen sources. Second, the believers have a deep ground of assurance that they have the life John is describing because they recognize the worldly values to be inappropriate. The one who pursues the will of God possesses eternal life, abides in or resides in it forever. Clearly, the term 'abides' is not a temporal state in this context.

How can we apply the truth of this section?
(1) It is important to realize that exhortations in the Bible function in two ways. They may be used to incite an action, such as the calls in the Bible to come to Jesus Christ and receive through Him the gift of divine life. God does not command those who are not His children to walk in His likeness that the indwelling Spirit endues, only to live their lives in accordance with common grace. A second goal of exhortation is not to encourage what does not exist, but to remind, promote, and confirm what does exist in our lives and can be enhanced. This is the function of the imperatives in John's letters; it is to encourage believers in what is already in them with a twofold consequence: first, virtues should increase and, second, the increase of virtues should be a ground of comfort and assurance that God, indeed, has done a transforming work of grace for us.

(2) Those of us who live in the Western world live in the most prosperous, vastly materialistic, culture on the earth and, therefore, we live in dangerous realms of disadvantage. Materialism is really not about the accumulation of things, though that is certainly a symptom. A materialistic lifestyle

is rooted in the desire to obtain physical advantage as the ground of security, fulfillment, and contentedness. Another way to manifest a materialistic orientation is the desire to retain things, hoarding things, with little or no thought that 'enough' can never be satisfied and that it has the potential of depriving us of the simple joys of life in our overstressing quest for more.

(3) Love of the world is like lust; it is not a passing glance that is quickly counterbalanced by the perception that it pays no dividends and is pursued at devastating costs. Passing glances, passing desires, are not habitual patterns; they are reminders that danger does exist, that repentance is the path to victory, and that we are God's children because He has granted us new perspectives, new delights, and new attitudes.

(4) While we are to love the world as God does (John 3:16), we are not to associate with the immoral, covetous, idolaters, revilers, drunkards, and swindlers of the world (1 Cor. 5:9-10). We are not to adopt their values. The quality of our separation from the world is relative to its motives, practices, and supposed virtues, not the world as a sphere of life. How else will people see the possibility if an alternative to naïve, destructive assumptions are not demonstrated? How else would we have an opportunity to explain the gospel if those about us do not see in us the transforming character of the invisible? There is a vast invisible world, more real in many ways than the physical one, but the only way to see that world is through this one!

(5) Materialism is evidence of love for the world's values. Do we really believe that this is the 'shadow land' and that our hearts and minds should be set on heaven? Do our values reside in things, position, and accomplishments? The one effective antidote to worldliness is to have one's heart so filled with the Father's love that it has no room for any love that is incompatible with it.

B. The test of fidelity to the apostles' teaching (2:18-27)

John's point in this section is that false teachers cannot permanently sway true believers away from the apostles' teachings. Believers can sense error and, at best, are only temporarily enamored by it, though its teachers may appear to be helpful, attractive, and persuasive. Believers' intuitive discomfort with error about the person and work of the Redeemer, the essence of their encounter with life through Jesus Christ, is evidence that they are God's children.

The use of 'children' (v. 18) seems to be an indication of a new section as does 'little children' (vv. 12, 28). Some scholars do not see a turn of subject, the beginning of the discussion of a new test, since verse 18 seems to be a further expansion of 'the world is passing away' (v. 17). I have chosen to see a new section beginning here largely because of a shift in tone and audience, though the flow of John's thought is notoriously difficult to outline at times. What is evident in this section is that John not only writes to encourage the believers ('you all know,' v. 20), but he blends with it warnings and exhortations. It is interesting to note the frequency with which John uses the term 'world' in the letter. Actually, it occurs twenty-four times in John's letters and seventy-eight times in the gospel, together constituting over half of the occurrences in the New Testament. Here it continues to be used in a negative sense.

1. The presence of false teachers stated (v. 18)

A most controverted concept in John's writing is the way to understand the 'last hour' (a phrase only found here in the New Testament, though parallel phrases are found elsewhere within it). We know that Christ ended an age, the 'Age of Shadows', and inaugurated a new one through His resurrection and ascension, a period of time between the advents, that will end in the Final Judgment. The New Testament writers view the entire new period, the era between the advents, as the final days, with the return of Christ for the last judgment and the renovation of the earth as the eternal dwelling place of the children of God when time shall be no more, a future reality only now emerging in a shadowed manner ('the world is passing away' [v. 17], when the paradise of God [Gen. 1] shall be restored. God will have crushed His enemies and a renewed paradise will emerge with God dwelling in the midst of a worshipping people – not merely a couple [Gen. 2], but myriads and myriads [Rev. 21–22]). It may be helpful to note that the phrase appears without the article ('a last hour') signifying a general time, not a specific time. This would suggest that John is describing a general characteristic of the period. While the 'antichrist' may appear at the end of the age in the final conflict between God and Satan, there are many pre-figurements of the final figure in his minions that have appeared periodically across the pages of history (and will continue to do so until the end of time). Boice has a helpful comment: John 'is saying that the spirit that will characterize the final antichrist is already working in those who have left his readers' congregations' (69).

Parenthesis 19: The Bible in a nutshell
1. The Bible is divided into two parts, an Old Testament and a New Testament.

2. The Bible begins in a garden and ends in a re-created city-garden (Gen. 1–2; Rev. 21–22).

3. The Old Testament contains what is described as the Old Covenant, the promises to the ancient people of God; the New Testament gives us the New Covenant, the promises to the new people of God. The Old Covenant is presented to us in Exodus 19 and repeated in Deuteronomy 5. The New Covenant is promised in Jeremiah 31 and instituted in Christ's death (Heb. 8).

4. The differences between the two great covenants are made clear in Hebrews, a book whose central concern is to explain the superior qualities of the New Covenant over the old one. In essence, the New Covenant is superior because it is based on better promises through a superior priest, Christ, and on His superior once-for-all-time sacrifice. The Passover is a figure of Christ, the true Lamb that takes away sin forever.

5. The Old Testament is a book containing shadows or figures that anticipate the promised seed of Abraham, Christ. In figure and ceremony, the Old Testament taught believers to expect a greater one to come who would bring a greater deliverance (for example, Lamech named his son Noah, saying, 'This one will give us rest from our work and from the toil of our hands arising from the ground which the Lord has cursed' [Gen. 5:29]. Noah proved to be a failed Messiah figure, but one eventually came who did not fail!). The Old Testament progressively reveals two things: first, details about who this

person would be; and, second, the description of how that person would accomplish the redemption, resulting in rest.

6. The New Testament tells us that the one promised in the Old Testament has come on behalf of His people (John 1:14). He is the long-anticipated one. First, it tells us who this one is, Jesus Christ the Lord (Matt. 1:21, 23). Second, the New Testament tells us that He did what was foretold of Him.

7. The gospels and the epistles of the New Testament tell us what Jesus accomplished and is doing now to return mankind toward a new garden; Revelation describes its completion. All the nations will be blessed in Abraham through his greater Son, who will reign over all peoples forever. Thus, the Old Testament is a book of shadows; the New Testament is a book of light. What was enfolded in the Old Testament is unfolded in the New Testament; what was promised in the Old has been revealed to a fuller degree in the gospels and epistles and completely in the Revelation.

8. The Revelation tells us how time will end. When Christ comes again, He will destroy His enemies and welcome His children into a final, forever rest. That period is the time of the ultimate fulfillment of the promises given after the fall of mankind (Gen. 3:15) and, more clearly, to Abraham (Gen. 12:1-3). To this day we 'see through a glass darkly', but in a future day we will see more clearly; yet the shadows are fading. The gospels and the epistles are filled with fulfillment and anticipation. Salvation has come; sin has been judged, but it has not been removed.

9. The Bible envisions three eras of history; scholars commonly speak of the Old Testament era, the New Testament era, and the kingdom; or, a period that was, a period that is, and a period that will be. Hebrews 1:1 speaks of a time long ago when God spoke 'to the fathers in the prophets' ('the times of ignorance,' Acts 17:30) and 'in these last days'. In the Hebrews passage, the writer is indicating that the Jews thought of only two ages: the former times and the latter times. They thought they were living in the former times, because they did not think the 'latter times' had come in the spiritualized kingdom inaugurated by Jesus. The 'latter times' are divided into two parts: the time between Christ's two advents and a period of His full, perfect reign after His

second coming. Hebrews 9:10 refers to the final phase of the 'last days' as the 'time of the reformation' or 'consummation of all things' (9:26). Peter, in his sermon recorded by Luke (Acts 3:19-24), says that the prophets from Samuel announced 'these days', the latter days, and that Jesus will not return to earth 'until the period of the restoration of all things' (v. 21), or the latter part of the latter days. The Jews envisioned only two eras in all of history, the former days, and the latter days, the promise of Messiah and the advent of Messiah. They saw that the Messiah would reign politically and religiously, but not be crucified and resurrected. They did not see the latter days in two parts with Messiah reigning most fully at its end.

10. The Bible has one central theme, the restoration of all things. The central motif in the Scriptures is creation and recreation. The Bible begins with a divinely created garden (Gen. 1–2), an image of the divine filling of all things. It ends with a restored creation, a new garden (Rev. 21–22). The Bible describes how the spoiled 'garden' (Gen. 3) is restored. That restoration will come about through the fulfillment of the promise to Abraham (Gen. 12, 15, 17) of a 'land, seed, and blessing.' Christ came in the first advent to accomplish the redemption, creating a new garden paradise; He is now building that garden (reversing the effects of the fall) and will bring it to fruition at His second coming when all creation will rejoice.

11. The storyline of the Bible can be conceived as a cone lying on its side with increased disclosures of redemptive knowledge as you progress from the 'tip' of the cone in Genesis 1 to the opening of the cone in Revelation 22.

• • • • •

It is a 'last hour' in that many opponents of Christ are appearing, though their appearance only anticipates the 'last of the last hours' when 'Antichrist',[1] the 'man of lawlessness' (II Thess. 2:3), the 'Beast' (Rev. 13), will appear. The nuance of the term 'antichrist' is more than simply one that opposes Christ; it is one that seeks to replace Christ. He, and his

---

1. The article does not appear before the noun here ['the Antichrist'], but it does in 2:22; 4:3; and II John 7.

minions, stand in antithesis to the true Christ throughout all of the 'last days'. John is unmistakably identifying his opponents with the antichrist figure (2:26).

It seems that some expected the momentary coming of the Lord (John 21:23; II Thess. 2:1-12), a misapprehension by both John and Paul's audiences ('momentary' and 'immediate' are not synonymous concepts). As stated above, the 'last hour' can be any time, since we do not know when the era will end. Every 'last hour' that passes is a shadowed fulfillment of the 'last hour' that will come. Opponents of Christ appear always, arising in every decade of the history of the Lord's people, and each prefigures the final one.

2. The failure of false teachers: sustained (vv. 19-23)

(a) Their origin (v. 19)

It is clear now that John's opponents once gathered with the community of believers, but had departed over teachings they embraced and cultivated to the fracturing of the peace of the church. Their errors seemed to arise over a misappropriation of the benefits of Christ's death, advocating a form of victory over the struggle with sin not warranted by the apostles' teaching (II John 9). Actually, it may be more accurate to say that they rejected the apostolic interpretation of the person and accomplishments of Jesus, not believing that He was 'the Christ', viewing Jesus as a man who revealed the way to God by His moral example. Says Boice: '…it becomes clear from the context that John is thinking of a confession of Christ's full divinity. It is the belief that God became incarnate in Jesus as the Christ' (72). They left the church of their own volition, but proved an unsettling force. John writes that abiding in the apostles' teaching is a sign of true faithfulness. The disturbers were never really a part of the assembly of saints in profession of faith. Continuance is a test of reality. Sadly, and likely not coincidentally, John uses the same verb for the departure of the secessionists that he used of Judas' departure from the Upper Room on the night of Jesus' betrayal (John 13:30). For additional comment, see the commentary on II John 9.

The proof of the heterodoxy of the opponents is in their failure to abide; their failure in this regard is evidenced by

their departure. Continuance in the apostles' doctrine is proof
of the possession of the apostles' doctrine. The implication
of this verse ('they were not of us,' 'they do not belong to
us') is made explicit in the following verse; they are devoid
of the Spirit.

(b) The contrast (v. 20)
It is quite possible that these false teachers claimed to have
secret knowledge or a special endowment from God that
afforded them insights unavailable to ordinary Christians.
John says that the truth of which he is writing is available
and known by all Christians ('you all know'). Says Law:
'He writes because they know the truth. His aim is not to
instruct their ignorance, but to arouse them to realize the
significance of their knowledge… quicken their senses of the
irreconcilable opposition of truth and falsehood…' (109).

The meaning of 'anointing from the Holy One' is the most
difficult phrase in the verse. There are only three occurrences
of this particular noun in the New Testament and they are in
this chapter (2:20, 27 [twice]); however, the verbal form occurs
five times. Once the verb is used metaphorically (Heb. 1:9) and
the other four occurrences mention the Holy Spirit (Luke 4:18;
Acts 4:17; 10:38; II Cor. 1:21-22). Whatever the anointing consists
of, it is something that all Christians possess, it is involved in
the concept of abiding (v. 27), and it is granted by the Spirit.
The result of receiving this anointing is an intuitive knowledge,
which in the context of the passage is Christological in content.
It seems to me that John is talking about the inward reception
and acknowledgement of the apostles' message about Christ
and eternal life given to each and every Christian by the
Spirit. You might call it a 'built-in spiritual instinct'. In 2:27
the 'anointing' is about intellectual content or knowledge that
requires no human instruction to obtain. I take it to be the
Spirit's witness to who Jesus is and what He accomplished
for us on the cross; it comes with the inward reception of the
gospel message. It may be the same as the reference to 'seed'
within us in 3:9. We are told in 3:24 and 4:13 that the Spirit has
been given to us. Thus, the meaning of the phrase, most likely,
has to do with the Spirit's indwelling and teaching ministry
toward us concerning Christ and His redemption.

It seems specifically that within the Holy Scriptures the 'anointing' here is most likely an allusion drawn from Jeremiah 31:31-35, the New Covenant: 'I will put My law within them, and on their heart I will write them…for they all shall know Me from the least of them to the greatest…' In that passage there is a direct statement as to the inward workings of God; the result of the anointing will be a sphere of universal knowledge within all believers and this knowledge does not require a human voice of instruction. One scholar has written: 'John reminds his readers that they are members of the new covenant community and therefore do not need a teacher who has put himself in a special place of authority (in the likeness of the tribal representative teachers of the old covenant) by appealing to some special revelation or knowledge' (Bass, 109).

The word 'all' has been quite thoroughly discussed because a textual variance allows it to be read in two ways. Should the text be read: 'you know *all things*' or 'you *all* know,' a statement of the breadth of knowing or a statement of the common knowledge of an audience? The weight of the evidence seems to be in favor of the first reading since in every occurrence of the verb 'to know' in John's gospel and letters it is always followed by a direct object. This would make it the more difficult reading, and generally the reading chosen in disputes like this. However, the latter reading seems to fit the immediate context better, as well as the allusion to the Jeremiah passage. I do not know that we have the data to come to more than a probable answer.

If the anointing is the indwelling or gift of the Spirit of God in His teaching, revealing capacity, who is the 'Holy One' who is the cause of the anointing? Three factors make it apparent that the 'Holy One' is a reference to Jesus Christ. First, John refers to Jesus with this title (Rev. 3:7) and as the 'Holy One of God' (John 6:69). Second, in 2:27, a second reference to anointing, the pronouns most clearly refer to Jesus. Third, John tells us in the gospel that Jesus sent the Holy Spirit (15:26; 16:7).

(c) Their teaching (vv. 21-23)
We can see the apostle's confidence in verse 21. A double negative ('not…not') emphasizes the point that John is

strenuously pressing the differences between the teachings of the secessionists and that of the apostles. He is clear that his audience can discern the difference. The most significant discussion in this verse is how to understand the three occurrences of the term 'that' or 'because'. As such, there is no direct object of the verb, 'have written.' It would seem best, therefore, either to take the first two in a causal sense and the third as expressive of content ('have written... that') or to take all three as indicating content ('that'). In this sense John is not stating two reasons and a fact, but three facts. This seems preferable and is parallel with the way John concludes the letter (5:18-20). Says Marshall: 'The writer is not giving instruction to his readers because of their ignorance (after all they have the anointing) but because he can build on the fact of their knowledge of the truth' (156, n. 28).

The error of the false teachers is addressed in verse 22. This is the first instance in the letter that John specifically explains their errors concerning Christ; it appears that in 1:6–2:2 he alluded to the implications of their perverted Christology and later identified their moral deficiencies, but here he extends his criticism of them. They are adversaries of Christ, the one his readers know intuitively; what they are doing is replacing the true Christ with a false one (the meaning of 'antichrist' is not only one who opposes, but seeks to promote an alternative 'Christ').

John connects together in this verse 'liar' and 'antichrist'. The false teachers are designated as 'antichrist' because they prefigure or foreshadow the 'Antichrist,' 'Beast' (Rev. 13), 'man of lawlessness' (II Thess. 2) figure of the last of the 'last days'. The phrase, 'the one who denies that Jesus is the Christ,' has caused enormous discussion. While these teachers seem to have affirmed the historic Jesus-figure, they denied His redemptive role, His divine substitutionary atoning work. While they affirmed His benefit, it seems, they disagreed on its nature, teaching that Jesus is a restorer of moral propriety through some unstated means (and supporting their claims based on some suggested higher spiritual insights). Another way to say this is that they denied that Jesus came from heaven to reveal to us the way of redemption and, by so doing, rejected the notion that Jesus is the Christ who came to show us eternal life by being our righteousness through the shedding of His blood to appease a righteous God for our sins. The error of these teachers is that they sought to deprive Jesus Christ of His uniqueness; to them He was a man that revealed the ways of God, not the God/man who came from God to reveal Himself as the way to God.

'Jesus' is our Lord's earthly name (Matt. 1:21); it means deliverer and is equivalent to 'Joshua' of the Hebrew Scriptures (Joshua was a foreshadow of Jesus). 'Christ' is the Hebrew equivalent of 'Messiah' meaning 'the Anointed One.' These titles have deep covenantal and redemptive nuances (Jesus is the promised one who came to deliver or save us!). As the terms 'Christ' and 'Son' speak of the same person, the terms 'Son' and 'Father' clearly affirm the ontological relationship between the two (distinct in redemptive roles and yet one in characteristics). These false teachers claimed to know God, but not through Jesus who is also the Christ. Jesus' role in their notion of redemption was that of an insightful prophet and moralist. To deny the identity of the Son with the Father is not to know the Father because Jesus came to reveal the Father to us (John 1:18).

The false teachers' doom is mentioned in verse 23. Since only Jesus has access to the very presence of God, and because of His unique knowledge, He alone can reveal the Father to us. Knowledge of God is only and exclusively available through the Son of God! Here is the apostle's clearest declaration that his secessionist opponents are not truly believers. It is simply impossible to know God in any other way than through Jesus, who is the Christ (John 14:6). Calvin's ability to write with literary clarity is wonderfully evident when he says that 'There is no right confession of God without the Father being acknowledged in the Son' (46).

3. The instruction to believers (vv. 24-27)

At this point John adds to his argument moral exhortation. The reoccurring word, 'abides' (five times), indicates the emphasis of the section; it is applicative rather than declarative. 'Continuance in,' 'residing in,' 'remaining in' the things of God is evidence of the possession of the things of God. Twice John speaks of what the believers had been taught from 'the beginning' (v. 24), clearly a reference to the apostles' teachings (1:1-4). John does not imply by his exhortation to continue in the apostles' teachings that a true believer can walk away from faith in Jesus as the false teachers have done, that redemption is somehow contingent upon continuance in the things of Christ. He is saying that we should continue in His ways and not follow those who say they have found better insights, but do so by denying the fundamentals of Christian faith. A true believer can suffer from the disturbing effects of momentary, temporal confusion; John's exhortations are about this stifling spiritual possibility, not suggesting by doing so that salvation can be lost.

No one, I would imagine, would teach that the eleven disoriented apostles that remained after Judas' departure were not beloved of Jesus. In our Lord's great prayer on the night of His betrayal He asked the Father to keep them through the turbulence ahead ('Holy Father, keep them in your name… I have guarded them' [John 17:11]. Though it would be unwarranted to think that Jesus would not have His prayer answered, therefore the disciples' keeping would be unquestionable, He exhorted the true apostles to abide or remain faithful ('Abide in me' [15:4]).

Moral exhortation and certainty are not antithetical. When God ordains an end, such as the security of all who believe in Him through His Son, He ordains means unto the end as well. The fact of means, in this case the presence of commands, is the human sphere of the ways of God. Human beings are not robots, the subject of forced determinism; we all have choices that must be made. To reveal right options, we have been given the commands of God. That we surrender our wills to His is evidence that the one we cherish more than ourselves is of greater value in shaping our lives than ourselves. Again the false teachers did not continue in the apostles' teachings because they found something more appealing than Jesus, who is the Christ, and thus demonstrated that they had never truly encountered Him. To embrace the greatest of all loveliness means never again to be deceived habitually by lesser loves!

Another way of thinking through the apparent dilemma of certainty and yet exhortation is an insight of Calvin's. He suggests that God commands us to do certain things so that we would recognize our helplessness and inability within ourselves and seek the guiding, protective enablement of the Spirit. While God speaks outside of us through His Word, the Spirit speaks through His indwelling presence to remind us of the right path and to dissuade us from a temporary deviation from it. We have been given two wonderful sources for our strengthening: the witness of God through His Word and the witness of the Spirit in our very beings. Clearly the written Word and the Spirit are always in agreement (John 17:17; I John 5:7).

John's readers are exhorted by him to continue in sound doctrine (vv. 24-26). In verse 24, he turns to speak to his readers as a whole, the 'you' being plural, resuming comments following the 'you' of 2:20. The command 'to remain or abide' occurs three times in this verse. The initial two refer to the apostles' teachings, the third refers to the unbreakable relationship that one possesses through being in the Son and the Father. The phrase, 'if what you heard,' is a repetition of the previous sentence in the verse and functions to emphasize John's point. 'If' does not imply uncertainty in this case, but certainty (if you remain, you will abide); it is about assurance of life through Jesus into fellowship (life) with the Father.

The word translated 'promise' in verse 25 only occurs in John's writings here, though it is found over fifty times in the New Testament. The context makes it clear that the meaning has to do with the content of the promise, not the act of promising. The content of the promise is the fact of eternal life through Jesus Christ.

Does the pronoun, emphatic by being doubled ('He Himself), refer to the Father or to Jesus? Most scholars seem to agree that it refers to the latter since the context surrounding it is about Jesus. The promise of Jesus is eternal life, which is synonymous with 'fellowship', knowing God, and abiding in and with Christ. Clearly, the promise of eternal life is connected to abiding, a quality of life his readers possess (5:12, 20).

One of John's purposes in writing is to prevent the destructive intrusion of the secessionists (v. 26); 'these things' likely refers to what John has written in the letter. The repetition signified by 'I am writing' is a literary device to emphasize his point.

In verse 27, John urges his readers to continue in submission to the Spirit. As in 2:20, the anointing refers to the indwelling ministry of the Holy Spirit. The phrase, 'from Him,' refers to Jesus, as stated previously (2:25), indicating from whom the Spirit is sent (John 15:27; 16:7). The abiding/indwelling/ anointing ministry of the Spirit is the believer's ground of assurance.

Scholars are not settled on whether the verse ends with a command or a simple statement of fact ('abide' or 'you abide…'). If an imperative, the exhortation should not be read as indicating the possibility that a true believer might choose not to abide or remain; instead it is a call to stay on the correct path and not be victimized by the false teachers. If a statement of fact, it emphasizes the reality of their assurance. 'Abide' in the imperative mood does appear in the next verse, making it unlikely to be an imperative here. Further, a statement of fact seems to have a stronger contextual warrant because the immediate emphasis is upon assurance, not duty.

There are some things we do not need earthly instructors to teach us because the source of the teaching comes immediately to us, as the redeemed children of God, by the Spirit of God. Earthly ideas may make something appear true, but only God can make it real in our innermost being. The 'all things' has to be an example of a restrictive 'all'. It is all things about the salvation that we possess in Christ. Clearly, the presence of a wide diversity of opinion over some religious matters (for example, the meaning of the presence of Christ in the Lord's Table or the continuation of certain spiritual gifts) is evidence that the Spirit has not revealed everything to all of us.

What can we learn from this section?
(1) The fact that we continue in the gospel message, however maligned by those who think it is foolish, is evidence that God has done a gracious work in our hearts (see John 6:66-68). It is not our smiles, experiences, position, or our words; it is our actions that are the truest barometer of spiritual life. Outward behavior reveals our understanding of what we most value

since the origin or motive for action is the heart, the innermost faculty of our souls.

(2) Leaving the apostles' teaching has dire consequences. However, it surely does not suggest that the promise that Jesus made to His children, the promise of eternal life, can be forfeited by human dereliction or by a change of mind on God's part; a divine promise is a surety. Therefore, when a person who once professed faith in the Savior subsequently adopts a habitually calloused, uncaring attitude toward the things of God, we can say that the individual had never received the Spirit's teaching ministry and consequently is not a believer, nor ever has been. Notice I did not say that leaving a particular church is a sign of unbelief, that struggling with sin is a sign of unbelief, or that temporal spiritual failure is a sign of unbelief or lostness; the evidence of lostness is durative, insensitive, and brazen callousness to the things of God.

(3) Eternal life is the promise held out to believers by God. It was the message which Jesus revealed to us throughout His life, which was procured in His death, and which is guaranteed by the resurrection, and which is now awaiting complete fulfillment when He comes once more to judge the world and reign fully among His people. This message is embodied, as has been made plain in I John 1:2, in the Son of God who is the center and circumference of the message.

(4) Can a person make a false claim saying he/she knows God and at the same time reject the person and work of God's Son? 'There is no other name given among men whereby we must be saved' (Acts 4:12). Salvation is only through Christ or it is not at all. Further, one can make no valid claim that he knows God if he rejects the person of His Son. According to the witness of Jesus to the apostles, a message conveyed by them to us, Jesus is the only way to God. A person can possess commendable moral qualities without Jesus, but they cannot possess the life of God except through Christ.

(5) Actions are a true barometer of the validity of our confession when combined with faith; they are false claims when lacking the evidence of action. The mark of the saints is that they remain, abide, reside in the apostles' teachings and hence know God, which results in eternal life and fellowship. The infusion of the love of God at our

redemption, the beholding of the magnificent beauty of our Redeemer, is so life-changing that it alters our priorities with ravishing delight in the object of them, the great God of heaven known only through the Lord Jesus. Such a spiritual experience alters our behavior. Because God is love, and we are given the life of God, we intuitively love those about us. Because God is love, and we are given the life of God, we intuitively depart from those who would turn us away from such great love.

C. The test of moral purity (2:28–4:6)

Scholars debate whether or not verses 28-29 should be read as concluding the previous section or introducing a new one (some see 2:28–3:3 as a parenthesis, meaning they cannot envision it as belonging to either what has preceded or what follows). An indication that the writer is introducing a change of subject in the letter is that he moves from the declarative and cautionary to the positive and exhortatory. Further, the words 'and now' suggest a new topic in John's literary style. The reoccurrence of 'children' in verse 18 seems parallel to 'little children' in verse 28 in introducing a new section. It seems that John's emphasis moves away from the grounds of assurance, though this can still be detected, to dealing with the believers' response to the false teaching of the secessionists. Also, John does use the words, 'last hour,' to refer to the end of times rather than the time between the advents, as noted below. Says Brown, 'In 2:19 the author wrote about the revelation of the Antichrists in the last hour, here he writes about the revelation of Christ' (380).

1. The basis of a life of purity: Hope (2:28-29)

(a) It provides confidence at His coming (v. 28)
The verb, 'abide' (remain, reside), in form can be rendered as a statement of fact or as an imperative (as in the previous verse). In keeping with the context of exhortation in this portion of the letter, it would appear that we should read the word as a command. John seems to want to forestall any further inroads by the false teachers. Continuance in the message of the apostles through Christ about God will

cause us to delight in the coming of Christ at the end of the age. We will not be shamed at His coming, but welcomed home!

John began the previous section with a reference to the 'Last Days' and returns to the same theme. However, there is a difference in nuance. He shifts from a general description of adversaries arising as characteristic of the period between Christ's two advents, the Last Days, to the last of the 'Last Days' when the Lord will return and crush the Antichrist in the Final Judgment, as opposed to the many antichrists in our days who are only prefigurements of him. The word that John uses here, translated as 'coming', is only found here in Johannine literature, though over twenty times in the New Testament.

There is a subtle word play in the Greek language; the word for 'confidence' and 'coming' sound quite similar to the ear. This appears as no accident. The return of Christ for the believer should engender great hope, delight, and confidence. Also, John may be suggesting that for the false teachers the opposite will be true when the apostles' message receives its final confirmation.

(b) It provides evidence that we are His (v. 29)
John's point is simply that fruit is related to a cause since a consequence partakes of the nature of its origin. 'As the root, so the fruit' or, perhaps, more apropos in this context, 'like father, like son,' are truisms. This is the second time that Jesus is referred to as 'righteous' (cf. 2:1), John using the same description for the Father also (1:9). Christ and God the Father share the same character qualities. This appears to have been denied by the false teachers who envisioned Jesus as only a superior human being. In context, the word 'righteous' refers to actions or behavior, again a not-so-subtle rebuke of the secessionists. In contrast, the believers 'know' him because they have remained in the apostles' teachings; 'know' in John means the possession of something as a fact revealed in experience (this word reflects a dominate theme in the letter appearing some forty-two times). The form of the verb 'know' can be read as either a statement of fact, or as an indicative, or as an imperative, a command. Rendering

the verb as an indicative is preferable since knowledge is something that John assumes of his readers (2:3, 5, 20, 21; 3:16, 19, 24; 4:2, 13; 5:2).

While antecedents of pronouns are difficult to determine in the letter at times, the pronoun in the phrase 'is born of Him' clearly refers to God the Father. This tells us that the Father is the one who brings us into God's family through the provision of the Son as applied by the Spirit.

2. A parenthesis: The love of God (3:1-3)

These verses form a parenthesis in John's argument, though there is a connection with 2:28-29 through the similarity of themes such as Christ's coming and moral purity. The comment that believers are children of God seems to fill John with such awe that he pauses to comment on the wonder of the implications of the Lord's return for them. It is as though the apostle loses himself in praise! Again, John may unwittingly be drawing a contrast between the abiding believer and the yet-to-be-judged false teachers.

Though John had once possessed a thunderous personality, willing to call fire down from heaven on Jesus' detractors (Luke 9:54) and still viewing life through several sharp contrastive dichotomies, he could also be called the 'Apostle of Love'. The word 'love' is found forty-four times in the gospel and forty-six times in this letter (in chapter 3 there are nine occurrences and in chapter 4 there are twenty-seven). Yarbrough makes some wonderful comments on the word. Love, in this instance, the manifest of 'God's love toward us and in us, is beyond compare because of its consequences; it makes us the children of God. The magnanimousness of love, its expansive grandeur, is seen in its purpose; it brings us into a new family. And, the greatness of this love is revealed in its quality; it stands in sharp, superior contrast to any other love' (175-76). The final stanza of William R. Newell's poem, 'At Calvary' (1895), captures the thought.

> Oh, the love that drew salvation's plan!
> Oh, the grace that brought it down to man!
> Oh, the mighty gulf that God did span
> At Calvary!

(a) The cause (v. 1)
The verse is composed of two sentences. The first is complex, being composed of a sentence with an explanatory clause attached to it, and the second sentence is straightforward, stating a reason. The clause explains the ground for John's statement that the believers are loved of God. The love that God has for them is proven by His mercies in redeeming them, allowing them to participate in His family ('and *such* we are'). Being in the family of God is an established fact for these people (this is a mightily comforting statement for a people shocked by those who once had been trusted teachers but who betrayed them – when the emphasis is upon perfection, or moral victory over daily struggles with sins, there is the consistent danger of overstatement, a promise of too much. There seems also to be an accompanying emphasis on idealized performance that minimizes reality by providing a redefining of sin).

It is interesting that the phrase 'children of God' occurs for the first time in the letter (3:2, 10; 5:2 also), which fits the more congenial hortatory tone of this portion of the letter. Unlike the apostle Paul, John does not refer to the believers as 'sons of God'; 'son' is only used for Jesus in relationship to the Father. Thus, the particular use of this term is unique to the apostle.

Because the child of God is born from above ('for this reason'), the world of unbelievers simply does not, nor can, understand believers. Each believer has experienced a sphere of reality, which is much more profound in its significance and beauty than the world of a blighted creation (Gen. 3). Unless one is 'born from above', to use the phrase of the Nicodemus account (John 3:3), she/he remains in a world that does not fathom Christians, they being at best shrouded in an obtuse mystery. Thus, unbelievers find believers somewhat odd; being ignorant of God the Father through Jesus, they are ignorant of His people.

(b) The realization (v. 2)
This verse is particularly intriguing in light of John's opponents who claimed some type or stage of perfectionism in the Christian life. His point is that only when Jesus appears (2:28) will perfectionism become a reality. Thus, he is not denying

the perfection of the believer, but he places it in the future, not the 'now', which is 'the not yet'. It is also interesting that 'shall be' is a future passive, meaning that what we will be will be entirely a work of God and not of human cooperative endeavor. Since believers are called God's children in the verse, the most likely referent of the pronoun is to God the Father (when John refers to Jesus he commonly refers to Him as 'that one' ['that' and 'that one' are different words]).

The term 'whenever', here and in 2:28, does not suggest equivocation as to the fact of the Lord's coming; it suggests that the time is unrevealed. The 'because' states the reason that 'we shall be like Him'. It is then, and only then, that we shall be clothed in His righteousness experientially with completeness. John seems to be saying that the not-yet experience of imperfection will end when we stand in His, the Father's, presence. The reason that we 'shall be like Him' is that a transformation will take place when this mortal existence shall put on immortality, when death ends and true life begins (remember, we live in a shadowed land at best, yet not forever!). Isaac Watts' poem, 'Behold the amazing Gift' (1709), captures the thrill of the experience of our final deliverance.

> Behold the' amazing gift of love,
> The Father hath bestowed
> On us, the sinful sons of men,
> To call us sons of God!
>
> Concealed as yet this honour lies,
> By dark world unbeknown,
> A world that knew not when He came,
> E'en God's eternal Son.
>
> High is the rank we now possess,
> But higher we shall rise,
> Though what we shall here-after be,
> Is hid from mortal eyes:
>
> Our souls, we know when God appears,
> Shall bear His image bright;
> For then His glory as it is,
> Shall open to our sight.

(c) The result (v. 3)
Those who have the hope (a word that only appears here in Johannine literature) of seeing God someday in all His glorious righteousness, those whose affections have been turned in that direction, begin immediately to conform to that ideal, however unsuccessful they may be. John appears to be confronting again the false teachers who claimed that sin for the believer is inconsequential. The concept of 'purifies' means to set apart for holy use. The instance of regeneration or rebirth commences a renovating process, called sanctification, a setting apart. Jesus came to reveal the Father to us (John 1:18), but that is not all. Not only did He make it possible for us to possess the life of God now and forever, Jesus is also our pattern for conforming us to the character of God now. 'Just as' should not be understood as a stage that can be obtained in this life (1:5–2:2), but as the goal of our striving in this life since we have been granted an expanded perception of reality and a new set of priorities and regulative principles.

Parenthesis 20: Sin, redemption, and the believer
The subjective experience of redemption involves the perception of the ultimate beauty and congruity of the perfections of God revealed by the Spirit, a focus on Christ as merciful in His provision of life, and grounded in the will of the Father who had sent His Son for us. While beyond description, having only finite words to describe it, it is an encounter with the triune God resulting in our being ravished by His character and, having a taste of divine glory, the believer experiences a transformation relative in priorities, delights, and designs. While the dominion of sin, its total and unrelenting dominance, has been crushed forever, the remnants of its once universality remain. Sin grieves the saints, filling them with longing for their final redemption, and longing for greater progress in conforming their lives to God's standard.

It is an instantaneous, miraculous event that creates a Christ-follower. All Christians are disciples; that is, they are followers. Sanctification is not the root of divine forgiveness, but forgiveness infallibly results in progressive sanctification.

No one can claim that they belong to God, if they do not long for continued transformation by God! While God is discriminatory when it comes to choosing upon whom He would reveal His saving truth (infusion being the life of God into our very beings), He seems also to grant degrees of sanctification relative to our struggles with sin. What is a 'thorn in the flesh' to one person may not be an issue with others; we all have our sets of issues. A particular circumstance may be an occasion to sin that it may not be in other contexts. The struggle we have with sin is evidence that we belong to a new master and that we have different priorities and affections because of this altered orientation.

• • • • •

3. The characteristics of a life of purity: Righteousness and love (vv. 4-13)

John is making the point that a life of sinfulness and the profession of Christian life are incompatible. While Christians sin, some more than others, but only at times (lacking in consistency of callousness), they are not characterized by it (2:1). It is something they regret doing and take no delight in it after the false illusion of any benefit disappears through the accumulation of guilt greater than any gain they might have obtained. To realize that temporary advantage has come at the cost of offending the greatest object of one's affections turns the 'advantage' into a grotesque abhorrence.

Stott has made the acute observation that this section of the letter contains a series of stark, unequivocal statements (121-22). Six of these begin with 'everyone who,' 'everyone that,' or 'no one' (2:29; 3:4, 6a, 6b, 9, 10b) and three times the phrase 'the one who' appears (3: 7b, 8, 10c). These references mark out John's use of universal statements as a favored literary device.

(a) The fact of the contrary (vv. 4-7)

To sustain the point that righteousness and love characterize Christians, John begins with a description of what does not characterize them, sin. Sin is the failure to practice the law of love, the 'old/new commandment' (2:7-11). It is interesting that the only travesty that John states specifically of his opponents is their failure to love. However, the root of the error is the failure to understand the person and accomplishments of Christ, as well as the transforming reality of beholding the beauty of God and understanding the reality of divine forgiveness. The false teachers chose to know God another way (or at least claimed they did), not as revealed through Jesus Christ, which was no way at all! Love is the outward evidence of an inward invisible reality. That inward, invisible reality is the result of the mercy of God in sending to us an atoning, substitutionary sacrifice. Thus, a failure to love is the result of having no knowledge of God through His divine Son, the Christ. Love, salvation, Christ, God the Father, and the Holy Spirit are distinguishable, but not separable! This is the fatal error of John's opponents.

John states *a universal truth* in verse 4. Clearly he has his opponents in mind when he makes a reference to 'everyone'. A lack of love (consideration or care of others) is a violation of the law of love. The opponents, by manifesting intolerance for the believers, as well as their moral indifference (that sin does not really matter for the Christian because of Christ's victory) and schismatic performance, live apart from the law of love or in lawlessness. Calvin made the same point when writing, 'Probably there were those at that time who extenuated their vices by this kind of flattery: "It is no wonder that we sin because we are human; but there is a great difference between sin and iniquity"' (54). The standard by which love is to be defined is the character of God (4:8, 16) and modeled for us in the self-giving of Jesus (3:16); the dutiful expression of love for the believer is found in 3:17-18.

How are we to understand 'lawlessness' in this verse? Does it refer to one who breaks the Law, the Mosaic Code? Is it about law and law-keeping (Paul uses the term this way in Romans 4:7)? Ironically, John does not use the term 'law' in this letter, and 'lawlessness' only occurs here in his writings, so such an interpretation seems contextually unexpected. Further, John never accuses his opponents of opposing the Mosaic Law or of living frivolously. They obviously are accused of violating the 'law's' intent, the promotion of love. For John, the 'law' is the law of love, a charge that he brings against the secessionists. Lawlessness, indifferentism, is how

John defines sin, which he in turn defines as a lack of love in social relationships.

John makes *an appeal* in verse 5. The emphasis on the word 'know' throughout the letter may be an indication that the false teachers claimed to be privy to information unavailable to the 'ordinary' Christian and to follow them is to enter into a superior religious experience with God. John desires his readers to know that they actually do possess an adequate knowledge of God through the abiding presence of the Spirit (3:24; 4:13; 5:7).

The purpose for the appearing of Christ was to remove sins. If the false teachers claimed that sin really no longer mattered (1:6–2:2), in this statement John would be addressing the central error of his opponents. Sin does, indeed, matter in one's relationship to God, the holy God, but it has been dealt with in the merciful sacrifice of Christ on our behalf. The fact that 'sins' is plural has led some to understand that the nature of the transgressions here is of the common and frequent variety.

The latter part of the compound sentence ('and in Him there is no sin') likely suggests that the secessionists taught that Jesus was not sinless at the time of His appearing, but reached a stage of perfection and thus became something of a model of it for us. John here is asserting that Christ was always perfectly sinless and that is why He could deal with our plight. It seems that these opponents taught a progressive perfectionism, defined away the true nature of sin, and thought of Jesus as a paradigmatic ideal to emulate, seeing the triumph of His death as the penultimate instance of His purity and selflessness (how many today only see in Jesus the best in all of us, if we would dig deep enough into our inner selves? 'To discover the real "you" is to find "Jesus" personified, without a cross!').

John provides *a logical deduction* in verse 6. With a surface reading of this verse ('no one who abides in Christ sins'), as well as 3:9 ('no one who is born of God practices sin') and 5:18 ('no one born of God sins'), you have the shock of what appears to be a serious contradiction. Calvin made the opposite point succinctly, 'No one can boast of having a clean heart' (66). John repeatedly has made the claim that the Christian struggles with sin, a truth challenged by his opponents (1:8, 10). 'If anyone sins, we have an advocate...' (2:2). Though scholars have approached this verse from various perspectives (the 'notorious crimes' view [Christians are incapable of the worst of errors], a distinction between ordinary and obedient Christians [a radical division into sets of independent characteristics, the carnal and spiritual states], a descriptive view [John is speaking philosophically, not realistically], or a willful or deliberate sin view [sin here being defined as the opposite of acts of omission]), it seems there are two sensible solutions (one hinging on the present tense of a verb and the other on the context). The most serious problem with seeing two-types-at-times of Christians (when we obey or are 'abiding' we do not sin, though a temporal state for all of us) is that John's polarities in the letter are between light/darkness, believers/unbelievers, and redeemed/lost; he does not speak of states of Christian behavior in the book.

A view that seems to have serious contextual warrant is the notorious sin view, but with a unique qualification or restriction. In the context of 3:6, 9 the discussion is about the possession and manifestation of love as the unique charac-teristic of the life of God, who is love, in the believer and its absence in the unbeliever, the false professor of divine life. So, the sin a Christian cannot commit is the failure to love, loving being the manifestation of the life of God, the character of God, implanted in our very beings by the possession of the Spirit of God who is divine love possessed. A Christ follower by definition is one who has come into possession of the life of God. Since God is love, and they have come to participate in the life of God, the manifestation of love is as an intrinsic and natural act as it is in God himself. They cannot not love! Support for the view is several fold. First, love is a major theme in the letter (the word appears some forty-two times in the letter). Second, it is only the sin, the failure to love, that John explicitly applies to his opponents as evidence that they are false representatives of the apostles' message de-rived from Jesus (2:4-5; 3:10-12, 14-15, 17-18; 4:20-21). Third, in the immediate context, John draws the contrast between love and hatred in the Cain/Abel episode making the point that Cain did what he did because he did not possess the love of God. Fourth, the term 'love' appears in this section nine times and in chapter 4 twenty-three times suggesting that John's blunt antitheses is in view with no middle ground or qualification. In his polemical confrontation, John sees not shades, qualifications, or nuances. Everyone who is born of God loves because they possess the character of God through the Spirit of God's indwelling presence.

However, the difficulty with this approach is that it does not match reality in the Christian's life. If all sin is a failure to love, and we all sin, as John makes evident, then we are unbelievers unless the issue is temporal instances as opposed to steady, habitual patterns. Christians are capable of hatred, non-loving of others, as the Scriptures abundantly suggest by the observation of such behavioral patterns and the many serious warnings to desist from such action (redemption does not cure the maladies of our human nature, death does!). In other words, I do not see how the notorious-sin view is an advance in understanding such stark absolutes.

Others have taken the perspective that the verb, 'sin,' being in the present tense, denotes continuous action ('practices'). Thus, Christians are folks who sin, but not with a heartless, habitual disregard for God and His holiness (the presence of struggle in the Christian's life, knowing that such action is offensive to the holy, benevolent character of the God who immeasurably lavishes grace upon them, is itself an evidence of the mercy of God in one's life). Instead of calloused continuance, we confess our shortcomings (1:9). The reason for our lack of habitual sinning is the Holy Spirit (3:9) and the protective mercies of God (5:18). The major support for this view is at least three fold: first, the tense of the verb can support the idea, though not strongly, of habitual action. Second, the view seems to have contextual support answering the apparent contradiction with cogency. Third, the view has theological and biblical support from many passages of Holy Scripture that suggest the reality of the believers' struggle (Rom. 7:14-25), and which is evidenced by behavior patterns of believers within Scripture (the inconsistency observed in King David's sins, yet he is said to be a man after God's own heart), as well as the many exhortations to curb aberrancy in all of us.

The weaknesses of the view, however, are several. First, it places more weight than perhaps is warranted on a verbal tense, that is, that the present tense implies durative action, when it is not altogether clear that such a pivotally important point can be derived from such subtle nuances of a verb tense when the range of possibilities are broad. Second, such a view would create a contradiction with John's comment in 5:16 where the present tense is used, but, if it means habitual action, it does not lead to death. It is for this reason that some scholars view such present tense statements as generic or universal statements. Such statements would then be read with the meaning that sin is not the norm for the Christian. Says Bass, 'The absolute statements therefore serve as a polemic aimed directly at the secessionists, in order to expose their indifference to sin and demonstrate the falsehood of their claims and the reality that they are actually children of the devil' (141).

It would seem that the two views expressed above are not that antithetical, that, while they can be distinguished, they need not be separated sharply. Scholars have argued that the use of the presence tense, expressive of habitual action, cannot be completely ruled out. In 2:1-2 John is seeking to comfort and reassure his readers; in 3:4-11 he is seeking to draw a clear line of demarcation between believers and false teachers. One is made to tranquilize and assure; the other is a polemic expressing John's pendent for stark dichotomies. Theology favors the use of the present to indicate habitual practice, while context supports the interpretation of such absolutist phraseology as heated statements in the furnace of controversy. Therefore, I would argue that both uses of the present tense are mutually possible (the meaning of tenses in John is often obscure!). Perhaps, what John is saying is that true Christians do not fail to love (this failure John attributes to his opponents [3:17]). Lack of love, evident in the false teachers by their conduct intellectually (denying that Jesus is the Christ) and morally (practicing deception and divisiveness), is the notorious sin, but no Christian can fall into it because it is the antithesis of the life of God in them, though all Christians do so temporally but not as a defining state or perpetual characteristic. Though sin does exist, only to be fully triumphed over in death (which is the beginning of life as it was meant to be before the Fall), we do not fail to love in the sense of a universal or general principle, though we all have our occasions otherwise, and regretfully so. I simply do not know how to avoid the truth of sin's continuance and antithetical statements like these in John than to view them by meshing the two views stated above, relying on context to provide the clues to meaning. At this juncture, I quite agree with Boice, though I do not interpret the sin as any inappropriate act, but a specific one, failure to love. 'The ... only adequate interpretation of these verses is that the sin which a Christian cannot commit is lasting or habitual' (88).

John's point is that words without complementary action render verbiage empty and false. Those who sin, a present active verb meaning 'goes on sinning', have no right to think that they are in the family of God. Anyone who demonstrates a habitual, non-loving attitude toward others without awareness that it is an offense against the very character of God in Jesus Christ is an unbeliever. One who possesses the life of God, the character of God, cannot do this (3:9)! Humility and confession mark the child of God expressed in love for others. Echoes of Jesus' comments in John 13:34-35 resound throughout this section of the letter.

Parenthesis 21: God and moral ethics
For the Christian, one who has experienced a deeper or more expansive perception of reality than what is accessible through the five senses, the meaning of significance and truth has changed (or is it that we have changed?). We have been brought into a world vastly larger, more real, and captivating than we could have ever imagined existed. God has come to us through Christ to reveal the existence and character of the true God. It has been a shocking revelation that turned what we thought was light and beauty into a shadowed existence that can degenerate into the grotesque. Seeing the utter beauty of God in the face of Christ has changed the object of our affections, our goals in life, and our priorities. The latter, priorities, because God has become our focus and His character our delight of emulation. In other words, God has become the ground, source, and definition of life; He has

become our definition of ethics, right and wrong. It is now about conformity to His character. Establishing ethics on the social level, such as utility or pragmatic verities, is simply horizontal and relative, being defined by changing contexts and perspectives; it lacks a vertical perspective entirely, abandoning God as a source of authority, leaving us with subjectivity and relativity. God is the ground of ethics; His character is the definition. His character is the ground of establishing what is praiseworthy and blameworthy.

• • • • •

John makes *a clarification* in verse 7. His point is the incompatibility of being a Christian and continuing in sin with habitually and callousness, acting inappropriately as a settled principle of conduct toward God and His children. There must have been people in John's day who contested his teaching and who were trying to mislead the flock. John repeats and amplifies the point in fatherly terms.

'He' is clearly a reference to Jesus as the pronoun used in this case, and others by John, exclusively refer to Him (2:6; 3:3, 5). Jesus is our model for ethical practices; He revealed throughout His life on earth the character of God (John 1:18, '...He has explained *Him*').

(b) The origin of the contrary (vv. 8-13)

John states *a fact* in verse 8, which is that sin is incompatible with the character of God, but is consistent with the devil whose character has stood in antithesis to God's from the beginning (John 8:44). Morally, the devil takes advantage of our natures, being bent to evil; physically, he can use the infliction of pain and disease; and, intellectually, he can seduce us with errant thoughts. John indicates that the one who practices the characteristics of the devil (deception, lack of love) lives in his realm. Christ's mission to earth was to undo the devil's grip on the world. The devil is still busy doing his wicked works, but he has been defeated and through Christ we can escape from such tyranny. The present active participle ('the one who practices [or does] sin...') suggests repeated action, which again is consistent with the devil's character ('from the beginning').

While it is not uncommon to think of 'from the beginning' relative to the devil or Satan as some kind of pre-creation blight of his character, the context, a reference to Cain's murderous act (Gen. 4), would suggest that John is saying that 'from the beginning' of the devil's recorded actions he has shown himself to be lacking in love, rebellious, and deceptive. This interpretation seems warranted by John's use of the phrase, 'in the beginning,' six other times in the letter with temporal significance (1:1; 2:7; 2:24 [twice]; 3:8, 11). Two occurrences of the phrase are disputed (2:13, 14). The devil's children act in the same manner as the false teachers; in fact, they are his minions.

The stated reason for Jesus' earthly ministry in 3:5 was to take away sin; here a corollary is given, to destroy or to end the evil occasioned by the devil ('that' most likely refers to the statement that follows, not to what has preceded, thereby explaining the content of His endeavor in coming). This is the first time in the letter that John speaks of Jesus as the 'Son of God', linking His humanity and deity together in His one person. Jesus is not merely human, a view that John's opponents are willing to grant; He is both the Christ, the Anointed One of God, and the Son of God, a view John's opponents are not willing to grant. At this juncture in the letter, John no longer refers to Jesus as 'the Son' (2:23, 24, 25), but as the 'Son of God' exclusively (4:15; 5:5, 10, 12, 13, 20). Is this nuancing, perhaps, not a literary device building his argument to a climax?

A *logical conclusion* follows in verse 9. Stated in John's rather absolutist manner, this verse can be disturbing. Not only does the believer not sin, he/she is incapable of sinning! John seems to expand the point he stated in verse 6. Here, however, he states two reasons for the assertion. On the surface, it looks like he is saying that Christians by definition are constitutionally incapable of sinning (a clear contradiction of 1:6–2:22 and the exhortations in the book). Some have suggested that there is a state of maturity or perfection obtainable by some, but John is saying that, regardless of what he means by the phrase, it is the universal reality for those who know God. Others would see the sin that believers cannot commit as being apostasy from the apostolic message, but apostasy is not the subject in the immediate context; it is love. 'Apostasy' would fall under the purview of the notorious-sin view, but what John is saying, it seems, is that a believer cannot fail to love (that is, the sin they cannot perpetually practice). The topic of verses 11-18, the immediate context, is love; thus, John would be saying that Christians, truly regenerate people, people infused with the character of God by the indwelling presence of the life of God, the Holy Spirit, cannot not love. While Christians can be unloving at times, and thus in need of their ever-faithful Savior and advocate, Jesus Christ, it is contrary to the life of God within them and, therefore, not a consistent characteristic of any of them.

The first statement is that the Christian does not sin. This, as stated above, suggests present, oncoming, calloused action. Can it be that the 'sin' here is a specific one? Can it be, according to John, that it is a failure to love? Since the character of God is infused in the believer, the essence of rebirth from above, John is saying that a Christian cannot not love. The usage of the present tense of the verb 'sin' demonstrates an exhibition of settled character like that of the devil (3:8). The second statement is that the Christian 'cannot sin'. This would clearly seem to conflict with the writer's statements in 2:1-2 and 5:16 (a believer sinning, but not unto death). Again, it is not an isolated act of sin that John envisioned, but the settled habit of it as indicated by the present tense verb (to do or to practice). Says Stott, 'Again, it is not the isolated act of sin, which is envisioned, but the settled habit of it' (126). I would argue that the topic is love and Christians by definition cannot fail to love. Again, the reason is twofold: the rebirth brings about an entirely new orientation (the life of God, not that of the devil) and the indwelling 'seed'. The 'seed' is the life of God in them, the indwelling of the Holy Spirit. We see evidence of His presence in the fruit of the Spirit, the very manifestation of the character of God (Gal. 5:22). The new birth and the new nature, which is the Holy Spirit, exert a strong internal desire towards holiness and an outward desire to show His love to others.

Parenthesis 22: Fruit or fruits of the Spirit (Gal. 5:22)
Scholars have struggled with the grammar of this verse because the subject is singular (fruit) as is the verb, but nine

things follow ('love, joy…' [the direct object of the verb should be singular]). The nine 'fruits' might be taken as a collectivity so that there is agreement with the verb and subject. However, it may be that the agreement is with the first fruit (love) and the other eight fruits describe and explain the first. Reading it this way, it would be something like this: 'The fruit of the Spirit is love [meaning] joy, peace…' This would make more sense in reading John and his emphasis on love, though John is not Paul!

• • • • •

John once more uses the perfect passive in describing the believer's birth ('is born' or 'has been born'), making it clear that God is the active agent and we are passive, contributing nothing causally, but responding willfully.

As stated in the comments at 3:6, there are two ways to interpret the notion that Christians do not sin in light of 2:1-2: habitual sinning (they cannot go on sinning) or lack of loving (though Christians show a lack of love at times). This, the latter nuance, seems a moot point, but a clarifying insight, since the meaning would be that Christians do not perpetually act out of true love for others. Both solutions still deal with habits or a settled principle in one's life as the defining negative characteristic. Is David a covenant son for not loving Uriah or unrighteously loving Bathsheba? Does an act define a disposition or does the callous, unrepentant, and repeated reoccurrence of an act?

The word 'seed' has caused some discussion as well. The Greek term used here is translated 'sperm' or 'seed' suggestive of a reproductive metaphor, the life of God being in the Christian. This would be consistent with the birthing metaphor in the verse ('is born'). The reference would then be to the Spirit's indwelling ministry. It is interesting in John that he chooses to use the birthing metaphor of the Father (a male image itself).

Verse 10 is a summary, a conclusion, to what has preceded and a transition to what follows. It seems to connect with 2:28-29 where the 'practice of righteousness' is mentioned paralleling the comment here and framing the section as a distinct unit of thought. The lifestyle of those in Satan's domain is vastly different from those in God's kingdom. This is evident in our social relationships, our regard for others.

It is somewhat difficult to determine the referent of 'by this'. Does it refer to what has preceded or to what follows? In this case, it seems to refer to what has preceded, though it is difficult to establish indisputable criteria for the choice since contextual links can be found in both sections.

4. The manifestation of love (vv. 11-24)

This section is framed by the occurrence of similar themes at the beginning and end. In verse 11 the command is to comply with the message they heard from the apostles; in verse 23 they are commanded to live according to the 'new commandment' which came from Jesus through the apostles (2:7).

(a) Love commanded (vv. 11-13)

The command is positively stated in verse 11. The instruction to love is not novel; from the first hearing of the gospel (1:5) through the apostolic message ('this is the message') the love of God, love for God, and love for His children was pre-eminent. This is the first of several references in John's letters to a command set forth from Jesus to love one another (3:23; 4:7, 11, 13; II John 5. See Jesus's comment in John 13:34).

The command is negatively illustrated in verse 12. Cain is an illustration of the opposite of love (here is the only specific Old Testament allusion in the letter. It is also the only occurrence of a name other than for God or Christ); instead of loving his brother, Cain slew him (Gen. 4:8). In the Genesis narrative, the word 'brother' occurs seven times (4:1-11), preparing the reader for the shock to follow with Cain's hostility. On the surface, the reason for God's response to the offering or tribute of Cain is unclear; certainly Cain's reaction was unwarranted. John here tells us that Cain was an evil man and Abel was a godly man of faith (see also, Hebrews 11:4 and Jude 11). The issue was not likely the outward offering that caused the hostility of Cain, but the inward attitude (the choices of life emanate from an inward impulse, the affections). This was sustained by Cain's reaction to God's rejection of his gift (Genesis 4:5: he became angry, not repentant, and evasive). Further, Adam was instructed to till the ground, so it would not have been unwarranted to bring the fruit of that labor to God (Gen. 1:29-30). This was the first act of murder in the Bible and likely the reason John chose it to illustrate the opposite of love with that particular episode. Says Brown, 'When the author evokes Cain, who belonged to the Evil One and so killed his brother (Abel), he is using the violent image of fratricide and diabolic machinations to express his view of the secessionists' (468). Since faith is always the appropriate response to God's commands and promises, we may assume that God had revealed His will to them. Love is the response of faith; hatred (defined as anger in Matthew 5:22), that is murder, the response of faithlessness.

In verse 13, John draws out an implication from the Cain episode. Since Cain is an example of hatred instead of love, he is a child of the devil, not God. As such, Cain belongs to the world and becomes an example of the treatment of believers by those who do not know God. We can expect hostility from the world because it is the realm of the absence of true love, the love of God. The implication is that the secessionists are not acting in love by disseminating deception and error, by destroying the unity of the community. (Could this help us to understand John's warnings to the churches in Revelation 2–3? Is the emphasis on triumph through struggle in Revelation related contextually to John's letters? Does Revelation further elucidate the letters?).

To restate the point, Cain is a prototype of the world (a parallel example would be 'the seed of the serpent [godlessness]' and 'the seed of the women [godliness]' in Genesis 3:15, and the promise of perpetual conflict between them). The 'world' is Cain's posterity; we are not to marvel at it. 'Cain' stands opposed to everything Christian. The problem was not in Cain's offering; it was in his heart! Cain was willfully disobedient (Jude 11); Abel acted in faith (Heb. 11:4). The life of the Christian is so vastly different from those of the world, not so much at times in external behavior, but in motive and object for acting (we do it out of love for God). See Matthew 10:24-25 and John 15:18-20. For the Christian, light, life, and love are intrinsically bonded together in inseparable unity, while in the world there is darkness, death, and hate!

Parenthesis 23: Two kinds of love

Stating that the world of Cain is without love and beauty can be misleading because there is love and beauty in this blighted world. In fact, some unbelievers at times exemplify love more intensely and completely than some believers. However, the virtuousness of an act is not determined by the act in itself, but in the motive of the action. Unbelievers possess the capacity for secondary love (concern for the creature as a creature, desire to be recognized as benevolent, interest in consequent benefit) and that is God's provision for social civility (what theologians call common grace). However, it is not the manifestation of love that is rooted in the interests of God simply because they do not know Him through Jesus Christ. Primary love is action based on love for God, not so much for the benefits He might bestow but because He is deserving of reverential obedience. Love by those of the world is worldly in motive because it is detached from a transcendent reference point.

● ● ● ● ●

(b) Love stated (vv. 14-16)

John describes *the consequence of love* in verse 14. The fruit of obedience expressed in the command to love is a ground of assurance of the life of God, eternal life (see also 2:3, 5), because we have evidence that there has been a fundamental reorientation of our lives and priorities. The 'we' in 'we know' is in the emphatic position in the sentence and thus the point of emphasis. Evidence of disobedience is revealed by a lack of love, and hence life, as John sees it with his use of stark dichotomies, offering no middle ground or compromise.

The verb translated, 'we have passed,' indicates an action that began in the past with continuing results. Clearly, John sees the recipients of the letter as genuine believers, those who have been delivered from divine condemnation. The reason for assurance is stated: 'because we love.' John, evidencing a propensity for stark contrasts, states the opposite: to be characterized by a lack of love is to be devoid of the life of God.

In verse 15, the comment that one who hates his brother is a murderer echoes Jesus' words in Matthew 5:21-22, murder being anger or hatred toward another whether or not the act is consummated. Smalley makes the point when he says,

'John clearly states that murder and hatred are synonymous' (191). The words used here are found in John 8:44 (there the devil is described as a murderer from the beginning, likely a reference to the Cain incident in Genesis 4:1-8). Those who manifest the character of the devil are, thereby, shown to be the children of the devil.

The translation 'fellow Christian' or 'brother' in this verse can be misleading. A person that habitually despises or hates another is clearly not a Christian in John's reckoning. No hater abides, remains, or resides in the sphere of life (see 3:14). John is speaking in blatant dichotomies and what he says must be read in context of the argument of his letter. No one with the heart of a hater will see life, but, by the definition of hate offered by John, a lack of concern for one in need (v. 17), no believer is exempt from this accusation. However, is their action habitual, accompanied with callousness and delight, or is their action infrequent and accompanied with repentance in retrospect?

Parenthesis 24: Murderers and heaven
In what sense can it be said that a murderer is excluded from eternal life? If hatred or anger is murder, who has not qualified as a murderer? If hatred leads to the act of murder, is there no hope for the man or woman on death row? Clearly, we may not be a literal murderer, but have we not hated? If to break any commandment of God is to break them all, we have broken them all. Further, Paul lists a litany of sins, several being a violation of love, though murder is not in the list (I Cor. 6:9-10), but then writes, 'And such were some of you, but you were washed, you were sanctified, you were justified…'

It does not seem that John is speaking about any particular act of sin, such as murder, but a settled habituality as a general characteristic of life. The difference between a saved sinner and a lost sinner is not the inability to do one or another awful act; it is that a believer intuitively knows it is wrong, his/her conscience warning them, the Spirit crying out to them. That the believers are not characterized by continuance in it, having remorse over it, and that the believers know that they have offended God by their action, are grounds that God has wrought a change of their affections in the gift of eternal life.

Murderers will be in heaven, but no one whose character has not been changed by the presence of the Spirit of God will.

Believers are not perfect; they understand wrong as an offense against God. They know the art of confession because they know, to some small degree, the depth of the twistedness of their lives. Christians are capable of doing anything an unbeliever may do, but the differences are stark (sporadic contrasted to habit, remorse contrasted to delight, Godward repentance contrasted to supposed human advantage, abnormal behavior contrasted to normal behavior).

• • • • •

John illustrates his claim in verse 16. The standard of love is the character of God; the revelation of the standard is the atoning death of Jesus Christ ('by this'). The verb 'laid down' or 'gave up' is only found here in the letter, though the concept of sacrifice is found in 1:7, 2:2, 4:10 and 5:6; the verb is used by John several times in his gospel (10:11, 15, 17, 18; 15:13). The point is that Christ voluntarily and willing gave His life for His children, and God's children should and must emulate the pattern. All of this is given in the context of hatred and murder as the antithesis. Since the Christian's origin is from above, and not from below, they are known to be such by the nature of their behavior; it bespeaks as being of divine origin. The wonder of redeeming mercies through Christ has been captured in Philip P. Bliss' poem, 'Man of Sorrows' (1875).

> Man of sorrows what a name
> for the Son of God, who came
> Ruined sinners to reclaim.
> Hallelujah! What a Savior!
>
> Bearing shame and scoffing rude,
> in my place, condemned he stood;
> Sealed my pardon with his blood.
> Hallelujah! What a Savior!
>
> Guilty, vile, helpless we;
> blameless Lamb of God was he;
> 'Full atonement' can it be?
> Hallelujah! What a Savior!

He was lifted up to die;
'It is finished!' was his cry;
Now in heaven exalted high.
Hallelujah! What a Savior!

When he comes, our glorious King,
All his ransomed home to bring,
Then anew this song we'll sing:
Hallelujah! What a Savior!

The preposition 'for' occurs twice in this verse forming a parallelism. As Christ laid down His life *for* us, we are instructed to lay down our lives *for* God's children. Clearly, as our Lord's life was spent as a sacrifice, we are commanded to live our lives radically and sacrificially for others. Says Henry: 'Here is the condescension, the miracle, the mystery of divine love, that God would redeem the church with His own blood! Surely we should love those whom God hath loved, and so loved; and we shall certainly do so if we have any love for God' (1079). This is true discipleship and so vastly different from the self-possessed interests of the false teachers. Using the analogy of John 10, they are ravenous wolves, not tender, caring shepherds of the flock.

(c) Love detailed (vv. 17-24)
John asks a question in verse 17. It is interesting that John closes verse 16 with the plural ('brethren'), but shifts to the singular ('brother') here. The basis for helping a 'brother' is to perceive a need, to have the willingness to respond, and to have an availability of resources to help. John has instructed these believers that the material world is illusory and transitory, though not without deep significance (2:15-17); here he explains what their attitude should be to material things. They are things not to be clutched, but used as tools for the benefit of others.

There is some discussion about the translation of the word 'heart'. Some translations translate it as meaning the faculty of action, the affections (heart being used metaphorically). In this instance, is the issue one of motive for action or an action? Following the latter option, some prefer to see the action itself as in view and, therefore, translate the term as compassion. This seems contextually preferable from what follows in verse 18, an emphasis on action.

The rhetorical question demands a negative answer. A lack of compassion for a Christian in need indicates a lack of the transforming infusion of the character of God through the Spirit. The Greek is even more vivid for it reads, 'How can God's love reside or abide in such a one?' Here is stated the most explicit charge that John makes of the false teachers; they do not possess the love of God!

In verse 18, John describes for us the actions of true love. The prepositional phrases form two sets of couplets, the first negative and the second positive. 'With words' is coupled 'with tongue' explaining how words are produced (here meaning words devoid of truth); 'in deed,' or works, are to be exercised in the context of truth. Here, again, the backdrop is John's opponents and their loveless schismatic, deceptive, and heretical actions and teachings.

John makes several applications in verses 19-24. The phrase, 'by this we know,' functions to apply the meaning of verse 18 to John's Christian audience. The absence of love, words without deeds, evidences ingeniousness of profession; deeds rooted in truth, not deception, evidence the presence of the life of God. In this structurally difficult paragraph, the author applies the fact of true love to the assurance one can have of life. Fruit indicates root, to use an agricultural metaphor. Poor fruit suggests a rotten root; good fruit suggests a healthy root.

Confidence
Believers can have *confidence before God* (vv. 19-20). A life of loving care within the community of faith evidences the fact that God has done a work of grace through His regenerative mercies. That an effect partakes of the nature of its cause or source seems to be John's argument. Since the origin of love is God, who is love in His very character qualities (4:8), those who have been brought to share in His life partake of those qualities as well. Consequent actions indicate the precipitating cause of the action!

The fruit of a loving orientation is assurance of life in God, the source of love. The tense of the verb 'convince' or 'assure' is future, suggesting that loving deeds have an ongoing function. The word 'heart' normally indicates the innermost recesses of the immaterial nature and has various nuances. In this context, though no consensus prevails, it seems to denote the faculty of conscience since the function is to render judgment (v. 20).

Though not reflected in some translations, the opening phrase of verse 20 is a conditional, dependent clause ('that if our heart condemns us'). John is saying that even in those situations when their hearts or consciences are stricken, failing to react as they should to fellow believers in need, there God knows their lapses and has a view of them that is more positive than their own. In the context of the passage, the sense seems to be the offering of hope to troubled or confused believers. Momentary lapses, regrettable moments, while not condoned, are not grounds for a lack of assurance that they are the children of God.

It may be helpful to pause and unpack these two verses from a grammatical perspective. We are again faced with the question of whether 'by this' refers to what has preceded or what follows. If it is a reference to what follows, it then is connected to one of the three occurrences of 'that' (one in verse 19 and two in verse 20), making it difficult to determine the referent. The 'that' of verse 19 can be eliminated because it explains the content of the verb 'know'. The first 'that' of verse 20 deals with condemnation and is the opposite of evidence of assurance and the second 'that' explains more fully the one before it. It would seem 'by this' is disjointed from the two latter instances of 'that', making a connection between them questionable. In this reading of the 'that' in verse 20, the first is explained by the second. This stated, it would seem preferable to connect the 'by this we will know that' of verse 19 with the preceding verse (v. 18). One's actions confirm one's relationship to truth. The deeds of the Christian are grounds for assuaging a troubled conscience. The NET Bible captures the meaning of the passage: 'That if our conscience condemns us, that God is greater than our conscience and knows all things.' There is here a beautiful trilogy: heart, mind, and God. When the heart or conscience acts as our accuser, our defense should be the evidence to the contrary that we have come to know God experientially, though imperfectly because of the corruption of all our faculties of perception that frequently corrupts our conduct. When this remedial step fails to assuage our fears, which it often does (a proof of our blighted capacities is that we trust our own perceptions more than God's declarations), we should turn to the true judge in the matter, the omniscient and all-powerful judge of all things, in trust that His Son is our ever-faithful Savior.

Is the reference to God's omniscience ('knows all things') to be taken positively or negatively? Is the allusion to the possibility of a severe judgment before God for dereliction? Since the context is one of pastoral care and assurance, this latter view seems unwarranted. The former seems most preferable; if there is evidence to the contrary, we should not allow our consciences to take away our confidence. There will always be reasons for having fear, but if there are evidences of a work of grace in our hearts, mainly love for others, we should trust God and lay aside our fears. Since God is the final arbiter of who should fear and who should not, and since the life of God is revealed through the expression of love, and since we have evidence of love through action, we should have confidence that we are indeed the children of God. Perfection is not the issue as the ground of assurance; it is through the God we have come to know through the mercies of Christ and the gift He purchased for us, the Holy Spirit, who is love possessed. Assurance and a condemning heart are not antithetical, because one greater than us is the final arbiter!

Parenthesis 25: The immaterial nature of mankind
The Bible tells us that God created man out of dust and infused in him 'breath' (Gen. 2:7). Thus, it is common to speak of mankind as two-part: material and immaterial. The immaterial part of mankind has many facets and can be likened to a single, though many-faceted, diamond.

Within the immaterial nature there are two inseparable categories: the mental faculties and the inclining faculties. The mind gathers, reflects upon, and processes data, but it is not a decision-making faculty. Decisions are made in the inclining faculties of the soul that are described in the Bible with such terms as conscience, affections, and will. Conscience is an evaluative faculty, affections the determination faculty (do I like it or not?), and will the acting faculty that leads to consequential behavior, the outworking of choices.

While this might seem reasonable, the immaterial nature of the soul and its faculties are impossible to delineate because the Bible sometimes uses these terms interchangeably, even at times rendering them difficult to distinguish. All I am able to suggest is a general lineal theory of decision-making, but it is far more complex than that, and there is constant reciprocation and interaction between the faculties. A Newtonian model of strict cause and effect is simply too naïve; a postmodern theory of interactive reciprocalism between the faculties of the soul, based on a Quantum Physics model, seems more helpful.

• • • • •

The mind is the guardian of the heart. If we love each other and share with each other in need, we should have confidence to the contrary when our consciences trouble us over our imperfections, entertainments, and doubts, sometimes causing us to question our relationship to Christ. The change that the love of God brings results in an objective test of our Christian profession, because self-sacrifice is not natural to man in his fallen state. The heart accuses, the mind defends, and God is our judge! How do you gain peace when your heart or conscience condemns you? Think about what you were like before God came into your life.

In verse 20 the 'for,' or 'that' in some translations, functions in an explanatory sense; it explains why we should not allow our consciences to condemn us. The answer is because God does not do so and He is the one we should listen to in these matters. God is omniscient; Christians suffer from myopia. It is, therefore, wiser to listen to God rather than to our blighted conscience. Here is the trust factor coming into play. Are we willing to believe the words of God, supplemented evidentially by an observable change in our conduct, or not? While assurance is not devoid of the element of faith and trust, assurance is also rooted on the absence of contrary evidence! It is based on trust in an object more beautiful than our fears and uncertainties.

Answers from God
In verses 21 and 22, John turns from the curse of the condemning heart to the blessings of a tranquil heart. In harmony with God (who is a God of love), a heart willing and sensitive to the extension of love to fellow believers is that of a person who can without fear enter the presence of God. It gives boldness in prayer (this is the first reference of making requests of God in the letter). An untroubled conscience is a confident one. The reason God answers prayers is not a heart at peace; it is a heart submissive to the will of God. If we live obediently before God, we can be assured that we will not ask promiscuously for things, but in accordance with His will, and, therefore, we can be assured that He hears us. Obedience is not the cause of answered prayer; it is the evidence of a relationship with and submission unto God. Obedience is not meritorious; it is not the cause of self-gain. Instead, fellowship, life in God, is the cause of obedience. Obedience is, at best, a secondary condition or cause, a cause that is caused. This is evident by the content of verse 23; the condition consistent with answered prayer is faith towards God and love towards others.

The 'and' that introduces the phrase, 'whatever we ask...' (v. 22), is explanatory connecting an untroubled conscience with answered prayers. The conditions for prayer-answers are twofold in these verses: a good conscience before God and obedience to God ('things pleasing or acceptable'). The 'commandments' in John can be summarized in the words, 'love one another.' The pronoun 'His' refers to God the Father.

Parenthesis 26: Prayer and universal language
How are we to understand the oft-stated promises of God that He will answer our prayers (3:22, 5:15)? For example, 'If you abide in me, and my words abide in you, ask whatever you wish, and it shall be done for you' (John 15:7). There are many mysteries in prayer, undisclosed sacred secrets, that appear to be only resolved in trust that the incomprehensibly all wise and sufficient God is also benevolent and acts according to His promises. I believe that God does answer our prayers and

the answers are one of three: (1) yes and here it is; (2) no, it is not in my or to your best interest; or (3) wait because the timing is not right, but I will answer. Stated similarly, it may be that the answer we desire is not what He deems as best for us so that, in effect, He replies in silence as a resounding 'no'. Further, it could be that unanswered prayer is rooted in false motives for praying; that is, prayer that is either selfish in nature, spoken out of insincerity, or simply rooted in temporal, passing exigencies that are devoid of the interests of God in the expansion of His kingdom. Lastly, the cause of the delay may be a divine favor to you for your greater good because the timing, for reasons, perhaps, but not necessarily so, clarified subsequently, are not best.

• • • • •

An explanation
It is interesting that in verse 23 John specifies what the commandment is, but in doing so mentions two things, belief in Jesus and love for one another, moving from the plural (commandments) to the singular (commandment). The pronoun 'His' clearly refers to God the Father since the divine focus becomes the Son. Here for the first time in the letter John explicitly connects faith and love; they compose a single duty, being distinguishable though inseparable. The pronoun 'He' in 'just as He commanded us' is a reference to the Father (the three pronouns in the verse refer to God the Father).

The object of our belief is Jesus Christ, God's Son (Jesus means deliverer and Christ, or Messiah, means the chosen or Anointed One). Jesus Christ is our appointed deliverer. There is something further to add. To believe 'in the name' is to accord deity, sonship, and equality of character to Jesus. All of this indicates that Jesus is the Son of God, deity revealed through the flesh (see John 1:14, where John calls Jesus 'the Word,' word meaning disclosure. Jesus is the revealer of God!).

John's conclusion
Assurance of fellowship with God the Father (the four pronouns in the verse refer to the Father) comes to us through finding the workings of the Spirit in our lives by His presence. Where there is obedience and love, there is the life of God.

Obedience to the Lord's commandments is not the cause, but the proof of His people's dwelling in Him. Assurance of life in God is evidenced by two things: belief (v. 23) and moral behavior consistent with the divine character (v. 23), which is brought about by the presence of the Spirit of God manifested as an abiding, habitual, moral principle (the second of the grounds of assurance).

Abiding, residing, remaining is a mutually reciprocal union between the believer and God by the Spirit (v. 24). This is the first instance in the letter that it is stated that we abide in Him and He abides in us simultaneously. Brown is helpful at this point. 'On our part the abiding is conditioned upon keeping the commandments given by God, but on God's part our abiding stems from His giving the Spirit, which is not conditioned. The same God who *gave* the commandment *gave* the Spirit that enables us to live out the commandment' (482). Abiding or remaining is not a temporal state for the believer any more than it is for God; it is not a state admissible of alteration. See also 4:13. God is love, the commandment is to love; Jesus is love revealed; and the Spirit is love possessed. What God commands of us, God provides for us! The issue is abiding or not; it is, do we have life or not? We know we have life when we have the love of God within by means of the life of the Spirit.

Here, also, is the first statement in the letter of the role of the Spirit, though the Spirit is the indirect person involved in the anointing of 2:20, 27 (the anointing by the Holy One [Jesus Christ] is the gift of the Spirit). The fact of the Spirit's presence, the living reorienting effect of it, is solid ground for assurance. The primary role of the Spirit is to witness to the person of Jesus Christ. Thus, such concepts as believing in Christ, being indwelt by God (the Holy Spirit), and abiding in Christ compose a single unity of complex ideas (the wonder of salvation) that cannot be separated or divided, though they can be distinguished. The Spirit's witness to Christ prepares John's readers for what is presented in the sentences that immediately follow; the false teachers do not possess divine authority for their message.

Parenthesis 27: The nature of the indwelling of the Holy Spirit
There is no doubt; all true believers are indwelt by the Spirit of God (3:24; 4:13). The question before us is the nature of

that indwelling, since the third person of the divine Trinity is not quantifiable by volume, shape, or proportion, being immaterial or spirit. If God the Father is love and Jesus Christ is that love revealed, the Holy Spirit is that love possessed. The Spirit in the wonder of human salvation performs a dual capacity: He applies the benefits purchased by Christ and He is the sum of those benefits. To possess spiritual life is to be in possession of the Spirit. Since the Spirit is an invisible entity, He can only be identified by the effects of His presence. Thus, the presence of the Spirit is intrinsically interconnected with evidence of His presence (no one has seen wind but we know when it is present by its affects, its 'visibility' so to speak). We know of His indwelling presence because His character is expressed in our behavior.

• • • • •

5. The discernment of truth from error (4:1-6)
This section, as well as 2:12-14 and 2:15-17, seems to defy a congruent place in the flow of the letter; it, like the others, appears to be a self-contained unit because it seems out of place contextually with what has preceded and with what follows. That confessed, it might be well to see these verses as continuing the theme of faithfulness, meaning belief in the Son of God and love for others, as the truest evidence of Christian profession, though it is cast in the frame of warning and exhortation. John appears to be helping his readers to see his mandate by emphasizing the dangers to its realization. Following what appears to be digressions in the flow of John's thought in 2:12-14 and 2:15-17, there is a warning concerning the danger of the false teachers, a discussion of the distinction between truth and error. This section seems to have parallels to 2:18-27 concerning the separation of truth from error, the apostles and the false teachers. In both instances, John's plea is for that of discernment.

(a) The existence of lying spirits (v. 1)
The connecting link between this verse and the previous is the reference to the witness or abiding ministry of the Spirit (v. 24). However, John must have realized that further comment and clarification was required to safeguard his

audience (apparently the false teachers claimed spiritual authority for their teachings). It is clear that John is not concerned with the issue of mere outward appearance, sincerity of presentation, and robust claims. The pronoun in the main clause is second person plural, indicating that John is addressing the community as a whole. The present imperative may be translated 'do not go on believing', suggesting the disturbance fostered by false teaching in the churches.

In contrast to naïve, indiscriminate acceptance, believers are to critically examine any message that they hear in order to determine its truthfulness. Since John later in the verse refers to the 'spirits' as false prophets, it seems valid to suggest that the correlation in his mind is Old Testament prophets, drawing a connection between them and his opponents. Such prophets claimed a special anointing and unction from the Spirit of God (the false teachers likely claimed a superior spiritual status as well). Two criteria served the purpose of evaluation: did the prediction or warning come true (Deut. 18:22)? And, did the instruction lead the people away from obedience to God, even if a miraculous sign or miracle accompanied the prediction (Deut. 13:1-3)? Since verses 2-3 relate the test to confession of 'Jesus Christ as come in the flesh', the second of the criteria is in John's view. A vivid example of a false prophet in the Holy Scriptures is Micaiah, the seer of Ahab, king of the Northern Kingdom, and his prediction of victory over the Syrians (I Kings 22). John specifically applies the test of Deuteronomy 13; it is idolatrous to lead people to a false Christ (perhaps a clue here to the meaning of 5:21). John identifies the false prophets who have 'gone out into the world' with his opponents who have left the assembly of the believers (2:19). They were seeking, unwittingly being deceived themselves, to lead others astray, away from Christ to worship a false one.

(b) The discernment of truth from error (vv. 2-6)
The teaching of the false prophets is described in verses 2 and 3. 'By this you know' alerts us to a forthcoming test for discerning truth from error; the test is a person's under-standing of Jesus. The phrase 'that Jesus Christ has come in

the flesh' has been read in a number of ways. It can read, as above, as a simple statement reflective of the incarnation, the phrase being the object of the verb ('confess'). It could also be read with 'Jesus Christ' as the object of the verb and with 'in the flesh' as a complement, so that what was denied by John's opponents was the incarnation. Another way to read it is to see the object of 'confess' to be Jesus and the complement being 'Jesus *Christ as* come in the flesh'. In this case the opponents are not so much denying the existence of Jesus, but His role as the Christ or the Anointed One.

The difficulty with the first view is that the opponents' error does not seem to have been relative to the incarnation, but to His accomplishments. Also, the term 'Jesus Christ' is not used by John elsewhere of the pre-incarnate, second person of the divine Trinity. So both views one and two seem unlikely. While the second and third views are viable options, the overall context seems to favor the third reading. John's opponents could confess Christ 'as come in the flesh', but probably would not say that Jesus was the Anointed One in the capacity John gives to Him in the letter, that 'Jesus is the Christ'.

In the following verse, John argues that the error of the false teachers was to deny that Jesus is from God though they might have confessed that 'Christ in Jesus' was from God (a power within Him, an anointing or empowerment effected at His baptism). The false teachers were denying more than the incarnation by asserting that the Anointed One was in Jesus, claiming that He was merely a God-inspired, insightful man. Here is more than a denial of the incarnation; it is a denial of the divine origin of Jesus and His role as our redeemer from sin through the atonement. For the false teachers, 'Christ' was within Jesus as with the prophets of old; but He was not Jesus who is the Christ. John's affirmation about Him is that He is Jesus Christ!

To further sustain the case some scholars point to John 9:22 where 'Christ' is clearly the complement of Jesus ('...if anyone shall confess Him to be the Christ'). Brown summarizes the interpretative point this way: '...there is no separation between "Jesus" and the "Christ," and the [single or one] individual involved must be understood in terms of his career in the flesh. It must be noted that the author says "come in the flesh," not "come into the flesh," and so the act of incarnation is not the point' (493).

The error of the secessionists is most clearly stated in the negative (v. 3); they deny that Jesus is from God though they are willing to say that He is the 'Christ', God's servant or Anointed One. Jesus, in their view, was a spokesman for God, but He was not from God as to His origin; Jesus was a uniquely endowed human being and nothing more. Such teaching is born of satanic deceit and by its very nature is 'antichrist', a person animated by interests opposed to Christ, the desire to replace the true Christ with a false one, being already in the world and resisting the spread of God's kingdom (2:18).

The term 'world' appears six times in this section (4:1, 3, 4, 5 [three]). It can mean the general sphere of human existence, though it seems to bear a negative connotation (the realm of opposition to Christ since the term 'antichrist' appears here). In verse 6 contrast is drawn between truth and error, the former attractive to Christ-followers and the latter endearing to antichrist-followers.

John describes the assurance of believers in verses 4-6. In verse 4 the tone changes from robust polemics aimed at preventing further damage from the false teachers to the comfort of those disturbed by them, therefore, resulting in the need of pastoral reassurance. The motivating and equipping power behind the secessionists, the devil, does not compare to the Spirit of God who 'resides, abides, remains' in the children of God (3:24; 4:13). The tense of the verb 'overcome' (or 'prevailed') indicates not only a past accomplishment, but ongoing consequences as well; the victory over the false teachers ('them') has been and will continue to be secure! What a comfort for the troubled conscience to hear the great apostle say 'You are from God...' The 'greater is He that...' is most likely a reference to the Holy Spirit than 'he who is...' to the devil, the spirit that animates antichrists, John's opponents.

Continuing the thought of the previous verse that the devil animates this world behind an invisible curtain, John speaks more pointedly of his minions, the false teachers (v. 5). They act out the devil's deceptive designs. Clearly the 'they' is a reference to John's opponents. Their origin, work ('speaking'), and audience is motivated by Satan and the sphere of their operations is the world (the realm allotted to the evil one's temporal authority, not the divine kingdom that is emerging in the same sphere). Brown surmises by John's statement, 'the world listens to them,' that the secessionists have been able to gather a large hearing (498).

In verse 6, John summarizes the point of the section. There are only two sources of knowledge for John: God the Father (as revealed by Christ and the apostles, who were instructed by Him and commanded to disseminate His message) and the temporal realm (the sphere of the spirit of deceit under the limited control of the devil and executed through his minions). The evidence of one's origins, the world or the apostles, is demonstrated by which source consumes our willing attention and priorities. The world listens to error; the believer listens to God. The audience we associate with reveals much about who we are!! If we are born of God, if we have been brought to see a greater, far more beautiful world than this one, we have entered the realm of truth. If we are unable and unwilling to see beyond the temporal and material, we exist in mistruth. Who we follow tells us who our leader is! By this we can know what is true and what is not. The litmus test of true fellowship with Christ, the state of abiding in Him, the realm of eternal life, is obedience to Him. The world is controlled by the 'spirit of error' (or 'deceit'), being either Satan himself or his ambassadors (antichrist figures), or by the 'spirit of truth', being the Holy Spirit or the apostles of Christ. It would seem that for John the 'spirits' are human beings under the authority of and energized by supernatural power, 'spirits' being identified with false prophets in verse 1.

How can we apply the truth of this section?
(1) Though we exist in a culture that lives for the immediate and the temporally satisfying, we should think often about the return of the Lord. It will remind us that the things we see now will not always be, that there is more to life than the next anticipated excitement that will fade with the dawn of another new experience, that life as we live it is at best a passing shadow of temporalities. Awareness of the Lord's

return should give us perspective on this world. Further, living in light of Jesus' return is a purifying hope; it should fill us with anticipation and delight, putting spring in our steps and delight in our hearts. Every pain we experience should remind us that this is the only 'hell' that we shall ever experience; every joy and delight that we have been given is a tangible, frail example of the eternal pleasures of dwelling in the presence of God forever.

(2) Those who profess to know Christ, but habitually act unlike Him, should seriously question the genuineness of their profession. While coming to Christ is an expression of willingness, it is far more than a mere intellectual decision. Salvation is a two-sided coin, so to speak. While what we are to do is appropriate, that is to believe the message that God has given in His Son, salvation is a divine work that transforms our character, focus, and priorities. Sadly, many believe that they have a right to make Christian claims for themselves because of a past experience, but have little evidence that the said experience actually changed their focus in life. It is not by their words, but by their priorities and affections, that the reality of belief is validated.

(3) A Christian is not a person who always gets it right; he/she is a person who confesses when they get it wrong. Murderers will be in heaven, but not one whose disposition to hate has gone unchanged by the Spirit of God. Liars will be in heaven, but no one whose lying is a settled habitual lifestyle with no fear of whom they disregard and dishonor by their behavior. Heaven is the hope of cleansed sinners who are still sinners, but regrettably and painfully so. It is for people who long to be delivered from their temporal bondage so that they can worship as they ought the Savior of the world.

(4) Fellowship, life in the sinless one, and indulgence in sin are a contradiction in terms. If you find persons who claim to be Christians, but who live an openly disobedient lifestyle in contradistinction to the commands of God with longevity and no repentance, there are only two options. First, it may be that such should seriously doubt that God has done a work of grace in them; they have no right to any ground of assurance of His mercies. Redemption brings a transformation that is slow and painful at times, but there

is still transformation. Second, if they are children of God, they will face the terror of His gracious chastisement. If chastisement comes, they should bow in repentance and thankfulness. If it does not come, they should doubt that God has ever been merciful to their souls.

(5) The realm of light and the realm of love are one and the same realm; it is the realm in which the children of God are united in their heavenly Father. The realm of darkness and the devil are the same; it is the world of deception, lies, and destruction. There are only two worlds; there is no interim domain for anyone. To walk in the light is to know the compassionate love of God through Christ; to walk otherwise is to be eventually betrayed and broken. These are serious days for all of us because the door to divine mercy through Christ is still widely ajar, but it will not always be so.

(6) No matter how charming, how plausible, or how eloquent a teacher may appear to be, the test of his/her witness to Christ and His truth is the criteria by which he/she must be judged. The test of truth is love because love is of God and everyone who truly loves is born of God. Integrity of character is the test of orthodoxy, not words or smiles. Miracle working does not validate truth because false prophets can do miracles (i.e., the Egyptian magicians). If the devil can imitate some things that God can do, doing cannot be the criteria. The devil can duplicate what appears to be righteousness, but he cannot do so with longevity or consistency because his very nature is otherwise. Time and observation is a great test of what is valid, true, and enduring. Do not be swayed by a meeting or a TV program when you know nothing of the character of those you watch!

D. The test of love (4:7-21)

The word that dominates this section is love; it appears as a noun twenty-three times and as a verb twice. John elaborates what he has presented in I John 3:16, which is that God has revealed Himself to His people through Jesus Christ's self-sacrificial love and they are called upon, as partakers of His life, to love also. Since God is love (4:8, 16,) and they are His children, they should love also (a result shares in the nature of its cause). When they love, they are like their Father who is love.

John returns to the theme of love that he developed in 3:11-24 (remember reoccurring themes expressed in an upward developmental pattern is characteristic of John's writing, both here and in the Revelation); what we have here is an expansion of the former discussion. That God is love and that we ought to love are intertwined, dominant themes in the letter, the former the cause of the latter and the latter the assurance of the experiential reality of the former. The only way to be a partaker of the divine nature, to use Peter's terminology (II Peter 1:4) for spiritual life, is to be in possession of the life of God through the gift of God, the Holy Spirit. This test in our passage can be divided into two sections, each beginning with the word, 'beloved' (vv. 7, 11).

1. The reality of love (vv. 7-10)

(a) The origin of love (vv. 7-8)
Stated positively (v. 7). John bases his argument on God's eternal character. God is the source and origin of all love. The life of the child bears the imprint of the character of the parent. Because God is characterized in His actions by love, being a loving person, those who display the love of God, the character of God in this sense, give evidence that they know God (a child shares in the genetic structure and similarity of appearance of its parents). Love here is not the cause of salvation as the tense of the verb 'is born' or 'has been born' clearly indicates. Love is a consequence, an evidence, not a cause (see also 3:9, 5:1). Birth by the God of love results in the manifestation of love because, through divine redemption, we have come to share in His character through the mutuality of indwelling.

There are three other predicate nominative statements in the New Testament concerning God and His nature: He is 'spirit' (John 4:24), 'a consuming fire' (Heb. 12:29 quoted from Deut. 4:24), and 'light' (I John 1:5). However, love is the most comprehensive of the statements and is repeated twice in our passage in the form of a subject-verb-object construction (4:8, 16). Love is an expressive attitude that invariably leads to action (the fact and the action are inseparable). Love, which calls for expression, as well as the other attributes of God's character, is the reason God created. It was not an external cause that motivated God to do so, but an internal, self-orienting cause; love delights in expression. The same is true of the life of God in the believer; an internal motivation is the spring of benevolence, the experience of the love that God has for Himself, now possesses the believer producing the same effect (expression).

Parenthesis 28: Obedience and love
Another important insight from this passage is that love is a command. We are to love because love is a fruit of being joined to God and the ground of our assurance that we belong to Him (a command from God does not imply something that is contingent; what God commands of us He accomplishes through us, even though its fullest manifestation will wait until glory. The commands of God are, therefore, statements of the divine will and instruction to encourage us in their implementation). What God commands of us, He provides for us. Obedience is our response to what God has given the ability to perform; it is an act of submission and ownership. The ground of all life and ethics is the inter-trinitarian love that God has mutually expressed between the members of the Holy Trinity (4:8). Love by its nature seeks expression and that, it seems, is why God created; that is, to express His love and receive it back. The experience of salvation entails the realization of God's great love and an innate consequential desire on our part to express it. We love God because He loves us (4:10-11). Love in the believer is natural because it is natural to God!

• • • • •

Stated negatively (v. 8). John's simplicity and clarity is hardly more evident than here. The absence of love is the absence of the life of God; the absence of the life of God is the meaning of being lost. The most discussed statement in this verse follows an indication of purpose or the statement of a reason ('for God is love'). What is most important to observe is that 'love' is without an article preceding it. This means that John is not saying that 'God is love' in the sense that 'love is God' (that God is a moral force or manifestation, not a person). When the article does not appear before a noun, the emphasis is on quality; so John is emphasizing the worthiness, purity, and greatness of God's character. All of God's expressions or extensions of Himself possess the quality of love. All of God's acts are, therefore, loving activities. If so, not to express love in our activities is not to possess love at all, having never experienced it.

(b) The manifestation of love (vv. 9-10)
In the first coming of Christ (v. 9). The first issue encountered in this verse is a persistent one throughout the letter of John. Does 'by this' refer to what has preceded or to what follows? Since 'that' follows the phrase and functions in an explanatory manner, it must refer to what follows. The sending of God's Son was both a revelation of His love and the essence of love itself. God's unique Son was God's unique gift of love to us! The term 'only begotten', known to most of us early in our life in God through John 3:16, means 'one of a kind' or 'unique'; in John's writing it is reserved by him for Jesus Christ. This is a clear denial of the assertion by the secessionists that Jesus is merely one of God's special agents, like the prophets of old; Jesus Christ is unique, one of a kind!

The motivation for the sending of God's unique one to us, the one who enjoyed intimate fellowship in God's presence as His equal along with the Holy Spirit, is that we might join in that community of the mutuality of love. The phrase 'love of God' can refer either to the love that God possesses, that God extends, or our love for God. It is clear that the former is the proper sense because it is connected with God's commission of the Son to bring redemption into the world (here the term 'world' is used in a neutral sense, as it is in 4:14, not with evil connotations). 'Only begotten' appears only here in the epistle, but four times in the gospel (See John 1:14, 18; 3:16, 18). Sometimes scholars translate the term as 'well-beloved'. The term indicates the uniqueness of Jesus; He is God, being the Son of God.

Parenthesis 29: The divine motive in redemption: primary or secondary?
It is worth meditating upon the subject of 'why'. Why did God determine to create all that once was not blighted by us? Why did God move to redeem the creatures that rebelled against

Him and the creation that still groans as a consequence? What can be said is that the motive did not reside in something external to God nor a deficiency in God. God is self-existent, needing nothing. The impetus to action on God's part must have been an internal, inter-Trinitarian motive. That motive, I believe, is the self-love of God and mutuality of delight to behold the absoluteness of His beauty.

Thus, God's primary motivation for His action is His own self-glorification. To multiply the perception of His beauty God created all that we see about us. Beauty is symmetry, duplication and proportion. God made a tree to reveal His beauty so that in beholding Himself by extension He is glorified and His value is perceived. God has willed to redeem fallen humanity for the same reason, that His beauty may be seen and reflected back to Him. To maximize the praise of His glory, He sent His glorious Son for us.

It is a wonderful thing to be secondary in God's purposes when, as secondary, we fulfill a greater purpose by being the recipients of grace, mercy, and life in God. We have been created for a purpose, and that purpose is to reveal the character of God secondarily to our world, but primarily to God Himself. It is fundamentally important to grasp that God has greater purposes for us than our mere existence; it is to reflect God's glorious person so that He can behold Himself. 'For from Him and through Him and to Him are all things. To Him be the glory forever, Amen' (Rom. 11:36).

• • • • •

(c) *In the redemption through Christ (v. 10).* The proof of any assertion is not in the wording, but in the evidence. The immensity of God's divine love for His children is revealed in the grandeur of the gift He bestows upon them. The apostle Paul describes Christ as 'God's unspeakable gift' (2 Cor. 9:15). Simply put: God is the definition of love. The proof of that love is Jesus Christ: His life, atoning death, and resurrection (the proof that death has been banished). It was divine love that moved God to extend mercy, not the depth of the need of humanity. It was not human merit that moved Him; it was His own love to extend His love that causes anyone to experience divine love. Stuart Townend's song, 'How Deep the Father's Love for Us,' captures the immensity of God's love as best as finite expressions of infinity are capable.

How deep the Father's love for us.
How vast beyond all measure,
That He should give His only Son,
To make a wretch His treasure.

How great the pain of searing loss,
The Father turns His face away
As wounds which mar the chosen one
Bring many sons to glory.

I will not boast in anything.
No gifts, no pow'r, no wisdom
But I will boast in Jesus Christ,
His death and resurrection.

Why should I gain from His reward?
I cannot give an answer.
But this I know with all my heart,
His wounds have paid my ransom.

The reference to Christ as the propitiatory sacrifice for us is the second in the letter (2:2). The term 'propitiation', meaning satisfaction, is also sometimes translated 'atoning sacrifice' for the sins of His children. In this regard, John is likely responding to his opponents' claims. Apparently, they believed in the 'historical' Jesus, but denied His redemptive role. Jesus was a real human figure who was anointed by God to deliver a message in their estimation, but they rejected the notion that He was heaven-sent and that He died a penalty-bearing death as a substitutionary sacrifice. Jesus seems to have been only a moral prophet in their view who revealed what they considered to be a superior existence in which sin may exist, but it is no longer relevant for the Jesus-follower.

2. The fruit of love (vv. 11-21)

(a) Indwelling love and obligation (v. 11)
This sentence is composed of a conditional clause, 'if God so loved us,' and is followed by the main sentence. The grandeur

of divine benevolence brings with it obligation; if God so loves us as to give His only Son to purchase us, we have a duty to love others. God is the ground of ethics! Clearly this verse echoes John 3:16, as does the whole section of the letter. God does not ask of us what He has not provided the means and strength to do. He loved and He gave; we have received and we should give!

Parenthesis 30: The mechanics of obligation
There seems to be three grounds of motivation in human experience. Sometimes people obey in order to acquire something they desire and sometimes people obey in the hope that what they have will not be forfeited. These motivations do not apply to the Christian because there is nothing of a spiritual nature that we do not already possess and there is nothing with human failure can cause its loss. If this is so, what is the Christian's motive for obedience? The answer is twofold.

First, it is the disclosure to us of the love of God, for us as unmerited or uncaused. Christians take obligation seriously because they have come to the realization that they are the objects of God's love and grace through Christ. They no longer live in fear that God will change His mind about them, nor do they live in fear that God would find in them something so disturbing that He would forget His promises concerning them. God's actions are always in conformity with His character; His character is consistent with His promises.

Second, love is an attribute of God that demands self-expression. Thus, the gift of love revealed and granted through Jesus Christ to us innately demands expression as well. The difference between the divine self-expression of love and our expression of love is that ours is not native to us; it is foreign; it is the gift of God. Divine love is natural to God; it must be given to us because in our fallen state it is not natural, but supernatural.

These ideas are the bases of the mechanics of obedience. Choices are a function of our values. What we choose is the truest evidence of our affections. What we value most, resulting in consequent behavior, is what we perceive as most lovely. Simply put, our choices are related to what we value most at the point of decision-making. Beholding the immense, incomparable, incomprehensible love that God has for us, revealed in Christ's atoning sacrifice, causes us to know the meaning of love in its most profound sense. Having come to know, even in a meager sense, that God is love has transformed our choices. We choose what is most compelling, most desirous. God's love, revealed in the beauty of Christ, has become our compelling motive in choice making. Redemption has resulted in a new set of priorities, value, and delights.

(b) Indwelling love and assurance (vv. 12-13)
The unseen made visible (v. 12). How can we be assured that what is not visible to us is real? While Jesus revealed God the Father to us by the Spirit, the prophets and the apostles as well, no one has actually seen God for the simple reason that He is spirit (not subject to volume, shape or proportion). The answer is that an effect not only presupposes a cause, an effect also participates in the nature of the cause. If we love, as blighted creatures, if we possess love for God, that type of love not being native to us can only be ours through a gift. We have been given love, the love of God. If we have been given love, a love so great that only God could orchestrate it through His unique Son, then you and I have visible proof that God indeed loves us. If God so loves us, the manifestation of what is not native to us, is proof that we are the children of God. John will repeat the assertion that no one has seen God in 4:20.

The dependent clause, 'if we love,' grammatically describes a condition that is expected, expressing something that may be perceived as hypothetical. Further, the phrase, 'His love is perfected in us,' is subject to some misunderstanding since the apostle clearly rejects the notion that Christians have risen above fault. The tense of the verb is passive in mood indicating that it is something that God does for the believer. The verb 'is perfected' means 'to come to fullness or completion'. Says Smalley: '... when we "love one another," the implication is that mutual loving is indeed the fulfillment of divine obedience...' (248). The meaning, then, is that when divine love is manifested through us, God's purpose in granting His love is fulfilled; that is, love is granted so that it can be revealed. It is a developing, growing reality for Christians. See also the comments on I John 2:5 and 4:17.

The unseen gives confidence (v. 13). Since the Spirit is the love of God expressed in us, and Christ is the love of God manifested to us, we have grounds of assurance when we love others that we know God. To possess the character of God, albeit in shadowed form and with inconsistency, since the infinite life of God cannot be fully evident in any finite endeavor, lends credence to our profession. To have only what God can give is to have assurance because of the character of the one who has made promises to us. John states the same thing in 3:24 with the exact terminology.

There is some discussion as to how to translate the term 'that' which occurs twice in the verse ('... we know *that*' and '...*that* He has given us His Spirit'). The NASB interprets the first as explanatory ('by this we know that we reside in God'); that is, the phrase following *that* tells us what we know. The second *that* can be a statement of reason or cause, in this case for what we know (as in the NASB) or it can be explanatory as in the first occurrence. If explanatory, it tells us how we know (by the indwelling Spirit). If causal, it tells us why we know. Though the difference is slight, it seems best to see the second 'that' as explanatory because of John's use of similar phraseology in 2:3 and 3:24. It also elucidates 4:27. The fact of the Spirit, not so much the effects of the Spirit, is the basis of assurance here. It is not the ongoing witnessing of the Spirit to us; it is the fact of His presence in us!

This verse makes it clear that the word 'abide' is not used by John to describe a temporal state of Christian life, times of experiential intimacy with God. The 'abiding' is the simultaneous state of the indwelling of the Spirit sent from the Father. Since by definition all Christians have been given the life of God, a life purchased by Christ and granted in the Holy Spirit, all Christians abide in Him. John simply does not know of temporally abiding Christians; either we have the Spirit and abide or we do not and are without the life of God. John's opponents may claim to know God, and even know Him in an insightful way, but, not possessing the gift of the Spirit, they do not. Morality is a secondary ground of assurance that we possess the life of God; the primary evidence is the indwelling Spirit. Morality is not a constant state for any Christian; indwelling by the Spirit is the constant experience of all Christians. Since morality is the consequence of indwelling, it must be secondary evidence. Otherwise, it seems that an effect becomes its own cause!

(c) Indwelling love and confidence (vv. 14-16)
Assurance and the Spirit's indwelling (v. 14). Though no one has seen God, God revealed Himself through His Son to the apostles as the redeemer. This verse seems to be a repetition of verse 12, a literary device John often uses to highlight his points. The 'we' seems to be a reference to the apostolic community recalling his introductory identification in 1:1-3. John uses the same verbal tense in 1:1 as here, but, more importantly, John speaks of something the apostles actually *saw* (this could not be true of the church to which he is writing).

The phrase 'Savior of the world,' appears only twice in the Holy Scriptures, here and John 4:42. In 4:42, the phrase is expressed by a group of men after the encounter of the Samaritan woman with Jesus at the well in Sychar to whom she tactfully witnessed. In the statement of the men, the connotation is that redemption has expanded beyond the Jews, meaning people groups rather than an ethnicity or mere geographics. This text may have significance in the interpretation of the phrase in John 2:2, 'sins of the whole world.' What can clearly be expressed is that in John's writings 'world' is not limited to geographics, but can express ethnicities. Perhaps Smalley comes a little closer to John's nuance when he writes, 'The "world" in this context means not only mankind in general, as the theatre of salvation, but also the world in *opposition* to God, in need of redemption' (253).

Parenthesis 31: 'The Savior of the World'
In what sense will Christ be the 'Savior of the world'? It is certain that if 'world' means all the people in it, the phrase, if taken in the sense of normal usage, would be a contradiction. Simply put, the witness of Holy Scripture is that all mankind will not be saved. The 'world' can mean sinful society estranged from God and under the dominion of the evil one. There will be a day when the 'world' will be composed of the

godly in the new heavens and new earth exclusively. At any rate, 'world,' has several meanings in Scripture:

a) An inclusive term for all those who are in the kingdom of darkness and have not been born of God (I John 5:19).

b) The present sphere of the extension of God's love and saving mercy (John 3:16, I John 2:2, 4:14), the now aspects of the now-and-not-yet kingdom.

c) Godless values (I John 2:16).

d) In the final restoration of the world, in the great regeneration after the Final Judgment, the effect of Christ's death will result in a cleansed, revivified dwelling in the new earth of only the redeemed. Christ will redeem the physical world delivering it from its groaning to become a renewed 'city'.

• • • • •

Assurance and faith (v. 15). A second ground of assurance is belief that Jesus is the Son of God. Boice has a pithy comment on the grounds of assurance: '…we may know that we have the Spirit because we have come to confess Christ and dwell in love' (118). It would seem that John's opponents embraced the historic personage of Jesus, but they would have been troubled with confessing Him to be absolute deity in the flesh. Those who confess Jesus as true deity in a human body (John 1:14) know God, 'abide' in God, and God in them (3:24). Once more, the concept of 'abiding' is the same as knowing God and being indwelt by the Spirit. By definition, all Christians abide in God; abiding is neither optional nor temporal.

Assurance through love (v. 16). The experience of the indwelling of God is the manifestation of His love in us; this love is the Spirit. It is the divine indwelling of God which alone makes possible both belief and love. By indwelling, God's very character shines through the believer providing assurance that 'the one who abides in love abides in God'.

Since the topic is assurance, not the origin of the message of assurance, it seems that the 'we' is John, the believing community he addresses, and all believers. Are 'knowing' and 'believing' separate acts or is John using two words to describe the encounter with salvation? The nature of knowing, being more than intellectual ascent, and believing also suggests that John is describing the same phenomena with two verbs. While the tense of the verbs indicates past action with continuing results, it does not necessitate a linear or sequential understanding separating the two of them. In other words, knowing is believing! No one can appreciate the wonder and beauty of God, a glorious purchase by Christ, and the free gift of life through the Spirit without either knowing about it or embracing it through faith.

The substance or object of knowing, believing, is the love of God. The prepositional phrase, 'for us', can also be rendered 'in us'. If translated in this fashion the emphasis would be upon the indwelling or presence of God in the believer, not so much the affection of God for the believer. Taking it either way is valid. However, the same phrase occurs in 4:9 and 12 and is rendered 'in us'. The end of the verse speaks of God abiding 'in' the believer.

(d) Indwelling love and consequences (vv. 17-18)
Verse 17 begins with another of those difficult 'by this' statements. Does it refer to what has preceded it or does it explain what follows? It seems best to take it as drawing out implications from the discussion previously of assurance. The mutuality of union through indwelling, God in the believer and the believer in God, leads to certain consequences. We ought not to dread His coming, nor to live in fear that we will be punished.

Surety in the Day of Judgment (v. 17). The indwelling love of God as a divine principle within is being 'perfected' in us. The tense and mood of the verb is significant. The verbal tense is such that it indicates an action instigated in the past with continuing results into the present. Further, the verbal mood is passive indicating that the action of the verb is a work performed by God, not the recipients. It is something the believer receives. The verb means to accomplish, to bring to a conclusion, to obtain the goal, or to complete. God's love, expressed by His indwelling presence, is brought to fruition in the believer, in fact in all believers! Brown is worth quoting: '…it is relatively clear that this outgoing love from

God reaches perfection [intended purpose or goal], from one aspect, when it produces children in whom love dwells' (526). Here John seems to be saying that the presence of God's love in the believer has the effect, a purpose reached, of granting confidence in the 'Day of Judgment', a phrase only occurring here in the letter; there will be no reason for consternation or dread. The reason for the confidence the believers possess ('because') is that as Jesus ('He' clearly refers to Jesus as in 2:6; 3:3, 5, 7, 16) is now in the presence of God fully accepted, so shall they be some day ('…when He appears we shall be like Him' [3:2]).

The phrase, 'the Day of Judgment,' is found only here in all of John's writings. The concept of a final judgment is not alien to John, even in this letter though the exact wording is not repeated (2:28, 3:2).

Lack of fear in life (v. 18). The love that spells confidence banishes fear; fear and love are mutually incompatible. The reason for this is that fear is rooted in the potential of punishment. The threat of eternal punishment has been banished in Christ by the Spirit. Christ has eliminated the cause of true fear. He took our punishment for us! One knows that love is mature when a relationship of trust casts fear away. Says Brown: 'It now becomes clear that for the author fear involves not only the absence of love but also the presence of the punishment that it anticipates. By detracting from love, which involves God's presence, fear is anticipating final punishment, which consists in the absence of God' (531).

There has been considerable discussion concerning the phrase, 'but perfect love casts out fear.' Is the love, the indwelling love of God in believers, the believers' love for God, or the believers' love for one another? It would seem contextually that it is most likely the first of these options. In 4:9, it is the love of God that sent Jesus to them; the consequence is that they love God and one another (4:19, 21). The love of God in believers, when it reaches its purpose of showing forth the Father, is so great that it triumphs over lesser realities, such as fear. Philip Doddridge poem, 'Now Let Our Cheery Eyes Survey,' captures the notion of the confidence the Christian has in the love of God through Christ:

Now let our cheerful eyes survey
our great high priest above,
And celebrate His constant care,
and sympathetic love.

Though raised to a superior throne,
where angels bow around,
And high o'er all the shining train,
with matchless honors crowned —

The names of all His saints
He bears engraven on His heart;
Nor shall a name once treasured there
e'er from His care depart.

Parenthesis 32: The nature of imperfect love
John has mentioned the concept of 'perfect love' in the believer several times (2:5; 4:12, 18). The concept is not so much that love is gradually acquired as sanctification progresses, though the implications of love might grow. If the presence of life in God is the very life of God implanted as a permanent fact in our lives by the residence or indwelling of the Holy Spirit, since there are not degrees of a relationship with God (one is either redeemed or lost), and since the perfectness of love is in God, 'perfect love' is a call for us to realize something; it is a ground of our assurance of life eternal. Love by its presence necessitates manifestation or revelation, not increase; accordingly, at the instance of redemption, which entails the infusion of the character of God, love accomplishes its implanted purpose when it is revealed. 'Perfect love' is not that of the creature; it is the life of God in the creature. If the opposite of 'perfect love' is 'imperfect love', what is imperfect love? It is the absence of the love of God; it is hatred; it is to be in the state of lostness! Brown's comment is pertinent: '… in Johannine dualism the opposite to perfect love may not be perfect love, but hate. To hold on to fear is to be on the wrong side of judgment' (532). The presence of love, being a state, a reality, is not a matter of degrees; it is all or nothing because no one possesses the life of God partially and no one is lost partially.

• • • • •

The indwelling love of God and fear that there is punishment yet to endure are antithetical. The nature of the punishment in this instance is that related to the Day of Judgment (v. 17), suggesting that it concerns an eternal reckoning. The verse seems to imply that when the love of God has not reached its fullness in the conscience of the believer fear is the consequence ('the one who fears is not perfect in love'). Fear in this instance is the result of not completely understanding the wonders of divine redemption and thus is quite unwarranted. In John's radical dualism the opposite of resting in the love of God is living in hatred of God; it is the state of the unbeliever. If the love in question is the love of God, not the affectionate response of a believer, that divine indwelling love means the end of a fearful punishment for unrequited errors. Mutual indwelling casts aside fear.

(e) Indwelling love and conclusions (vv. 19-21)
A truth disclosed (v. 19). The great privilege of all Christians is that they share in the life of God. Since God is love, we love. It is interesting that this sentence is without a direct object (it simply reads, 'We love.'). Should 'God' be supplied as the direct object or should 'one another'? Within the larger context both are appropriate (John is easy to read, but the meaning is often clouded in obscurity). If one had to choose between the options, both being viable, the following verse places an emphasis on the mutuality of human love. Also, the pronoun 'He' is clearly a reference to the Father (4:16).

A clarification stated (v. 20). Love excludes the disregard of others. It is incontrovertible! Says Smalley: 'Love for God, as said in verse 12, is expressed in love for others. To withhold the one is to render the other impossible' (264). Clearly, the pronoun 'He' refers to the Father (4:16). His love is revealed in the sending of the Son of God to be our redeemer (4:9, 10, 14).

The structure of this verse (a claim, a circumstance, a condemnation, and a justification) should remind the reader of similarities with 1:6, 8, 10 and 2:4, 9. As in the previous parallels, John seems to have his opponents in view. They make a claim to love, but their actions betray their profession. Love of God, knowledge of God, life in God, and abiding or residing in God are mutually inclusive; the life of God possessed is the life of God expressed. It is impossible to have the character of God within through the Spirit and not to show love on a human plane that is a response to the love of God. Redemption changes haters of God, and thus haters of mankind, into lovers of God, and, thus, lovers of mankind. Says Brown: '…in Johannine dualism neither indifference nor insufficient love is the opposite of loving – that opposite is described as not loving at all (4:20d) or hating (4:20b)…' (533).

Parenthesis 33: A fundamental claim
One of the most important insights one can have is simply the ability to differentiate between what is cause and what is effect. This is a most persistent error in human experience; often we confuse the two, accrediting to an effect the function of cause. This is fatal in the Christian faith because a fundamental assumption of the faith is that it is supernatural in origins and cause. Christians are convinced that 'salvation is of the Lord', that it is a free gift from God mediated through Christ and given through the Spirit of God, and our response to the disclosure of God's grace is not the cause of God's grace in salvation. The cause of salvation for anyone is the unexplainable, discriminatory mercy of God (if salvation were based on human merit of any kind, even a response on our behalf, it would make God obligated to us and salvation becomes something due us, a wage, something acquired by us). Thus, love is not the cause of salvation; it is the result of salvation. The quality of love in redemption is divine; it is infinite, not finite. Finite love can only result in finite love (a consequence participates in the nature of its cause). God cannot be obligated or necessitated; He acts without external contingencies. It is the desire of God to manifest His very character that accounts for salvation, as well as creation.

● ● ● ● ●

A commandment reiterated (v. 21). Because God is love, He commands us to love. We should not separate what God joins. In the structure of the verse, the second half explains the nature of what is commended in the first half (the 'that' is explanatory); the commandment is to love. What is unique in this verse is that John connects love for God and people positively whereas in verse 20 it was stated in the negative. The pronoun 'Him' in the verse is a reference to God the Father (there are two different pronouns that John employs and they are translated in the same way; however, by virtue of their structure and usage one refers to the Father and the other to Jesus Christ). The immediate context supports the reference to God the Father as well.

How can we apply the truth of this section?
(1) A consuming passion for the well-being of others has its wellspring in the character of God. We love because God first loved us! To know the God of love means to express love, which is the love that God has for us. Just as God's character demands expression intrinsically (love having the internal need of expression as does divine glory), so does the characteristic of love from within the redeemed.

(2) God showed us the meaning of love when He gave us His Son; the Son showed us His love when He died for us on Calvary's tree; the Spirit is the love of the Father and the Son expressed in and through the believer. 'While the origin of love is in the being of God, the manifestation of love is in the coming of Christ' (161), said Stott. The experience of love is the Spirit.

(3) The Spirit is the love of God in us (vv. 12-13). Since the Spirit is immaterial, not subject to perception and having no form that is observable, His presence can only be seen in the consequences that result from His presence in us. God's presence is more than a mere moral principle (admittedly something beyond words to adequately explain), the evidence of His presence is revealed in morals, both attitudes and actions.

(4) A lack of love makes one's profession of knowing God suspect. If a person makes a claim to know God, but the consistent pattern of their behavior is contrary to the character of God, their profession is empty. When God saves, He changes those He saves in attitudes, priorities and actions. All Christians, having the remnant of sin's once universal dominion as a present reality in their lives, are not perfect, nor can they be until the final redemption in the great day when Christ returns to judge the world and all that is in it.

However, the pattern of the life of Christians is discernibly altered by the divine presence causing them to long for holiness and to grieve over their imperfections.

(5) Christians can have an assurance of God's redemptive mercies. This assurance is grounded in the presence of the indwelling Holy Spirit. Consequently, Christians need not live in fear that God will punish them for some wrongdoing because Christ died for them, paying the penalty for all their trespasses and has ascended to heaven where He acts as their great advocate. To know the love that God has for them, evidenced in the sending of the Son and the Spirit, is to no longer live in fear that something in their past (or today or even tomorrow) would prevent their full acquittal at the bar of divine justice!

(6) The section begins and ends (vv. 7, 21) with the command to love one another. It seems that the Liberal Tradition of Christian faith is correct in emphasizing the love of God and the necessity of love for one another. However, where they often err is in not according Jesus Christ the absolute perfections of deity. That tradition sees Jesus as more or less human, the flower and best of humanity's true prophets, who came to disseminate a message of self-giving, exemplifying it in His own sacrifice of quiet forbearance of injustice, not of a dying and atoning Savior but a grand example of human self-emptying for others, a humanitarian. John makes it plain that it is impossible to know God except as He is presented to us through the Son of God (vv. 9-10, 15). There can be no true Christianity without a truly divine, substitutionary atoning, Jesus Christ. Only through Jesus is the love of the Father revealed, purchased, and possessed. Love is not defined by mutuality of reciprocation on a human level; love's real meaning is found in the character of God revealed in the character of Jesus Christ and granted to us by the divine Spirit. The Liberal Tradition makes much of God's love, but it is without a biblical foundation and thus becomes at times little more than the support of prevailing cultural values in the name of 'love'. This statement, however, is not to disparage or leave unrecognized the enormous humanitarian efforts of that tradition to extend love for mankind. Mankind's love for mankind is important, but it should not be denominated

Christian love, the revealing of the love of Christ, when the person and work of Christ is denigrated!

E. The test of faith (5:1-12)

Of the five tests of genuine profession, the apostle comes to faith or belief last; it is the apex of his argument. Faith, love, and obedience are the natural fruits of a supernatural rebirth just as faith, love, and obedience are the evidences of the mutual indwelling of God with His people.

It is not a matter of consensus among scholars that 5:1 marks out a new section. However, the basis for this choice is what seems to be a change of topic to belief. The word 'believes' occurs six times in these verses, faith once in verse 4, and 'receiving a witness' four times in verse 9. In addition, in verse 12 there is a near parallel expression in 'He who has the Son...' It, therefore, seems that a new theme has been introduced.

1. The evidences of faith (vv. 1-4a)

(a) Love (vv. 1-2)
The fact (v. 1). The origin of divine redemption is God through Jesus, the Anointed One of God. Since the consequence of that redemption is love, because every effect partakes of the nature of its cause, a Christian is one who innately loves both the giver and the provider since they share mutuality of love (as parent, so child). The content of saving faith is 'that Jesus is the Christ' (here, John uses 'Christ' as a title, rather than as Jesus' fuller name [as in 4:2, 'Jesus Christ']). Calvin makes the same point when he writes: 'This title... designates the office to which our Savior was appointed by the Father' (87). John's opponents would have embraced the fact of the historical Jesus, but they would have had problems with the claim that Jesus was the Messiah (the Christ), the promised one of God. They seem to have viewed Him as a prophet-like human person only, who arose to deliver a message from God similar to the prophets before His time. Thus, they denied the apostolic message that Jesus was God in the flesh, that He came from heaven, that He is deity, and that He was God's chosen redeemer. So in 4:2, 'that Jesus Christ has come in the flesh

is from God,' the point of dispute, is not so much that Jesus is human; it is that He came from God (the incarnation and preexistence of Jesus who became the Christ). '...it becomes clear that their Christology involved a denial that Jesus Christ is the Messiah, God's Son, come in the flesh, and whose death was both real and necessary (4:2-3, 15; 5:1, 6-8)' [Kruse, 170].

Parenthesis 34: John's claims concerning Jesus
What John says of the person and work of Jesus is interesting, providing a composite picture of the apostles' Christology: '...His Son Jesus Christ' (1:3); '...Jesus His Son... (1:7); '...Jesus Christ the righteous' (2:1); '...Jesus is the Christ...' (2:22); '...in Him is no sin' (3:5); 'The Son of God...' (3:8); '...that Jesus Christ has come in the flesh' (4:2); '...His only-begotten Son...' (4:9); '...Jesus is the Son of God' (4:15; 5:5); '...Son of God...His Son' (5:10); '...His Son' (5:11); '...the Son of God' (5:13); and '...the Son of God...His Son Jesus Christ...' (5:19).

What Jesus accomplished was more than delivering a self-help, self-awareness message to buttress self-esteem. He came to purchase salvation through His substitutionary sacrifice: '...the blood of Jesus His Son cleanses us from all sin' (1:7); '...we have an Advocate with the Father... (2:1); '...and He Himself is the propitiation for our sins...' (2:2); '...He appeared to take away sins...' (3:5); '...we might live through Him...' (4:9); 'He...sent His Son to be the propitiation for our sins' (4:10); and '...this life is in His Son' (5:11).

• • • • •

The verb 'is born' is perfect tense and passive voice, suggesting that the action commenced in the indeterminate past with continuing results. The mood of the verb implies that regeneration or rebirth is the work of God; it is something done on our behalf without our participation as to its cause. This perfect, passive verb occurs seven times in the letter (3:9 [twice]; 4:7; 5:1, 4, 18 [twice]). Further, the perfect tense verb is connected with a present tense verb, 'believes.' This suggests that believing is a consequence of the rebirth or regeneration. Says Stott: 'It shows clearly that believing is a consequence, not the cause, of the new birth. Our present, continuing activity of believing is the result, and therefore the evidence, of our experience of the new birth by which we become and remain God's children' (172). The literary eloquence of Robert Law makes the point even more lucid: 'The fundamental Johannine position is that the whole redemptive process has its origin, not in any conscious human act, but in a sub-conscious activity of the Divine life in man; and the first fruit and manifestation of this activity is the power to "see," "to believe" on him who is Light, to "know" God whom He reveals' (63). It is interesting that the Father, using a birthing image, is cast in the role of mothering.

When John uses the word 'believe', it is often in reference to Jesus Christ; that is, Jesus is the object of saving faith (3:23; 5:1, 5, 10, 13). It is not without significance that John only uses 'belief,' meaning a truth system once (5:4) while it appears in New Testament literature over 240 times. John's emphasis throughout the letter is upon a person, rather than a coterie of assertions about the person.

Parenthesis 35: The sequence of regeneration and faith
There is considerable discussion within theological circles, clearly divisive in demeanor and consequence at times, of the relation of the action of the Spirit in regeneration and the human act of faith. Which causes which is the issue? If regeneration precedes faith, how do you handle the many texts of Holy Scripture that state that salvation is a consequence of belief – for example, 'Believe on the Lord Jesus Christ and you shall be saved...' (Acts 16:31) or '...as many as believe on Him, to them He gave the right to become children of God, even to those who believe in His name' (John 1:12). The very call of the gospel seems to indicate that faith precedes regeneration.

However, a text such as this one (5:1) is equally clear that regeneration, the rebirth, takes precedence sequentially over faith. A solution may be found in understanding that the two occur without sequence, instantaneously. How can this be so since you cannot have two events happening at the same time in normal experience? The answer is that the rebirth and faith, the action of God and the response of faith on our part, are components of a single miracle. A miracle is comprised of many events that occur instantly (this is why an unbeliever can see a miracle and contribute it to circumstantial factors and, consequently, believe that it did not happen!). Logically, regeneration must precede faith because an effect is not a cause. If faith is the ultimate cause of salvation, then salvation is a consequence of a human endeavor. Thus, in this scenario, salvation would be a wage, a work, and meritorious (clearly not the case, as Romans 4:1-5 and Ephesians 2:8-9 witness). In such a view faith becomes, in function, a Protestant form of a Roman Catholic sacrament. Simply stated, no one can make a choice that they do not perceive as a choice in the first place. An object must be perceived, in this case the beauty of the atoning Savior, before a choice of that Redeemer can be confessed.

What we have is the failure of finite language; language confined to explain events in a linearity of cause-effect sequence that is incapable or cannot explain the multiplicity of events in a miracle without distortion. Those who do not accept divine authority leave God out of the equation seeing natural causes behind unexplainable events; the Bible explains the miracle of regeneration from the divine viewpoint and a human viewpoint. The failure is that we do not hold these in tension; the approach taken by many is to downplay the witness of some verses claiming that others take precedence over them. One is the perspective of heaven and the other the approach of human explanations. It would seem wiser to believe all that the Holy Scriptures declare, and simply be left with fewer answers, though we wish more, than to have answers that do not value some texts as are warranted. We are not people with all the answers; we are people who have met the one who is the answer and we desire to speak of Him to any and every one. It is wisdom to realize that God has revealed Himself truly, but not completely. How can finite creatures, even redeemed ones, grasp the infinite God whose wisdom has only been partially disclosed to us?

• • • • •

The last part of the verse, 'whoever loves the Father loves the child born of Him,' seems to be an axiomatic saying (parental affection implies sibling affection since an effect partakes of its cause). The opposite of love is hatred (4:20) and this is the charge that John claims of his opponents; they lack love because they have never had an authentic encounter with God through Christ by the Spirit. Therefore, they do not know the Father for, if they did, they would love the Father's children. And, they do not.

The test (v. 2). Just as in redemption, when the life of God is expressed in divine love received and residing as an abiding moral principle within our innermost beings, so the principle of affection emanates outward from its recipients in a loving appreciation for God and a respect and regard for His children. Love is more than a feeling or mental attitude; the invisible translates into the visible. This is a valid test that we have been born of God. Do we share His character? This is how, John would say, that we know that we know God.

We have noted the phrase, 'by this,' several times as it appears throughout the letter (2:3, 5; 3:16, 24; 4:2, 6, 13). The difficulty arises in understanding whether it refers to what precedes or what follows. It would seem that we should take it with what follows ('By this [love of God's children], we know that we love…'). Again love is expressed in tangible ways to John; it is when we obey what God dictates as proper behavior toward others. Yarbrough makes an interesting point at this juncture: 'First John 5:2 rules out that common oversimplification of Christian faith, which contends that how we treat other people is, in the end, all that counts' (273).

Parenthesis 36: Love and others
The Bible makes it clear that all believers have an obligation to love one another. However, how are we to fulfill this commandment, one that is both new and old (2:7-8), when we know so very few in the global body of Christ?

In an intricate web of cause-effect relationships, well beyond finitude to grasp, in some kind of redeemed second-Adam unity, we serve those we do not know by doing what is proper and, equally true, we dishonor those we do not know when we disobey the Lord. Simply put, obedience has ramifications none of us will ever grasp.

• • • • •

(b) Obedience (v. 3)
1) The test (v. 3a). The verse begins with the word 'for' which indicates that the author is drawing an inference from what has been stated previously. This verse reiterates and develops what it means to love God, to embrace God's redemption. Love of God, meaning our love for Him (the evidence for saying this is the 'we' subsequently in the verse, the subject is our love, not God's love for us), is expressed in obedience, not mere words of testimony that such is the case. The 'that' in 'that we keep…' introduces an explanation of what we 'know'.

Parenthesis 37: Motivation for obedience
In the previous verse (v. 2) John spoke of the love that God has for His children; here he speaks of His children's love for Him expressed in obedience. As human motivation is grounded in our quest to maximize what we consider pleasurable while minimizing what we consider painful, the criteria of what we consider good or bad becomes the issue. Choices are made from this perspective by all of us. The difficulty is not that the unbeliever has no ability to make choices; it is that he/she has only an earthly viewpoint on their options. By the infusion of the life of God into their souls, believers have been given new priorities because they have been introduced to an overwhelmingly compelling object here-to-fore unknown to them. This vision of God and heavenly delights does not change the mechanism for freely making choices; it redefines what is pleasure and pain. Things once loved pass, while things unknown to love come and remain. Knowing the utter beauty of God through Christ is so renovating that our ethics are radicalized in comparison to what was once considered pleasure and pain.

• • • • •

The Bible does not say that obedience is easy (it does state that it is not 'burdensome'); it says that obedience is a 'delight'. Because we have come to know a love that is beyond description, being infinite, our perspectives toward others change in conformity to that revealed, unexpected affection. The word 'burdensome' means grievous, difficult, or irksome.

Regeneration (v. 4) simply is a reorienting gift from God; it is the state of having found a world far more 'real' and meaningful than the passing shadows of this 'real' world. The phrase 'of God' can either indicate our love for God or God's love for us. The context makes the latter most probable.

Some of our translators see two sentences in this verse, the first ending after 'commandments' (the NASB places a semicolon there while others place a period). In either option, the sense remains the same. What is interesting, even amazing, is that while the grammar is often difficult to understand, the meaning is not!

(c) Victory (v. 4)

The 'victory' John speaks of here is not empowerment for an exceptionally successful, spiritual life. It is about triumph over the worldly system of values, particularly in the context of the issue of the care and prioritizing of the needs of others; it is the lot of every Christian simply because faith is the lot of every Christian. We are able to keep the commandments of God for two reasons: first, the rebirth that brings a new perspective on our values and, second, persistent faith. Our faith in God has caused us to value less what we once esteemed highly in many instances. The verb 'to overcome' or 'to conquer' is found also in 2:13-14 and 4:4. In the former, the reference was to victory over the evil one and in the latter verse the reference was to John's opponents. It seems most probable that John is referring to victory over error with the use of 'world' twice suggesting worldly values or teachings.

The reason ('for' or 'because') that the commandment to love is not troublesome is that our priorities have changed by virtue of a new object of affections. John most likely also has in mind the true believer's unwillingness to follow after the false teachers. Love is not only a command; it is a ground of assurance. The perfect passive verb 'is born' suggests a past action orchestrated by God, something done to us, not by us, with continuing consequences into the present (3:9 [twice]; 4:7; 5:1, 4, 18 [twice]). The fact that the rebirth by God has continuous results is why the believer is an overcomer! John H. Yates' poem, 'Faith is the Victory,' captures something of John's thought:

Encamped along the hills of light,
Ye Christian soldiers, rise.
And press the battle ere the night
shall veil the glowing skies.

Against the foe in vales below
let all our strength be hurled.
Faith is the victory, we know
that overcomes the world.

His banner over us is love,
our sword the Word of God.
We tread the road the saints above
with shouts of triumph trod.

By faith, they like a whirlwind's breath
swept on o'er every field.
The faith by which they conquered death
is still our shining shield.

Faith is the victory!
Faith is the victory!
O glorious victory that overcomes the
    world!

Note in these verses that John repeats the phrase, 'overcomes the world,' three times. It is present tense; it is an ongoing reality. What does he refer to as the cause of our overcoming? Our rebirth! We now see the world of false values that once glittered like gold as tarnished fool's gold!

The ground of victory is stated in verse 4b. The way to avoid the deception of the false teachers is a matter of object of alliance. However, the faith of anyone is only as valid as the object unto which it is expressed. John tells us that the proper object of overcoming faith is Jesus, the Son of God (4:5) or deity in the flesh. Faith or trust in this one delivers us from the deception that is present in the world.

What precisely is the object of this faith or trust that delivers from the deception present in the world? Is it our faith? Is it the object of our faith? What is the object of faith, if it is faith? The most cogent answer seems to be the salvific accomplishment of Christ through His death for us

(John refers to Jesus in this manner in the gospel [16:33] and in the Revelation [3:21, 5:5, 12:11]). The false teachers would not object to the notion of allegiance and deliverance through Jesus, but they would be troubled in according Him the status of equality with God. The opponents of John claimed that Jesus was a prophet-like instructor, but not the Redeemer from sin through His atoning, substitutionary sacrifice.

A logical question emerges at this point because of what appears unclear, the meaning of the use of the past tense 'has overcome'. John goes on to specify that 'our faith' is the cause of victory that has been secured. It appears to be a past, completed action. To what does conquering faith have reference to in this instance? Does it refer to 'our faith' in the accomplishments of Jesus? However, John only says that it is 'our faith'; he does not specify its content. Does it refer to the inception of faith, the time they came to faith-conversion? Though it is impossible definitively to determine the issue, it seems contextually warranted to define the content of 'our faith', faith that resulted in some type of accomplishment, as the recognition and defeat of the secessionist attempt to pervert the apostles' teachings. John's recipients seem to have realized the danger and he writes to encourage them in the aftermath of the disturbance that had been caused in the churches. This seems to respect the credibility of the past tense over the other views. In 2:14 and 4:4 the conquering or victory is an ongoing process (the perfect tense of the verb is used to signify continuous action), not a completed action. Here it seems that what is envisioned is completed action.

The grounds of victory are reiterated in verse 5. A rhetorical question is stated and answered for emphasis by John; Jesus, the Son of God, is the object of conquering faith. John often uses the literary method of repetition to make a point explicit. True, biblically warranted, and overcoming faith, is in Jesus who is the Christ (5:1), the Son of God (4:15)! John combines these two titles for Jesus; He is both God's anointed deliverer (the Christ) and deity (the Son of God). John's opponents would have embraced the concept of the historical Jesus, but would not accept that He was deity in the flesh.

2. *The object of faith (vv. 6-12)*

The previous paragraph (vv. 1-5) begins and ends with the same topic, belief or faith. This paragraph states the historic grounds of our faith. There it was stated that faith overcomes; it brings triumph over the world of false values. Here John turns to the object of this victorious faith, the identity of Jesus Christ specifically.

(a) The object of faith: stated (vv. 6-8)

John begins by identifying the ground of the believer's victory, 'Jesus…the Son of God' (v. 5), Jesus Christ ('this is the one…') whom he verifies by two instances of His coming, 'water and blood.' The emphasis seems to be upon the second of the identity marks of Jesus because John writes, 'not by water only.' It can be conjectured that John's opponents would not have objected to 'water', but it seems they did His blood (that is, if they viewed His baptism as the referent to water and identified the significance of it as the time the Christ, the power of God, came upon Jesus to energize His prophetic-like ministry). As noted earlier, the false teachers did not deny that Jesus was a historical figure; they believed in His physical historicity, but denied His equality with God, as deity in the flesh. 'Jesus is the Son of God' is John's claim (5:5; 4:15), '…that Jesus Christ *has come* in the flesh' (not simply Jesus, but Jesus as the Christ *had come*, 4:2). The issue with the false teachers is not Jesus, but Jesus Christ (the Messiah, the term having a redemptive nuance) and the verb 'has come'. They argued that Jesus was flesh, yet nothing more (not the Christ).

The most difficult phrase to interpret is 'by water and blood'. Some have understood John to mean that His adversaries rejected the humanity of Christ so that the point of the phrase is to declare His humanity, interpreting the phrase to speak of His baptism and crucifixion, the beginning and end of our Lord's earthly ministry. Thus, in this view, the false teachers were some sort of proto-Gnostics, dualists embracing a docetic or mystical view of Christ's flesh, denigrating any material aspects of His life and elevating the moral/spiritual instead, and John is combatting that notion here. However, they believed that Jesus was only human, not deity in the flesh (the assumption that John's opponents denied the humanity of Christ does not seem warranted, the assumption being without textual affirmation). They denied that Jesus Christ had come in the flesh, not that Jesus possessed humanity. Their assertion was that He only possessed humanity. This particular view, then, takes the prepositional phrase as a general affirmation of Jesus' humanity, and the particular reference is to His baptism and crucifixion as held by many scholars.

Yet it would seem that the least problematic interpretation, and the most textually consistent Johannine approach, is that the phrase looks to a single event – the death of Jesus, and not to two events in His life (if two events were envisioned, separated by some time, one would expect two prepositions, not one). In this instance, the conjunction 'and' governs 'water' and 'blood' as a unity. John elsewhere indicates that 'blood and water' flowed from the pierced side of Jesus (John 19:34). While the phrase in the gospel is 'blood and water', John may have reversed the order here to stress the point of his disagreement with his opponents, the atoning blood of Jesus. The secessionists might have been willing to identify water with Jesus' baptism by John the Baptist, but would have rejected a salvific meaning to His death ('not by water only, but by the blood and the water'). Kruse makes the point succinctly: 'It was the reality and atoning significance of Jesus' death that the secessionists denied and that the author is compelled to assert' (178). Further, the only other reference to the blood of Jesus in the letter is to His atoning sacrifice (1:7).

John ends the verse by reiterating the basis of authority for writing as he has. The validation of the witness of the water and blood, the death of Christ, is by the Spirit (the assumption being that 'that' is to be rendered causally ['because'] as in the NASB, though it could be declarative ['the Spirit bears witness that the Spirit is truth']. Believers know that these things are true because they have received divine affirmation through the anointing of the Spirit, something inherent in the miracle of regeneration and, hence, requiring no teachers (it is a reality that accompanies the miracle of redemption). The Spirit is truth, the unquestioned authority regarding the meaning of the things of God. John may once more be hinting at the error of his opponents. In all likelihood, the false teachers believed in the Spirit of God, being pneumatists (spirit-people), but they misinterpreted the Spirit as being a power or force in Jesus' life as He was in the lives of the prophets (remember, it seems that their model of Jesus and His ministry was that of the Old Testament prophets exclusively). John would then be saying that the witness of the Spirit is to Jesus as the Christ, the Son of God. In essence, John would be indicating that his opponents are wrong on both Jesus and the Spirit, though they claim the latter's empowerment and possession of a prophetic role themselves (4:1-3). See also, John 21:24.

Some have pondered why the Spirit is introduced as a third witness at this juncture (v. 6b), though it is not specifically stated that the Spirit is an additional witness, John having stated that there are two witnesses in the previous sentence. A possible answer may be found in John 19:34 and its context. In 19:35, John speaks as an eyewitness of the crucifixion with wording that is somewhat parallel to what we have here, except that here John accredits what he saw to the Spirit. There is no instance in the New Testament Scriptures where the Spirit witnesses to Himself; the function of the Spirit is to bear witness to Jesus Christ. Thus, the witness of the Spirit is to the evidence provided by the 'water and blood'. The Spirit substantiates John's witness to Jesus' atoning death (Jesus is the Christ, Jesus is the Son of God, meaning one sent from God as His equal and, thus, fully capable of procuring our forgiveness through His atoning sacrifice as evidenced at Calvary in the spilling out of water and blood, His very life). The reference to plural witnesses may be an allusion to Deuteronomy 19:15; there it is stated that a claim is to be substantiated by two or three witnesses.

Though truth is to be confirmed by two witnesses, John mentions three (vv. 7-8). Having mentioned the Spirit as a witness in verse 7 and the water and blood in verse 6, it would seem that John, by using three witnesses, is making the point indisputable. The repetition of the connective 'and' and the definite article before each makes the three witnesses parallel and equal. Together, the witnesses point to the truth of Jesus' redemptive death, something John's opponents would have denied. The subject of verse 5, Jesus' death, is continued in verses 7-8.

(b) The content of faith: verified (vv. 9-12)
John adds a fourth witness to the sacrificial death of Jesus,
and the witness is God the Father (v. 9). The tense of the verb,
'has borne,' indicates an event with continuing validity; God
bore witness to His Son and the witness continues. God's
witness to Jesus surpasses that of human witnesses! The
'witness of men', being surpassed by God, most likely does
not refer to the Spirit's witness nor to the inspired prophet
John the Baptist, since John's ministry was inspired by the
Spirit and, hence, divinely sanctioned, but to what believers
say about Jesus (John was a man, not 'men', and the witness
is singular, so what we have here is a collectivity seen as
a unity). It could simply be a generalized truism (God is
more truthful than men), without reference to any particular
person or persons. Some have suggested that 'the witness
of men' is a reference to John's three witness-passages to
Jesus in the gospel (1:32 in reference to John the Baptist's
testimony; 3:31-33 the apostle's testimony; and 5:36, Jesus'
witness to Himself before the nation's leaders). However, the
witness of God and the witness of Scripture, being the voice
of God written, are authoritatively equal (since God's witness
is recorded in Scripture with absolute correctness, He being
the author of it himself, and the witness of men is cited with
the same absolute correctness, guided in its accuracy by the
superintending providence of God, they are equal witnesses
since God's witness is His Word). The 'we' seems most likely
to be a reference to John and Christians in general.

Because another view, not entirely unlike the one above,
has warrant I will offer it as well. If, as some have suggested,
the 'witness of men' is that of John the Baptist, with 'men'
being used for humankind in general, at the instance of the
beginning of Jesus' ministry (John 1:29-34), then he would
be saying that his opponents are quite wrong in their
understanding of the baptismal event. With this view of
the misreading of the significance of the event, it would
make sense of his saying that Jesus came 'not by water only'
(v. 6), meaning that God verified at Jesus' baptism that He
was more than a special, prophet-like person; He was God's
Son. John recorded John the Baptist's very words: 'Behold
the Lamb of God that takes away the sin of the world' (1:29)

and '...I have seen and bear witness that this is the Son of God' (1:34). The apostle's witness was to His deity and His atoning death ('not by water only'), not simply that He was a prophet-like figure. John is saying, in either case, that the witness encompasses more than Jesus' baptism as to His person; the person of Jesus is defined by His death also. The witness of God, John tells us, is that He procured for us eternal life through His Son (v. 11).

The 'that' which introduces the final clause in the NASB is rendered in an explanatory sense; that is, the translators see the succeeding clause as further elucidating the content of the witness of God. However, it can, and most likely should, be translated as a relative pronoun ('which') telling the reader the object of God's witness – His Son. John employs the same relative pronoun in the next verse (v. 10b).

Parenthesis 38: The role of faith
A logical question to pose at this point is this: why does John emphasize faith to such a high degree? It seems that the answer is twofold. First, faith is the only approach to God commended by the Scriptures in the context of receiving spiritual life – redemption. Faith is not a cause of redemption because faith merely accepts what first has appeared as a delightful object. Faith always has an object; faith is a response to an object. Faith cannot cause salvation because faith is not a power; faith receives only what has become apparent. It does not create! Faith closes with Christ; it approves as altogether beautiful what is seen. Faith is a gift from God in at least two ways: faith is a gift in terms of the object unto which faith is exercised (what is infinite cannot be grasped by the finite because the finite cannot ascend to the infinite without divine grace and mercy first). Further, because human faith is capable of grasping only the finite, our faith must be strengthened by the Spirit to grasp the infinite beauty of Christ. Faith must be lifted above the mundane to an object otherwise unknown in redemptive depth.

Second, faith is so emphasized because it alone brings total glory to God in granting the redemption that is through Christ Jesus. If faith is merely a human expression capable of divine approval without divine enablement, it would not profoundly make the point that salvation is all of grace unto the penultimate goal of the glory of God alone. Meritless faith is the subjective channel of eternal life because only meritless faith glorifies God ultimately. The apostle Paul would state the wonder of redemption this way: 'For from Him and through Him and to Him, to God be the glory forever! Amen' (Rom. 11:36, NET).

• • • • •

Verse 10 seems to be a parenthesis in John's argument, which is resumed in verse 11. The person who embraces God's redemption possesses the witness within him (that is, the Holy Spirit); those who refuse to believe do so simply because they have not found the witness compelling or attractive. It would seem contextually that John is drawing a comparison between his readers and his opponents. They belong in two different worlds, possessed of two different objects of affection. It is interesting that in this verse 'believes in' occurs twice, each time referring to either Jesus Christ, or to God's witness to Him, yet in regard to those who do not believe, the preposition is absent. A truly saving faith does not merely have as its object factual data; it entails acknowledgement and trust or commitment as well. See also 5:13 where 'believes in' occurs for a third time. Says Brown: 'The difference between the believer in 5:10a and the nonbeliever in 10b...involves the acceptance vs. refusal of a Christological evaluation of the historical Jesus as the Son of God' (589). The rejection of a witness is commonly based on the assumption that its source is not credible or unreliable, that God is untruthful (this charge John brings upon his opponents [1:10, 5:10]).

Resuming the argument (v. 11) after a brief hiatus, the testimony of God given in verse 9 is explained ('that' is explanatory). The witness of God is to eternal life and that life is through His Son (1:1-2). 'God has given' implies that faith is a free gift to us. It seems that John is making three points in this verse: first, eternal life is not a prize to be won (it is not an achievement) – it is a gift; second, eternal life is only found in God's Son – it has been achieved for us; and, third, this gift of eternal life is a present possession – it will always be ours.

To know God as He has revealed Himself in and through Christ is to possess the life of God. What John links, with simplicity in contrastive couplets, results in clarity. How can life be stated with greater profundity? Life is in God's Son; to be without the Son is to be without life in God. John's opponents are woefully wrong in their judgment of Jesus. The context of the verse can be as simply stated as this: there are only two spiritual realities, life through the Son or life without true life without the Son! Embracing the testimony of God to his understanding of Jesus is the penultimate ground of assurance. John's opponents have made the fatal error of separating the written or witnessed-to word from the Living Word; they have failed to conceive that the words of the apostles are the words of God. The errorists have mishandled the testimony of God!

What can we learn from this section?
(1) Our faith in God is a gift from God (5:1). We did not believe in order to be saved. God revealed His Son to us, and we believed. It was a miracle whose sequential parts cannot be chronologically arranged because they occurred together and immediately (in the context of a miracle you can have multiplicity simultaneously). The miracle of redemption cannot be accurately described using finite, linear or sequential terms.

(2) In what sense is the exercise of faith a gift from God if it is a personal responsive act on our part? How is faith a gift if faith is something exercised by all people in their lifetimes regardless of their spiritual condition? Faith is not the sole commodity of believers, experience attests. Faith is a gift from God in at least two senses.

First, the gift of faith is in the giving of the object of faith. A person cannot exercise faith in an unknown object or person. Faith always has an object; however, all human objects are finite while the envisioning of Christ in the miracle of redemption is an infinite perception. That which is natural is natural; it is not supernatural (John 3:6). Seeing the beauty of the infinite Christ must be, accordingly, granted to us.

Second, faith is a gift, and yet ours to exercise, in that God strengthens our weak, finite faith to embrace someone entirely infinite. In allowing us to behold an infinite object of pleasure, something absolutely beyond our grasp to do, God performs a miracle both in perceiving an object and in the ability to embrace it (the latter is the realm of the action of faith). It is our faith that embraces the Savior; it is not our faith that causes the Savior to appear to be precious to us (5:4).

(3) There is an immense web that interconnects all believers in Christ, the family of the victorious second Adam. We are indeed a family even though we are separated by miles, cultures, and circumstances. In a way beyond anyone's grasp, our individual conduct, whether praiseworthy or blameworthy, has an effect on the entire community of faith. Simply stated, there is a cosmic dynamic to personal conduct. By disobedience we can harm those who are in 'our family', but we can also do them good by our obedience. We can fulfill the command to love one another in this way.

(4) To say that one loves another implies willingness of submission for the other's greater good. This is done in the marriage ceremony in the exchange of vows and promises. The coin of love is two-sided; one side receives and the other side gives. To make an argument that one loves another without any evidence, only what is contrary to it, invalidates the claim; it makes up what we call a false profession. To say we love God, but do not act in a submissive way to His will or fail to do good to His other children as commanded is falsity of profession.

(5) The surety that promises will be fulfilled rests on the quality of the character of the one who makes them. Some people have valid intentions, but lack power and circumstance to fulfill them; others are evil and have no intention to keep them. God neither lacks the ability nor is hobbled by circumstance to fail in His promises. Further, being absolutely holy in character, God can never act in a deceptive manner (what He says, what He commands, He will do!). If we embraced the message God has given of His Son through His death and resurrection, and by the witness of His Spirit, we can be assured that we are His children.

(6) All Christians are overcomers because faith is the victory. Victory over the world is in knowing that its glittering values are empty and destructive. Victory comes through

acknowledgement and acceptance of one whose values, provision, and character are vastly of a different sort. There are simply no Christians who are not victorious Christians. Christians are those of faith in a supernatural person who provides supernatural benefits to them through the gift of His Son's sacrificial, substitutionary, atoning death. Faith in Christ is conquering faith. Troubles we all have, deficiencies we must endure, but victory is in Christ and we possess Him! He is risen!

F. Epilogue (5:13-21)

The expression, 'These things I have written' (5:13), is a bookend to the similar statement in 1:4; the two statements combined frame the main body of the letter. The 1:4 statement is forward-looking to the body of the letter; 5:13 looks back summarizing the content of the letter. In 1:4 the verbs suggest present action ('write'); the verb in 5:13 suggests an action in the past ('have written'). Just as 1:4 serves as a transitional statement from the prologue (1:1-4) to the body of the letter, so 5:13 functions as a transitional statement to the epilogue (5:14-21). 'Joy' in 1:4 is knowledge of 'eternal life' in 5:13.

1. One summary statement (v. 13)

John has written the letter with a purpose. He wants his readers to know that they possess eternal life, though the false teachers proved to be disconcerting. Ironically, the purpose statement here parallels a similar statement in the gospel (20:31). John seems to be affirming what he wrote in the previous verse, and throughout the body of the letter. Christians can know that they have life, eternal life presently, in God's Son through trust in His provision and character. I think Smalley is helpful when he writes: 'This verse is transitional, in that it looks back to the subject matter of verses 5-12, and also provides a summary conclusion (to I John in its entirety) which leads to the closing remarks in verses 14-21' (289).

2. Four affirmations (vv. 14-20)

John draws the letter to a conclusion by reiterating four sureties that provide evidential comfort for the believer that he/she has been born of God. The passage has a triumphal tone to it. The verb 'know' occurs six times and 'confidence' once. Clearly the author desires to emphasize the fact that we can truly know God through Christ.

(a) Confidence in prayer (vv. 14-17)
John's point seems to be more that Christians have access to answers to our requests as children in His family than simply to prayer itself. He says that prayer to God, and His bountiful responses, is a ground of assurance that we truly know Him, that we have discourse with God, and that we turn to God in our needs. The fact that He entertains our presence is evidence that we know Him. If we did not truly know God through Christ, we would not have intimate interaction with Him, yet Christians do, evidencing the fact that they know Him. They would not turn with such heartfelt affection to Him if they did not know Him, if they did not see Him as altogether beautiful. A little known poet, C. Austin Miles (1868-1946), has captured the sense of intimacy in prayer in a hymn made famous in the early twentieth century and entitled, 'I Come to the Garden Alone' (1912).

> I come to the garden alone
> While the dew is still on the roses;
> And the voice I hear falling on my ear
> The Son of God discloses.
>
> He speaks, and the sound of His voice,
> Is so sweet the birds hush their singing,
> And the melody that He gave to me
> Within my heart is ringing.
>
> I'd stay in the garden with Him
> Though the night around me be falling,
> But He bids me go; through the voice of woe
> His voice to me is calling.
>
> *Refrain*
>
> And He walks with me, and He talks with me,
> And He tells me I am His own;
> And the joy we share as we tarry there,
> None other has ever known.

The use of the term 'confidence' in John's letter indicates that when he prays, the Christian has assurance of a positive outcome in his asking. It is used with this nuance (i.e., surety) relative to the Lord's return in judgment, that we should not see it as a fearful, terrorizing event for us (2:28, 4:17). When we pray we are assured that He hears us and this implies that we have a relationship with Him; we are family members.

If our requests conform to His will, they will be answered (the 'if' in verse 15 is a statement of fact, not of contingency or uncertainty; it is called a first class condition and could be translated 'Since we know that...'). A parallel passage to this in the letter is 3:20-21 where the word 'confidence' is also employed. In 3:20-21 the reason for answered prayer is obedience; here it is asking according to God's plan and determinations. If we are obedient in our behavior, we will not be asking contrary to the divine purpose of God.

The essence of verse 15 is that, if we possess assurance that God hears us when we pray, we will know also that He will answer us. God is a prayer-answering God, because we are His children!

Parenthesis 39: The meaning of prayer
Prayer is not a convenient device for imposing our will on God or bending His will to ours, but it is the prescribed way of subordinating our will to His. It is in prayer that we see God's will, align with it, and rest in it. If we pray according to His will, the certainty of answers is immediate; the actuality may be in the future.

• • • • •

Verses 16 and 17 elucidate two things stated in the previous verses: God hears prayer and God answers prayer in accordance with His will. Not every prayer gets a positive answer, although they are all answered. There are some things that we should not ask for, yet the things that we can ask of God are many.

An example cited (v. 16). The verse is composed of two sentences. The first concerns a believer who sins and the awareness of it should lead us to prayer with the assurance that God will intervene on that person's behalf. The second sentence states that there is sin in some lives that we should not speak to God about because the answer we would desire is outside His will. One immediate observation is that in the first sentence the sin is in relation to the actions of a Christian; in the second sentence such is not stated. I find myself agreeing with Kruse when he writes: 'It is the "brother" whose sin is not unto death for whom the readers are commanded to pray. This suggests that the sin that does not lead to death is the sin of the believer. If this is the case, then the sin that does lead to death is most likely that of the unbeliever' (194). The substance then of praying for one whose error is not impossible to cure is to ask for a change of attitude which will be answered in the case of a believer because the sinning of a believer is not habitual and calloused; there is hope.

One of the most significant problems in the verse is to determine the subject of the third person, singular verb, 'will give or will grant.' A clue is found, perhaps in the 'if'; it alerts us to what should be considered as expected under certain circumstances. This is verified by the main verb. Most translations supply the subject, though the text itself does not. From the standpoint of the grammar, the most likely reference would be the person making the request; however, that is impossible because God alone forgives sin, not the one who prays. A second option would be to supply the word 'God' as the subject of 'will grant' and understand the 'to him' as a reference to the one who asks; however, while we may ask God to forgive another, the answer comes only when that person seeks forgiveness (God does not forgive a person because someone else asks Him to do so; it requires a repentant attitude on the part of the violator). A third option is to see the subject of 'will grant' as God and the 'to him' to refer to the sinner. This seems most probable, even though the grammatical presentation is at best difficult.

The other difficult interpretative problem in the verse is the phrase, 'sin not leading to death'; the issues are twofold: what is the nature of the 'sin leading to death' and what is the meaning of 'death'? Concerning the second issue, some see it as physical death and finding support both in the Old and New Testaments where the death envisioned for sin is physical in nature rather than spiritual (see Acts 5:1-11;

I Corinthians 11:30; and II Corinthians 5:5, for examples of death in a physical sense). This would make sense because the sin involved is that of a believer, a 'brother'; a Christian can only sin and consequently experience remedial punishment in the physical, temporal realm.

Some scholars, however, believe the reference here is to spiritual death. The word 'life,' found thirteen times in the letter, refers consistently to spiritual life. Since life and death are juxtaposed in verse 16, the nuance of both would seem to be spiritual. The only other occurrence of a reference to 'death' is in 3:14 where clearly the connotation is to spiritual death since the readers are told that they have passed from death, though living previously in the state of it. Further in the gospel by the same author, spiritual life and spiritual death are interconnected (8:51, 11:26, and 12:24).

The issue of the nature of the 'sin leading to death' has spilled a lot of ink! There have been three approaches to the issue. The first is to identify it with a specific sin ('the sin'), sometimes alluded to, though not necessarily (Matt. 10:32-33), as the 'unforgiveable sin' (Matt. 12:32; Mark 3:29). However, in the view of the fact that God defines sin as a violation of His character, can a distinction be made between more serious and less serious sinning? It may be argued that the gravity of sin is defined by the number of people it effects; however, sin is not defined by its ripple effect, but by the holy character of God. All sin, small or large, is a violation of the divine character. Also, if we are not to pray for a sinning believer, what is the criteria?

What is clear is that we should pray that a believer who falls into sin will repent and come to his senses as did the prodigal son. However, the text does not state that the person, who should not be prayed for, is a believer. Further, the statement of a sin 'leading to death' is actually parenthetical or ancillary to John's main idea of confidence in prayer as a ground of assurance. The sinner who does wrong 'leading to death', we should not petition for, is most likely not a believer. In the broader context of the letter, the 'sin unto death' would have reference to the apostasy of the secessionists and those carried adrift in their wake. Those that 'went out from us for they were not of us' (2:19) should be left to their worldly deserts. 'Anyone who goes too far and does not abide in the teachings of Christ' (II John 9) should be left to their worldly ends. Brooke says it this way: 'The form of expression would seem to indicate that the author is not thinking of one particular sin, definite though unnamed.... The whole phrase thus indicates a "kind of sinning"... rather than any definite act of sin, which leads inevitably in a certain direction' (146-47).

However, and to elucidate further, should we not pray for unbelievers? Since we are commanded to pray for all people, it must be that John has a particular group of people in mind. The most probable answer is that John forbids prayer for the false teachers, the secessionists, whom he considers as without faith (2:19) and belonging to the world (4:1). The sin that leads to death is Christological in nature; it is the rejection of the redemptive work of Jesus Christ, the Son of God. Those who embrace secessionist opinions are without the life of God and, additionally, they are arraigned in knowledgeable opposition to him. In John 17:9, the apostle records Jesus' pointed comment in His prayer that even He did not ask for the world, but for those given of the Father to Him out of the world. The denial of Christ need not be a permanent state, but its continued affirmation is a rejection of the only hope of forgiveness. It seems harsh, and even unloving, but there are some people that should not be on our prayer list; while yet living, some bear the eternal wrath of God upon their souls. Yet it must be remembered that this is not a major point to John; it is actually ancillary and nebulous. Boice's point is well taken: 'Whatever interpretation we give to the exception, therefore we must always bear in mind that it is the *exception* and that the burden laid upon us by John is to pray for any believer we see falling into sin' (143).

Not willing to leave aside the importance of intercessory prayer for sinning believers, John reiterates sin's gravity, but makes a vital distinction (v. 17). What is the sin in question here that is not fatal? First, it should be noticed that the error is not specified. Second, the reason the sin is unstated is that it could be any sin that is not practiced with habituality, without repentance, and with delight.

(b) Security in God's provision (v. 18)

A second ground of surety, bringing solace to the troubled believer, is the keeping power of God. John's point, that the children of God, those fathered by God, do not sin is as shocking as it was when we encountered similar comments in 3:6, 9. It would seem most probable that the sin that a believer cannot commit is that of the error of the opponents, the sin being a denial of the salvific mercies brought singularly through Jesus Christ. What Jesus did, according to the secessionists, was to show that sin is not a serious matter and can be eradicated by believing that Jesus revealed through His moral example how to manage one's life well. John would be saying, on the contrary, if this interpretation is valid, that for a believer to sin against God by denying His provision for sin is incompatible; in fact, a believer cannot sin after the similitude of the false teachers.

There are two bases for the security of believers in the latter part of this verse: God's preservation and the prevention of the devil's evil intent for them. The most difficult words to interpret in this section concern how to read the phrase 'he who was born of God keeps him'. The question is this: who does the keeping? Some have been willing to interpret 'the one fathered of God' as Jesus. However, the mention of Jesus appears unexpected contextually. John does not refer to Jesus as 'born of God' (every other appearance of the phrase in the book refers to believers). Others interpret 'the one' as the believer, meaning that 'the one born of God keeps himself', but such a wording seems foreign (while 'keeps' is found twenty-five times in John's writings, he never follows it with a reflective pronoun as the direct object) and unexpected. Further, this section deals with divine assurances of the believer's security, not an action required of the recipient. Also, some read the passage as the believer, 'the one fathered by God holds on to God', yet this view faces the same criticisms as the previous and the verb rarely has the meaning proposed. Perhaps the most plausible reading would be this: 'the one fathered by God, He (God) keeps him.' This reading is consistent with the theme of the passage, the surety of the believer in God.

(c) Understanding of false values (v. 19)
John shifts from the third person singular ('one') to the third person plural ('we'). Though God is the source of our spiritual lives, the world of other values, or the realm of our temporal existence, is in the lap of the evil one. John envisions that there are two 'worlds' within one; all persons are in one of those two worlds, believers are in both. There is no 'third world' in this world. The phrase, 'the whole world,' occurs here and in 2:2; however, in 2:2 John is speaking of the realm of the family of God, those who are the objects of Christ's satisfaction. Here, the world is the sphere of values controlled by the evil one.

(d) Apprehension of the truth (v. 20)
If 5:13 sums up the point of John's rebuttal of the secessionists or false teachers (we can know that we belong to God's family though He is absolute perfection; His standards of acceptance are His perfections; and we are not without discounting the gravity of sin), this verse sums up the ground of John's argument for his assertion. The words 'know' (twice), 'understanding' (once), and 'true' (three times) suggest John's emphases in the verse; it is about the surety of things.

God sent His Son so that we might know God (v. 20a). It is interesting that John does not say that 'Jesus has come', but that the 'Son of God has come'. The false teacher would consent to Jesus as a human being, an insightful prophet, but not accord to Him the status of absolute equality with God. The intent of His coming was to reveal the Father to us (John 1:18). No one else could possibly do so since only one came from the presence of God.

We have come to know God through Christ (v. 20b). The phrase 'we might know him who is true' refers to the Father. John says that this has become a reality through the placing of the believer in Jesus Christ, 'His Son.' Since the Son is truly God, and they have been joined to him, believers possess the life of God.

In knowing Jesus Christ we have eternal life (v. 20c). The antecedent of 'this' or 'this one' is difficult to determine. Does it refer to Jesus Christ or to the Father? The closest antecedent is Christ, though in John the closest antecedent to a pronoun is not always the referent. The words 'eternal life' seem to refer to Jesus since the Father in John's writings is not the lifegiver (1:1; see also John 11:25; 14:6). Also in 1:2 in this letter, John states that life came from the Father through Jesus Christ.

It seems more than probable that 'this [one] is the true God and eternal life' is a summary of John's claims concerning Jesus Christ. He is God sent from God to bring to us the life of God. Thus the epilogue has several similarities with the prologue of the letter. The one attested by the apostles at the beginning of the letter is affirmed at the end of it.

3. One exhortation (v. 21)
John does not tell us the referent to 'idols', so it must be surmised from the content of the letter. Though some interpreters take the term literally, referring to various cultural idolatrous practices, the view seems to be unexpected given the argument of the letter. It is preferable to see the term metaphorically as a command to avoid the false teachings and practices of the secessionists concerning Christ and the world. The letter has several warnings in this regard (2:15; 4:1-3; as well as II John 10). Stott quotes a scholar's transliteration of the phrase: 'Do not abandon the real for the illusory' (196). The Greek word for idol means 'false appearances'. Marshall states the meaning in this way: 'John urges his readers to have nothing to do with false ideas of God and the sins that go with them' (355-56).

What can we learn from this section?
(1) The Christian message concerns the claims that Christ made concerning Himself and was passed on by the apostles and centuries of Christ-followers down to today. We proclaim that Jesus, though His name signifies earthly origins, came from the presence of God to the earth as God's anointed one, the Christ, the Messiah. Jesus Christ came to reveal the Father to us in His earthly sojourn that culminated in His sacrificial, substitutionary, and atoning death for us. He now lives today as proof that He accomplished the intent of His coming and He will yet come once more to bring His kingdom to

completion through the judgment of His adversaries and the gathering of His people.

(2) That faith, and faith alone, without human merit is the proper and only true response to the revelation of God's mercies in and through Jesus Christ. It is a travesty to God to denigrate the accomplishments of His Son. He, and He alone, procured access to the Father by becoming that access through His atoning death and priestly advocacy. How can any human endeavor contribute to what God alone can do? The mandate upon all human beings from God's perspective is that they must believe in the message delivered by His Son. It is not by doing something that necessitates the favor of God that one enters into the life of God; it is by believing in the revelatory accomplishments of His Son.

(3) It is possible on several counts to know that we have entered into the life of God: first, because of the indwelling presence of God in our lives by the Spirit witnessing to the beauty of Christ; second, because by God's grace we have embraced the message that God sent through His Son; and, third, because God's renovating work of conforming us to the life of God is evident in the changes redemption has brought in our changed perspective on the person of Jesus Christ, our radically altered priorities and attractions, and our attitudes toward others. John makes the point that we can know that we know God, not so much by what we have done, but by what He has done in our lives.

(4) God desires us to firmly know and rejoice in the fact that we are securely under His protection and that He will bring all of His children into His presence on the final Day of Judgment and redemption. As daily evidence, God answers our prayers, so assuring us that we are His children, and also protects us from the destructive assaults of the devil. Thus, God's daily benevolent care for us and giving to us, which is beyond finitude to grasp, should bring us great confidence in our relationship with God, a relationship that is real and true though beyond anything that we can otherwise experience in this world.

(5) John reminds us that we live in a world of false values perpetuated by illusory appearances and twisted truths. Though the kingdom of God is emerging, it has not reached

its fullness; it is 'now', but 'not yet'. It will only be destructive to our walk with God to find our deepest values in the world. As beautiful as the world truly is at times, there is a very dark side, a side controlled since the fall of Adam by other than God (though the reign of the devil and his minions is temporal and limited in extent). Are we too enamored by the values of the world? The world of false values is not the 'world' where we should find our values.

(6) False teachers are going about with their false understandings of Christ and His accomplishments, and their pleasant words and promises entangle many. The way to spot false teachers is twofold: their teachings and their moral conduct. All falsity twists the message that God sent through His Son by denigrating His person (denying His deity) and minimizing His work (denying His blood atoning sacrifice, and so making Him merely into a wise instructor of our duties). All false teachers somewhere accept the values of the world (its false pride, its advantage seeking). By their conduct and their words we can surmise their validity. Be careful what you value! An eighth century Irish monk Dallan Forgaill wrote a poem to honor the life and ministry of the celebrated St. Patrick. The words of his tribute, 'Be Thou My Vision,' speak much to what we should most value.

> Be Thou my Vision,
> O Lord of my heart;
> Naught be all else to me,
> save that Thou art.
> Thou my best Thought,
> by day or by night,
> Waking or sleeping,
> Thy presence my light.
>
> Be Thou my Wisdom,
> and Thou my true Word;
> I ever with Thee
> and Thou with me, Lord;
> Thou my great Father,
> I Thy true son;
> Thou in me dwelling,
> and I with Thee one.

Be Thou my battle Shield,
Sword for the fight;
Be Thou my Dignity,
Thou my Delight;
Thou my soul's Shelter,
Thou my high Tower:
Raise Thou me heavenward,
O Power of my power.

Riches I heed not,
nor man's empty praise,
Thou mine Inheritance, now and always:
Thou and Thou only,
first in my heart,
High King of Heaven,
my Treasure Thou art.

High King of Heaven,
my victory won,
May I reach Heaven's joys,
O bright Heaven's Sun!
Heart of my own heart,
whatever befall,
Still be my Vision,
O Ruler of all.

2 JOHN

Introduction

Unlike I John, this second writing of the apostle, as well as the third, in structure generally fits the pattern of a first century letter composed on a single sheet of papyrus (6.5 inches by 8.5 inches). A typical letter of the period was tripartite: an introduction, the body, and a conclusion. In the case of II John, the introduction (vv. 1-4) contains a reference to the sender and the recipient followed by a greeting and a note of thankfulness (there is no health wish which is common; instead there is a church greeting). Following the body of the letter (vv. 5-12), a correspondence of this type would end with a repeated health wish and a final greeting (v. 13; in this case there is a greeting, but no wish of health).

The background issue that has generated some discussion is in the relationship of this letter to I John. Do the two letters deal with the same issue threatening the life of the churches? It would seem most probable that the answer is affirmative. Simply put, the issue in each book seems to be the same and the manner of treatment the same, with the reoccurrence of words and phrases pointing in that direction.

First, in both writings there is the recognition that schismatic secessionists have disturbed the recipients. In I John 2:19 there is mention of a rending of the church by false teachers who have separated from the believers. The same is stated by the writer in II John. In both cases an unspecified number have left.

Second, in both cases, John refers to the false teachers as 'antichrist' figures (I John 2:18; II John 7), states that they have departed from the faithful ('they went out from us' [2:18] and 'gone out into the world' [II John 7]), and calls them deceivers (I John 1:18; 2:26; 3:7; II John 7).

Third, not only are the actions of John's opponents described in the same way, so is their error. In both instances they denied the deity of Christ, affirming only His humanity (they seem to have no problem with Jesus as 'come in the flesh', but were unwilling to affirm 'Jesus Christ as coming in the flesh' [II John 7]). Further, in both instances, John makes it clear that one cannot know God without also confessing Jesus Christ. That is, Jesus Christ is the only person through whom one can truly know the Father. Without knowing Jesus, God's appointed revelation of Himself, any profession of knowing God is empty (I John 2:21-22; II John 9).

Fourth, many of the key words found in I John are repeated in II John, such as reference to a 'new commandment', which is to love (I John 2:7-11; II John 5) and a command 'from the beginning' (I John 2:7; II John 5, 6). In both letters there are references to fullness of joy through the recipients' abiding in the apostles' teaching (I John 1:4; II John 12), the gospel.

In conclusion, it seems that John is writing to a church or group of churches fearing the infiltration of the secessionists, and that their disruptive effect has already proven to damage the churches through their false teaching concerning Jesus. The letter to this unspecified church is a warning that the erroneous teachings of some travelling itinerants might be repeated. 'Watch yourselves…' (II John 8). 'If anyone comes to you and does not bring this teaching, do not receive him into *your* house, and do not give him a greeting (II John 10). John's concern is the health of a church ('for the sake of the truth…' [v. 2]) and the prevention of the spread of a deadly doctrinal virus! The imperatives in the letter are only two: 'watch' (v. 8) and 'do not receive him' (v. 10). The instructions, implying duty, are also two: 'that we love one another' (v. 5) and 'that we should walk according to his commandments' (v. 6).

The dominant themes in II John, as well as III John, are those of the first letter: truth and love or doctrine and life-style. In this letter 'truth' is found five times in the initial four verses and 'love' four times (vv. 1, 3, 5, 6). 'Truth' appears six times in III John (vv. 1, 3 [twice], 4, 8, 12) and 'true' once (v. 12). 'Love' appears twice (vv. 1, 6). 'Truth' is found in the apostles' instructions concerning the person and accomplishments of Jesus Christ and 'love' is the ground and evidence of true fellowship in the apostles' teachings.

Commentary and Comment
(II John 1:1-13)

A. Introduction (vv. 1-4)

1. The author (v. 1a)

The initial issue in this personal letter is the meaning of the term 'elder'. The options are three: the term can refer to a church officer within a local assembly. In this case, John would be indicating that he is serving in a nearby church with an official designation. While John appears to be known to the recipients of the letter (v. 12), mutual greetings being exchanged between the churches (v. 13), the only instance of an apostle using the term as a self-designation is Peter (5:1) where he addresses briefly the leadership in a local assembly and identifies with them in a similar capacity.

A second option is to take the term in a non-official administrative sense, though literally, suggestive of John's advanced age at the time of the writing (most likely John is the last of the original apostles living).

A third possibility is to see John's use of this title in the broader context of his writings and suggest that the reason for not using the title, apostle, was his reluctance for self-identification. Since the churches operated in the first century under the direction of a plurality of elders (the shift to a single leader in each church coming in the early second century in Syrian Antioch), it is strange that John would speak of himself as 'the elder' if he meant an office in the church. For example, John does not mention himself in the gospel account, preferring to speak of himself only as 'the disciple whom Jesus loved' (19:26). However, if this interpretation is valid, it is interesting that he does not use 'elder' as a self-designation elsewhere. There is no definitive answer, though the latter option appears most viable.

2. The recipients (vv. 1b-2)

(a) The addressed (v. 1b)

The major issue here is that of the meaning of 'elect lady and her children'. Some have surmised that the letter was addressed to a lady by the name of Electra; however, this is unlikely since the word 'elect' is an adjective, not a proper noun. Others, such as Jerome and Athanasius, early churchmen, recognizing that 'elect' is an adjective, thought the letter was addressed to a female named 'Lady' or 'Lord'. Still others see the expression metaphorically as equivalent to 'Dear Lady'. However, when John did address a particular person in a letter (III John), he did not use the plural pronouns when referring to them. The difficulty with identifying the addressee as a single person here is the pronouns and verbs. John refers to the recipients using the second person plural ('you,' vv. 6, 8, 10, 12), except in the concluding verse (v. 13). 'Children of your chosen sister' (v. 13) seems to be a reference to the church from which John is writing and thus is parallel to verse 1, both being metaphorical references to a local assembly of believers. Says Edwards, '… the letter is still written to a church even if the "elect lady" is taken to be an individual' (128).

It seems preferable to understand the recipients of the letter as a local assembly of believers, 'elect lady and her children' being used metaphorically, and that John wishes to alert them to the spread of a potent danger. Another possibility emanates from the observation that 'chosen lady and her children' lacks the prefatory article (the), thus 1:1 would be read as 'an elect lady and her children'. This would perhaps indicate that the letter was circular, being written to several churches (in verse 13 the greeting is sent from 'children'. Are there two ladies of the same name with children?). We do know from I John that the false teachers had enacted an itinerate ministry to propagate their views, lending further speculative credence that this may have been a circular letter.

(b) The addressed described (vv. 1c-2)
The recipients of the letter are described as genuine believers, those who have embraced the truth concerning the person and accomplishments of Jesus Christ ('in the truth'). This regard for the truth (a term used three times for emphasis in these verses) is the sphere of John's fellowship or mutuality of love (I John 1:3) with the entirety of the Christ-followers. The abiding principle John has in mind is the indwelling of the Spirit, promised upon our Lord's departure (John 14:16-17), teaching by His presence the truth and protecting believers in it forever.

It is interesting that John tells us that in genuine believers the truth about Jesus Christ is an 'abiding' truth with eternal duration. 'Abiding,' as John uses it here, is not a temporal state, but an enduring state. This understanding of John here should shed interpretative light on John 15 suggesting that the exhortation there to remain faithful is in light of Judas' departure and the impending crises for the remaining disciples. A command expressed can be a promise declared; a promise expressed, undergirded with surety, can be an exhortation as well.

3. The greeting (v. 3)
The greeting is consistent with first century letters. What is important to grasp is John's emphasis on the Father, the Son, truth, and love. This may have been stated as a response to John's opponents from the inception of his writing. The interconnection between Jesus Christ and the Father is denied by the secessionists who argue that the Father can be known apart from according the title 'the Christ' to Jesus (the errorists being willing to believe in Jesus, but not that He is the Christ (I John 3:22-23, 4:2-3; II John 7). John emphasizes the unity between Jesus and Christ by combining the titles or names together, Jesus Christ, and also by referring to Him as 'the Son of the Father'. The statement connecting truth and love (one preposition governing two nouns emphasizing their interconnectedness seems to be a reply to the false teachers that truth can exist without love). John argues that the criteria for recognizing false teachers is twofold: their failure to abide in the truth (I John 2:19, II John 9) and their failure to manifest love in social relationships by keeping the commandments (I John 2:3-5; 3:12, 19; 4:21; II John 4-5). It is interesting in the

greeting that John uses the word 'mercy' for the only time in his writings. The sequence of the words ('grace, mercy, and peace') is noted by some commentators as indicative of the sequence of God's redemption from a linear perspective; grace (God's unmerited favor) leads to the extension of mercy and results in peace.

Parenthesis 40: Redemption, truth, and love
John makes the assertion that apostolic truth and love are inseparably linked, the former as the cause and the latter as the effect. He makes the bold statement that without truth there can be no biblical love and without biblical truth there can be no love. How can this be true and without exception? The answer is found in the nature of regeneration, the miracle of rebirth. Salvation comprises a reformulating of all human faculties with a common focus in all the facets of immaterial natures. While salvation is far more than intellectual perception, a change of mind, it entails a change of beliefs and attitudes. It alters our affections from alienation toward divine interests making them a priority within a renovated system of values. Salvation brings about a new focus, new priorities, and new motivations. Further, because salvation entails the infusion of the character of God into the life of the believer, it brings about necessitated expression. Simply put, salvation is the free gift of God granted solely by unnecessitated grace and mercy and that it always bears the consequence of changing the objects of that divine redemption. No one can say that they love God and not long to conform to His image; conformity is the fruit necessitated by love (not so much our love for God, but the revolutionary insight of His great love for us!).

• • • • •

4. A commendation (v. 4)
The circumstance for writing of the letter appears to have been knowledge John became aware of concerning this particular community of believers; however, John does not tell us how he accessed it. The most difficult word to interpret in the verb is 'some', a word supplied to smooth the translation. Does it suggest that 'some' only were walking in the truth? This seems unlikely since the immediate context is positive.

It would seem that John is saying that he met 'some' from the church and that inspired him to write. It could be that John had heard that there was a cause for concern, though the church was doing well, and he felt the urge to write. Generally speaking, it can be said that the church was holding fast to the apostles' teachings about Jesus Christ and John wrote to exhort them to continue.

5. The exhortation to love (vv. 5-7)

(a) The fact stated (v. 5)
Instead of an imperative, which would be expected, John begins the body of the letter with an exhortation in the form of a descriptive commentary (the subject of the letter in John's mind is not doctrinal error, but the moral implications in reaction to a theological danger). While the word 'love' is not in the imperative mood, it has that nuance by virtue of being identified as a commandment. The commandment that these believers ('you' is singular indicating that he is viewing them as a group, not as individuals, which lends to the probability that 'Lady' [v. 1] is to be read metaphorically for the believers) heard is elucidated by the phrase that follows 'that'; it is to love one another. 'From the beginning' is likely not a reference to the message these believers heard from those who brought to them the gospel, but the message that came from Jesus Christ in His earthly ministry and conveyed to the apostles ('one which we have had…'). It is the message that rang in the apostle's ear in John 13:34 and John wrote of in I John 2:7-8. The essence of love is manifested in obedience (I John 5:3) or 'walking in it' (v. 6).

(b) The fact explained (v. 6)
The content of love is described in the phrase following 'that', meaning love expressed, as it must be, in obedience. Love by its nature consists in obedience to the commandments of God. The manner or content of obedience is explained following the second occurrence of 'that', 'that' being a reference to the new commandment of verse 5. Love, by its nature, is a settled or habitual principle of caring for others expressed through our lives as Christ-followers. The referent to 'it' at

the end of the verse is most likely 'the commandment', the nearest antecedent, though some take it to be love, found at the beginning of the verse. To John, however, to love and to keep the commandments, summarized by love, is all encompassing; the two are synonymously intertwined. Thus, it would seem that when John speaks of 'commandments', but then explains it as a 'commandment', he is suggesting that all the commandments can be summarized into one, love. This commandment, with its many applications, these believers heard from the very beginning of their Christian experience.

(c) The fact threatened (v. 7)
The reason for the exhortation to love is captured in the 'for' that begins the sentence, indicating an inference drawn from the discussion of love. The threat posed by John's opponents that, while rooted in theological error, is manifest in moral perversion (penultimately, a failure to show love). Poor doctrine always results in poor living! Poor living makes one susceptible to bad doctrine! The 'for' could also be translated as indicating a reason from what has preceded. If so, the reason would be the lurking danger that is antithetical to the manifestation of love in the assembly of saints; it is the potent threat of false teachers. Either option leads to a similarly interpretative conclusion.

The 'many deceivers' clearly has reference to John's secessionist opponents (I John 1:8, 2:26, 3:7); the word 'many' indicates that the threat is serious (I John 4:2). Not only have the false teachers caused turmoil in one church; they have departed from the assembly of believers (I John 2:19) and are offering the portent of a disruptive movement in the churches. The essence of their teaching is the same as in John's first letter; it is Christological (they deny 'Jesus Christ coming in the flesh', not the historical, human Jesus). Again, the false teachers seemingly would have affirmed the historic existence of Jesus, but were unwilling to see Jesus as the Christ, God's anointed one. The error concerns 'Jesus Christ', the person and the role. Jesus, they would affirm; Jesus Christ, they would not!

The present participle 'coming' can be read either with futuristic connotations referring to the second coming of

Christ, suggesting that the false teachers are denying the Lord's return, or as a historic present referring to His first coming. Almost certainly the reference is to the latter; there is no hint in John that his opponents quibbled over the second coming. Further, this is consistent with John's comment on I John 4:2. Again the error of the false teachers is not that they failed to embrace Jesus; it is that they did not see Jesus as the Christ. They saw Him as more of a human prophet-figure than God's anointed one to deliver us from the penalty of sin.

At the beginning of the verse John speaks of his opponents in the plural, but at the end he speaks in the singular. The best way to read the singulars is metaphorically (the ultimate figure is rendered by something that temporally prefigures it), that the actions of the deceivers prefigure that of *the* deceiver, Satan, and that the actions of the deceivers prefigure that of *the* master Antichrist figure, the one seeking to replace the true Christ.

6. The exhortation to watch (vv. 8-11)

(a) The fact stated (v. 8)
The danger posed by the false teachers to this gathering of believers seems to be serious, though John has indicated that many in the group are doing well. In spite of this, the danger is real, as 'yourselves' seems to imply. Unlike the situation in I and III John, it may be that John is writing to warn a church or group of churches before the danger posed by the false teachers penetrates into them, since the exhortation is to awareness.

The most pressing issue in the verse is the meaning of the phrase 'that you lose what we have accomplished'. Simply stated, what is it that these believers have the potential of losing through the invasive errors of John's opponents? It does not appear that John is warning of the potential loss of eternal life for several reasons: first, that subject is not the issue in John's letters and contextually a foreign notion. Second, John has assured his readers that they are in the truth (v. 1), truth that abides or resides in them ('with us forever' [v. 2]). Third, the Holy Spirit, the expression of the abiding presence of God, is a gift to the believers (I John 3:24, 4:13, 5:7).

It would seem that the best contextual approach is to understand 'reward' in a corporate sense of the peace, harmony, and spiritual vitality of the believers. If the secessionists have their way, they will disrupt the life of the church, sowing seeds of discord and limiting the witness of the church to the gospel. Smalley notes this when he says, 'The elder refers… to the pastoral and missionary work which has been undertaken and accomplished in the community and beyond, and shared with his orthodox church members …' (330). Note that the imperative, 'watch,' is second person plural and the 'you' in 'you may receive a full reward' is also second person plural. Clearly John is speaking to a group, not to individuals; he is speaking to the corporate assembly about a collective matter. Even if a person could somehow forfeit personal salvation, the concept of that possibility for a church is never broached (remember: however you read 'some of your children' [v. 4], even in the worst of cases it cannot mean the totality of them).

What is the 'full reward' that is a possibility of not being received? It would seem to be in context the joy of a productive, outreaching, mutuality of fellowship in the fruits of gospel ministry. In I John 1:4 John spoke for all the apostles when he urged unity in the faith that 'our joy may be made full'. As this letter draws to a close, John repeats much the same idea saying, 'That your joy may be made full' (v. 12). It seems that what is threatened by the false teachers is the unity of the assemblies through a false gospel so that reference to reward would be corporate, the churches regarded as entities.

(b) The fact explained (v. 9)

The reason the false teachers are a dangerous commodity to permit in the churches is that they refuse to abide in the apostles' teachings about Christ, God's Anointed One, the Savior of the world. They are described here with a double participle ('goes too far' and 'does not remain') governed by a single article; the verbal actions are complementary. They have progressed beyond the limits of apostolic truth and have refused to remain in the company of true believers.

The 'teaching of Christ' is a difficult phrase because it can mean two things: the teachings about Christ or the teachings of Christ. Is it what the apostles' taught that Christ taught or is it what Christ taught? It seems that the former of the options has more textual weight. John mentions the apostles' teaching about Christ, derived through His earthly ministry, in the first letter (1:1-4). The distinction between Christ's own teaching and the apostle's teachings which they learned from Him is not at variance with this; the interpretative choice is simply a matter of the most cogent contextual fit.

To think, according to the apostle, that one can claim a relationship with the Father other than through His Son, Jesus Christ, is impossible. To claim to know God apart from Christ is deception. On the contrary to remain, reside, continue in the teachings of Christ, revealed to the apostles and conveyed to believers throughout the centuries, is to truly know the Father. Jesus, who is the Christ, God's appointed servant, came from the realm of God to reveal God to us. He accomplished this through His words, His teachings, and His works, particularly His death on the cross. The Christ not only described God to us; He also became the way for us to God by dying our death that we might live!

(c) The duties enjoined (vv. 10-11)
The initial issue to resolve is whether 'house' refers to a literal house, and thus the instruction pertains to entertaining itinerants, or to an assembly of believers that met, as many did at that time, in a private home. The most decisive argument against the house-church view is that the gender of the word, 'house,' is feminine while all the other instances of the term in the New Testament are masculine (though none of the other references are in John's writings).

It would seem, however, that the broader context would favor the latter interpretation. First, if, as we suppose, 'elect lady' (v. 1) and 'the children of your chosen sister' (v. 13) refer to churches, it makes sense to see 'house' in the same light. Perhaps what we have here is a literary particularity of the writer. Second, the strident urgency not to help an itinerant promoting such errors, as John's opponents promulgated, would apply to either situation. Third, it would seem in keeping with I John 2:29 that this letter was written to a gathering of believers. It could be, as in the case of III John, that the letter was written to a person who was prominent in the church with the view that the church was to receive the message. Fourth, 'elect sister' is likely the church from which John is writing. As stated above, the beginning and ending references to 'children' seem best to be taken metaphorically. Fifth, John writes to the 'children of the elect sister', not to the 'sister'. If 'sister' were to be taken literally, why would John not send a greeting to her from the local church where he is residing? Certainly this letter would have been read in the church. Ultimately, the data is insufficient for a decisive decision and either approach does not alter the meaning of the instruction, merely the sphere of application.

The dependent introductory clause, the 'if' statement, presupposes that the infiltration of itinerant false teachers will make inroads into the church. In the earliest churches, instruction in part depended upon traveling preachers, such perhaps as Demetrius (III John 12). John's second letter is a warning to a church not to accept itinerants with teachings contrary to the apostles; his third letter, at least in part, seems to have been written because of the over-application of the instruction by Diotrephes (III John 9) who wanted to refuse all itinerants ('strangers' [v. 5]) and who seems to have gone about addressing a serious problem in the wrong way and expressed the concern with improper motives.

The instruction is clear; the recipients of the letter are not to allow false teachers to promote their teachings among the believers nor are they to be recognized as fellow believers. Thus, they are not to be 'greeted'. The standard of determining an itinerant's validity to teach was conformity to the teachings of the apostles concerning Jesus Christ. In John's view, the false teachers are clearly not believers; they are prefigures of antichrist. They refuse to embrace faith in Jesus as the Christ, the revelation of God to us, and, therefore, do not know God because He is only known through Christ. Again, Smalley is helpful at this point. 'In these verses John is not saying, "do not love others." Nor is he forbidding all contact with the heterodox.... Rather, the presbyter is warning the members of his community against the dangers of entertaining their views in such a way as to strengthen and develop their erroneous position, and so compromise the truth [cf. v. 4]' (334).

To greet a person, an itinerant, in this setting is to condone and express sanction for their instruction, thereby indirectly sharing in the promotion of error (v. 11). The meaning of 'evil deeds' is not specified though contextually it most likely encompasses the promulgation of Christological perversion and consequential behavior malfeasance, a failure to truly love the brethren.

B. Conclusion (vv. 12-13)

The urgency of the situation, the impending danger posed by itinerants promoting false doctrine, caused John to write a letter, but he wanted to visit personally, though that would likely take more time than to get his message to the churches (John repeats the same line in III John 13). His arrival, and their fellowship together, will bring forth a delight created by personal interaction that a letter cannot engender. Joy is the result of fellowship with each other in God the Father and God the Son by the Spirit.

John's intent ('that' [v. 12] suggests purpose) is that the churches will remain stable, not racked by the disruptive teachings of John's opponents. The 'joy' would be that of harmony and unity of purpose that comes from doctrinal agreement. See verse 8 for a discussion of the meaning of 'reward'.

John ends the letter with a greeting from the church that appears to be where he is residing (v. 13). He seems to assume the pattern that he takes up in Revelation 2–3, that of monitoring the nearby churches. It may be that John is writing from Ephesus, even as he will later write from Patmos to the churches, including Ephesus.

A clue to the nonliteral rendering of 'elect lady' (v. 1) is the difficulty of reading it literally in light of the final greeting from John. The address is not to the 'lady and her children' from John, but to the 'chosen sister' of the children. It would seem that the 'lady' and 'children' are paralleled to 'children of your chosen sister'. Therefore, it would seem that the least problematic solution, and most natural way of reading the texts, is to interpret the 'elect lady and her children' as a local assembly and the 'children of your chosen sister' as the church from which John wrote. Peter speaks of a church in similar terms in I Peter 5:13.

What can we learn from this letter?

(1) The interconnectedness of right belief and right conduct is integral to Christian faith. The former is the cause of the latter; the latter is proof of the former. Persons who claim to know God, but who consistently reveal behavioral patterns and priorities contrary to the moral ramifications of knowing Christ, should, in the least, pause to ponder if indeed their profession is little more than words or consider the positive implications of the Lord's mercy through chastisement.

(2) Clearly John has made the point that the only way to God is through the sacrificial, atoning mercies of the Christ, the Messiah, the Anointed One, the Son of God. Contrary to much contemporary speculation, there are not several or many ways to God, Jesus Christ being only one of them. If individuals do not come to God through Christ, they cannot make the claim of knowing Him, according to John. Jesus said it this way: 'I am the way, the truth, and the life: no one comes to the Father but through me' (John 14:6). To embrace this teaching is to know the Father (II John 9).

(3) Allowing or abetting the promulgation of false teachings among Christians is a very serious matter. False teachers are a disaster in the making within an assembly of God's people. Being deceived themselves, they have the capacity to lead others astray, thinking that what they are doing is actually helpful. Instead of positive outcomes, the toleration of doctrine contrary to the apostles' teachings promises discord, division, and the weakening of the church.

(4) While heresy is a serious matter that ought not be trafficked in the church, one must be careful not to allow mere personal preferences and insights legitimacy for pressing one's private agenda either. If one defines the apostles' doctrine, what the apostles' learned through their personal contact with Jesus Christ, it would concern His person and accomplishments. By this, the apostles would have meant the absolute deity and oneness of the Father and the Son, the mission of the Son to reveal the Father, the atoning death of Jesus Christ as the purchased price for our sins, and the just and righteous declaration of the Father of our acquittal thereby. The heart of the apostles' teachings according to John is about Jesus Christ and the divine salvation procured

through Him, declared so by the Father, and granted through the Spirit of God who is the gift that Jesus purchased.

(5) If the teachings of the apostles remain foremost in the life and instruction of the churches, they will experience harmony, unity, and productive outreach. When the center of the churches' proclamation and delight is Jesus Christ, the believers will possess true joy and full reward. Joy for Christians is not to be found in the exercise of personal freedoms that they have in Christ merely; it is found when His interests and passion become that of the church as a collectivity.

(6) Deception by its very nature does not come to us with a sign or badge saying, 'This is bad; this will harm you.' It comes wrapped in pleasant circumstances, enticing words, and alluring promises that there is another way, even a better, truer, way. It comes structured around teachings that flatter natural instincts and interests; it questions things once received by others through suspicion that there are better options than what those who are perceived as intolerant and narrow profess. The false teachers taught that Jesus was a revealer of a self-help theory by saying that sin was not sin, as they had been instructed, and that you can know God without a dying Christ.

(7) We have often heard people say that love makes the world go around. Religiously, liberal teachers and theologians have made much of the importance of Christian faith and love, but in manifesting an unwillingness to abide in the teachings of the apostles have grotesquely twisted the meaning of love by detaching it from Jesus Christ, the Son of God. The secular poet, the spinner of lyrics and melodies, as well as the religious teacher, are right in emphasizing it (John would have no disagreement with them on the importance of love). The problem is that love is defined with a horizontal bias, as pragmatics or mere sensitivity. God is love in His very character. God is the criteria of love. Jesus Christ is the love of God revealed. The Holy Spirit is the love of God possessed. Care for others is the love of God demonstrated. The love of God for Himself is the ground of ethics. God is what love is and love is what we have been redeemed to reveal!

(8) John offers a valuable clue to the strategies of false teachers when he tells us that his opponents refused to remain in the apostles' teaching and had gone beyond them (v. 9). He offers a strident warning about listening to those who claim to

have 'advanced or mature' knowledge that will make a person a better Christian. If you find a person offering interpretative 'keys' to biblical knowledge, you should pause and ask yourself, 'Is this additional teaching apostolic?' 'Does the new teaching conflict with what you know about Jesus?' 'Will any of these "new insights" improve on the old, old story?' Eugene Bartlett's 1939 poem 'Victory in Jesus' captures the timeless truth of the apostles' teachings.

> I heard an old, old story, how a Savior came from glory,
> How He gave His life on Calvary to save a wretch like me;
> I heard about His groaning, of His precious blood's atoning,
> Then I repented of my sins and won the victory.
>
> I heard about His healing, of His cleansing pow'r revealing.
> How He made the lame to walk again and caused the blind to see;
> And then I cried, 'Dear Jesus, Come and heal my broken spirit,'
> And somehow Jesus came and brought to me the victory.
>
> I heard about a mansion He has built for me in glory.
> And I heard about the streets of gold beyond the crystal sea;
> About the angels singing, and the old redemption story,
> And some sweet day I'll sing up there the song of victory.
>
> O victory in Jesus, my Savior, forever.
> He sought me and bought me with His redeeming blood;
> He loved me ere I knew Him and all my love is due Him,
> He plunged me to victory, beneath the cleansing flood.

3 JOHN

Introduction

III John has the distinction of being the smallest in size of any of the books in the New Testament writings. It has twenty-six fewer words than II John, its nearest competitor for brevity, though in the number of verses it has one more. The book, more properly the letter, contains 185 Greek words. Though small, it is a gem among fine stones! Further, it is the only writing of the apostle John's that is written to a specific individual, a man by the name of Gaius (the name being rather common in the first century). It is a blunt letter that moves along quickly (perhaps due to dire, foreboding circumstances); there are no references in the letter to Jesus, Jesus Christ, or Christ (nor to the Spirit).

The letter is typical of first century formatting, written on a single piece of parchment. It has a somewhat standard introduction composed of the identity of the sender, recognition of the recipient, and a wish for wellbeing, though it does lack a greeting (vv. 1-4). After the body of the letter (vv. 5-12), there is a conclusion that includes a benediction and greetings (vv. 13-14). Unlike other writings by John, this is the only one addressed to a named individual. With this stated, of the letters of John this one most exactly conforms to the format of private letters of the time. The differences are: (1) the author is not specified by name, (2) the normal word for greeting is omitted, (2) the health wish is unique in that John distinguishes between physical and spiritual health, and (4) the concluding salutation is of peace rather than an expression of hope of continued health.

The letter itself can be conveniently organized around four personages: the author of the letter who identifies himself as 'the elder'; the recipient who is Gaius, a godly man supportive of the message of the apostles and an intimate of John's; a troublemaker by the name of Diotrephes who is hindering itinerant ministry in the church; and Demetrius who appears to be the opposite of Diotrephes as a worthy itinerant. John writes to commend and encourage Gaius in his support of the itinerants, expose the high-handedness of Diotrephes, and commend Demetrius to service in the church as an itinerant.

A crucial question in the approach to the letter is its relationship to I and II John. Is the topic in each of the three generally the same? It would seem that the answer is 'yes'. The issue is the troubling presence of false teachers that have propagated a perversion of the apostles' teachings. They have rejected the notion that Jesus is the Christ; that Jesus is God's divine revealer sent from heaven to explain the way to life in the Father. Instead, these opponents of John see Jesus as a human moral instructor who taught that one can come to a place where sin no longer matters in the Christian's experience, that Jesus came to *show* the way, but not to *be* the way. They offered a salvation without sin and, therefore, without the necessity of the cross. Their teachings caused serious disruption in the churches, the very nature of the gospel being at issue, as well as the nature of authority, leading to a secessionist movement (I John 2:19) that threatened the churches. Further, the opponents were organized to the point of sending out itinerants to the scattered churches promoting their views. III John appears to have been written to alert a church to the gravity of the situation and warn them not to allow such itinerants to gain access to a teaching ministry (vv. 7-11). John's instruction is that such teachers are not to be permitted in the church or sanctioned in any way (vv. 10-11).

Further, this letter appears to be addressing an unwarranted reaction to John's warning about the danger of itinerants. A person of influence in a local assembly, having personal spiritual and moral issues, took the position that all itinerants should be excluded from trafficking through the churches. John writes to condemn the view as unwarranted extremism and commend the practice of receiving itinerants into the churches if they are properly certified in the apostles' teachings. He commends Gaius for acting rightly in supporting the itinerant missionary endeavor, seeking that he accept Demetrius as one among them, and condemns the overzealousness of Diotrephes. What seems to be clear is that the issue is not doctrinal aberrancy, a departure from the apostles' teachings as explained in I John, but the according of hospitality and, thus, sanction to itinerants. It seems that Diotrephes wanted to resolve the portent of dangerous intrusions into the church by cutting out all outside influences. A secondary issue is the manner of Diotrephes' ethical response to his extreme solution (John claims that the underlying motive for Diotrephes' position was arrogance and a power quest).

Commentary and Comment
(III John 1:1-14)

A. Introduction (vv. 1-4)

1. The writer (v. 1a)

In the previous letter, and in this one, the Apostle John refers to himself as 'the elder'. As indicated in comments in that letter, the term is either a reference to his agedness, also suggestive of his spiritual maturity (though this hardly requires saying), or a self-deprecating identification. The latter fits with his unwillingness to make much of himself throughout his writings and, thus, perhaps is the better choice (though it is uncertain).

2. The recipient (v. 1b)

Because Gaius was a common name in the first century, he is impossible to identify. What we know of the man must be derived from the letter itself. First, he is a godly man who associated with the apostle in the faith propagated by the apostles ('walking in truth,' v. 3). Second, John views Gaius affectionately ('beloved' [vv. 1, 3, 11], 'I love,' [v. 1], 'my children' [v. 4, likely a phrase suggesting spiritual care over rather than spiritual origins]). Third, evidence of this man's commitment to the apostles' teachings is his support of the itinerants sent out by John to the nearby churches (v. 5). John considers Gaius a valuable asset in the defense of orthodoxy. Fourth, Gaius is on friendly terms with the church of John's residence and there are people in Gaius' church that share in his regard for John's (v. 14). What we cannot know, because data is unavailable, is if Gaius held a position in a church, if his home was a meeting place of the church, or if he was simply hospitable.

Is Gaius in the same church as the authoritarian Diotrephes? It seems that we do not have enough information to make a decisive judgment. It is reasonable that Gaius knew Diotrephes in some manner, but it would be difficult to understand that, if they were in the same church, why he had to be informed of a letter to the church (unless Diotrephes suppressed it and Gaius was unaware one had been written). Further, Gaius' action of accepting itinerants would have brought Diotrephes' censor (you would think that John would have instructed Gaius to anticipate it). Would Gaius need information about Diotrephes' arrogance if they were in the same church? Gaius seems distant from Diotrephes in terms of the gatherings they attended. Perhaps they were in nearby, but different, house churches. With this said, there seems to be a connection between the two men since John seems to have made the assumption that Gaius knew of Diotrephes, though the manner is unstated.

'In truth' is John's manner of expressing unity in the apostles' teachings and may be rendered 'in *the* truth' as in II John 1. Truth is a crucial concept throughout John's writings; the term is used six times (vv. 1, 3 [twice], 4, 8, 12) in this short letter. Gaius is an individual who is one with John in the propagation of orthodoxy in the churches.

3. The greeting (v. 2)
John's health wish is that Gaius' physical health be as robust as his spiritual maturity. While first century letters often included a physical health wish, John extends the wish in recognition of Gaius' spiritual vitality. The word 'soul' is interesting. It refers to Gaius' immaterial wellbeing. John prays that his physical health be as solid as his spiritual health. Does this suggest that Gaius may be older with health needs? Could it be that his health prevented him from participating in the church, making him unaware of Diotrephes' conduct, though he was still able to extend hospitality to John's itinerants. There is no textual evidence in this regard; it is speculative. The reason that Gaius' spiritual health is vibrant is that he is walking in the truth (v. 3).

4. The circumstance (v. 3)
The impetus for the letter, at least in part, is that John has heard reports from some believers, likely itinerants that John

sent to the churches, who witnessed Gaius' embrace of the apostles' teachings and his practical behavior in promoting its proclamation. The emphasis as a result of the report is upon Gaius' extension of kindness to them. By 'walking in the truth' (vv. 3, 4), John is saying that Gaius' life style, or manner of living, unlike Diotrephes', is consistent with the truth. It is a point not to be missed that John connects spiritual health with 'walking in the truth', right thinking about Jesus and spiritual vitality being interconnected.

5. An axiomatic statement (v. 4)

This appears to be a general statement ('children' being plural) concerning those who walk in the apostles' doctrine, rather than a statement that Gaius came to Christ through John literally. This nomenclature ('my children') is found in Paul for a spiritual father-son relationship, but it is not found in John's writings. Gaius is simply among his spiritual children because he sees him within the sphere of his care.

B. Body of the Letter (vv. 5-12)

1. The Commendation of Gaius (vv. 5-8)

(a) The declaration (v. 5)

John commends Gaius ('you are acting faithfully') for the support that he provided for the itinerants that John had sent to the nearby churches, though to Gaius they were 'strangers' (the plural may be an indication that itinerants travelled about in teams as was the practice of Paul as well as of Barnabas following their separation [Acts 16:36-39]). What is stated generally in the previous verses is here particularized; the evidence of Gaius' spiritual health is his grasp of the apostles' teachings and the practical manifestation of it in the extension of care. These itinerants are likely those ('brethren') who brought back a good report to John (v. 3) of Gaius' provision and support of them ('they bear witness to your love before the church' [v. 6]).

(b) The basis (vv. 6-8)

As stated above, the itinerants, sent out by the church of which John is a part, have returned with a glowing report of Gaius' assistance; this prompts John's letter. John, though likely the last remaining original apostle, is a member of a local church. The church apparently sent out the itinerants because they reported back to the church. Here we may have insight into the structure of authority in the earliest churches, a pattern discernible from the Book of Acts. There were leaders in the churches, elders, yet the action of a local group of believers was viewed as corporate (Acts 15:22).

John commends Gaius' support and requests its continuance, though there will be a Diotrephes. This suggests also that more missionaries were on the way to the churches in Gaius' area ('you will do well to') and they will need his continued benevolence, perhaps the reference is to a team led by Demetrius (v. 12). The practice of the earliest churches was to provide for the itinerant missionaries by supplying their physical needs while in a church and also by helping them to move on to the next one (Rom. 15:24, I Cor. 1:16, Titus 3:13).

One commentator has speculated that because of Diotrephes' attitude toward itinerants, the original team John sent out had been turned away and Gaius graciously provided for them (thus the notice of the report, vv. 5-6). This is intriguing, though speculative. It does suggest that we lack sufficient background information to answer our questions at times.

These itinerants depended upon the churches for support, having no other sources of revenue (v. 7). Because they would not accept money from unbelievers, for reasons unstated, the goal of the itinerants appears not to have been evangelization, but to strengthen the churches (the source of help coming from those helped! Unbelievers would not be expected to help propagate a religion they despised). The word translated 'Gentiles' only occurs here in John's writings, and only three other times in the New Testament. It would seem that John would not prohibit support from believing Gentiles, since they constituted a significant portion of the churches, so that the referent must be to unbelieving Gentiles. Why they should not accept help from appreciative pagans is not stated. Some commentators have speculated that the acceptance of help from pagans would identify them with many other itinerants that did not share their views, whereas others say that to accept money from non-believers would suggest that Christians were unwilling to support their own cause. A lack of evidence precludes a definitive answer to the question.

Somewhat disputed is the referent to 'the Name'. Of the possibilities the two most likely are as follows. One is that it may refer to God. This is supported by the use of the definite article (*the* Name) and that God is mentioned at the end of the previous verse (the nearest antecedent). Second, it could refer to Jesus Christ. In I John 2:12, for example, the writer says, 'your sins are forgiven for His (Christ's) Name's sake.' It is interesting that John places emphasis on the prepositional phrase 'for His name's sake' by putting it first in the sentence. Additionally, John never uses the name 'Christ' as a designation for Jesus in his writings (he does use Jesus Christ, but not Christ without Jesus). However, and with all of this stated, it is probable that 'the Name' does refer to Jesus Christ here (John often uses 'Christ' as a title [the Anointed One] rather than one of His names, which it is in other writers). 'The Name' is used as a synonym for the Old Testament term Jehovah, which, in this case, is Christ.

Inns or overnight lodgings were available throughout much of the empire in the first century (post houses and inns were placed at some fifty mile intervals along the great Roman roads and were supervised by provincial governors), but they were notoriously unsafe being the haunt of thieves. Lice and insects were prevalent in bedding, accommodations dirty, infectious diseases rampant, food often poor, and moral standards decadent. Travel by foot for long distances was infrequent in Roman society and hazardous. Thus, it was imperative that Christians entertain their traveling teachers with the basics for sustaining life and ministry.

In verse 8, John draws a deduction from the previous verses ('therefore') and uses the first person plural for the first time in the letter ('we') identifying himself, Gaius, and believers generally in the need to provide support to orthodox, sacrificing itinerants. The purpose of the support is rendered by the 'so that'. Those who sustain missionaries share in the ministry with them. More specifically, the phrase 'with the truth' suggests the sphere of cooperation. Further, the Spirit is referred to in John as the Spirit of truth (I John 4:6,

5:6). Thus, in helping missionaries, they not only participate in their work, but they are also co-workers with the Spirit.

2. The Condemnation of Diotrephes (vv. 9-11)

(a) The context (v. 9)

John wrote a letter to 'the church' concerning itinerant support, now lost, perhaps through the dereliction of Diotrephes, who prevented it from being read and, by doing so, rejected apostolic authority. It is interesting that John said 'he wrote to the church', suggestive that Gaius was not present at its reception and was unaware of it. More than one commentator has suggested that the suppressed letter was II John, though there is no collaborating evidence for the assertion.

Are Gaius and Diotrephes in the same church or merely acquainted? What can be deduced is that Gaius knew Diotrephes since there is no introduction in the letter to him. This would indicate that Gaius knew him, but was unaware of his bully-like deportment in the church (Marshall speculates that Gaius may have been prevented from attending the assembly of saints due to health issues [v. 2] and was ignorant of Diotrephes' belligerency [89]). It could also be that Gaius lived a distance from the church and simply assisted itinerants along their way. Whatever the circumstances may have been, John writes suggesting a distance between Gaius and the church by referring to the church in a way that separates Gaius 'from them' (v. 9). However, this does not explain why John wrote Gaius unless the sphere of Diotrephes' shadow extended to some distance, explaining Gaius' ignorance of the situation. The difficulty is that this view does not take into account that John is writing to more than Gaius ('friends,' v. 14; 'the church,' v. 9) and the reference to John's personal coming seems to suggest the close proximity of the two men.

The identity of Diotrephes can only be gathered from John's comments in the letter to Gaius. He seems to have been able to exercise significant authority in the church, perhaps the leader, but John tells us only two things about him here, and more in the following verse. First, he is on a personal quest for significance in the church, being arrogant in demeanor to acquire it. Second, in suppressing John's previous correspondence, Diotrephes has rejected apostolic authority, being unsubmissive, self-promoting, and haughty. For some reason, he refused to help the itinerants sent by John and the church (I have speculated that the motive may have been a good one [to eliminate the possibility of poor, intrusive teaching in the church or that he simply used the potential circumstance to promote his own self-interests]).

(b) The consequence (v. 10a)
If John gets the opportunity to visit the church, he says he will confront Diotrephes for his inappropriate behavior toward authorized itinerants and his abandonment of apostolic authority. The 'if,' being a third class condition, expresses uncertainty that John will visit, but he makes it certain what he will do if he does visit; he will reveal the injustices of Diotrephes' conduct.

(c) The reasons (v. 10b)
The charges that John would bring against Diotrephes are four: (1) that he has lied, spreading untruths about John's efforts as well as those of the itinerants; (2) that he refuses to sanction and help the itinerants sent out by John and the church; (3) that he will not recognize those who accept the missionaries (that is how he would treat Gaius, if he could); and (4) that he casts those who do support the itinerants out of the local assembly. These accusations concern Diotrephes' actions, while in verse 9 John spoke of his character and his repudiation of authority.

(d) An axiomatic statement (v. 11)
Here we have the first command in the letter. Though addressed initially to Gaius, it is clear that John is addressing a church ('friends'). This suggests that Gaius may have exercised some degree of leadership role, but that is only probable. Concerning Diotrephes' behavior, John implies that he is not a genuine believer ('one who does evil has not seen God' [I John 3:6, 10; 4:20]), the absence of Christian character implying the absence of Christian truth! The lack of care for others in the family is an indication to John that the uncaring one may not be in the family. The point is that Diotrephes'

action is unwarranted and orthodox missionaries are to be supported by the churches.

3. *Commendation of Demetrius (v. 12)*

After the report of Diotrephes' rejection of missionaries sent to the churches, John writes to Gaius requesting that he would support another team sent out, this time led by a man named Demetrius and, again, a 'stranger' to Gaius. As such, the letter would serve as an introduction of Demetrius to Gaius of the propriety of support in his efforts; Demetrius is an example of one who 'went out for the sake of the Name' (v. 7). It may be that Demetrius carried the letter to Gaius.

Demetrius is described with a threefold impressive testimony. First, he is well spoken of by everyone, his testimony being validated by all. Second, his testimony is confirmed by the truth itself; the Christian genuineness of Demetrius did not need human witness. It was self-evident. He professed truth and lived out the truth he professed. Third, 'we also speak well of him.' John is probably referring to the authority he carries as 'the elder' speaking for the church as a whole that he is attending.

C. Conclusion (vv. 13-15)

John anticipates a visit to Gaius in the near future (vv. 13-14), most likely at the time that he plans to deal with Diotrephes. John's final comment about a visit, rather than a letter, is similar to his wording in II John 12.

A benediction of peace (v. 15a) is interesting in light of the turmoil that the author and the churches are experiencing, with the threat of false teachings disturbing them with their intrusiveness, as well as the troubles within the churches from the likes of Diotrephes.

The closing greeting in verse 15b is similar to II John 13. That John speaks of sharing greetings among 'friends', and not 'the brethren' or mentioning of specific people, may hint that John and the churches are not well acquainted. Another clue to sustain this is that one of the reasons for the letter is to garner support for Demetrius, a person with whom Gaius is most likely unacquainted, and his team as well, by verifying their worthiness ('we also bear witness and our witness is true' [v. 12]).

What can we learn from this letter?

(1) Every church is blessed when it is filled with Gaius-types. Here is a person whose beliefs matched his conduct. He understood the need to participate in the outreach of the church and the importance of a vital and orthodox teaching ministry for the churches. He gave willingly to those who sacrificed for the health of the church and, in doing so, shared with others in the work of the Spirit of God. Though the church is in need of Demetrius-types, they cannot exist without Gaius-types.

(2) Sadly there are Diotrephes-types in our churches as well. These are people that want to control the direction of the church and in the process cause enormous damage to its health. John's condemnation of Diotrephes is forthright and clear; his reasoning is concise and accurate. These types in our churches must be confronted and the sooner the better. The quest for power and the presence of pride are powerful tools in the destruction of a work of God.

(3) To reject the authority of the apostles is a very serious matter. If it is true, and it is, that Jesus Christ became the incarnate God so as to reveal God to us; if it is true, and it is, that Jesus passed the message He came to deliver to a trusted band of men who have passed it down through the centuries, then it is a message that rests on the highest authority, the authority of God. It is not a message to be trivialized, distorted, or used for selfish gain. It is the message of God! It must be preserved, taught in the churches, and proclaimed throughout the world!

(4) Conduct is the barometer of truth; how one lives is evidence of what a person truly believes and values. One may not catch the presence of error upon the first hearing of it, the message often being couched in familiar terms but with unfamiliar meaning, but if you observe a person's misconduct you should sense disconnect between what they truly believe and their mere words. The minions of the devil can imitate righteousness, but they cannot do so with duration. 'All that glitters is not gold' is an old saying; with time the true nature of a metal becomes apparent when it tarnishes. Diotrephes may look shiny, but his behavior proved his message was a lie.

(5) Faithfulness to the things of God is important and even more so when evidenced by longevity. Gaius has a 'good report' for his conduct toward the missionaries sent out by John and the church. Gaius was a man whose lifestyle matched his professions. He valued the work of missionaries and demonstrated it by his financial generosity and hospitality. He is a model for all of us who value the work of godly missionaries.

(6) This little letter provides a wonderful description of the spiritual integrity of those who have been called to labor in the mission fields as itinerants. They are people who value the preciousness of their calling, not counting the cost or the danger it may involve. The truest mission-motive is Jesus Christ ('they went out for the sake of the Name' [v. 7]). It is for Him that they accept the perils of dependence and run the hazard of meeting rejection and hostility from 'Diotrephes'. It is for Him that they set aside financial security to live dependently upon the grace and gratuity of others. They are a hardy band of women and men that should be helped 'in a manner worthy of God' (v. 6).

(7) The work of Christ is an endeavor that requires a team of contributors. If all Christians were sent out as missionaries, they would go out without support. If all stayed in their churches, who would go out? We need both operating together in order to accomplish the God-ordained task of developing healthy churches. Mission work is not an option; it is a duty and a privilege. It is a duty because God has commanded that all churches should engage in reaching out; it is a privilege because we thereby share in the greatest enterprise in the world, the building of the body of Christ. There is simply no greater joy than participating in the proclamation of the wonder of Christ's redemption and the offer of salvation without cost or merit.

Concluding Thoughts

As this particular study draws to a close, it seems profit-able to gather together some of the thoughts that have emerged. The profundity of John's thoughts, the simplicity of literary expression, the difficulty of the grammar, and the clarity of his message lend a majestic sweetness to his letters that leaves the reader amazed and humbled. That we might know the God of whom John speaks through the Christ that he describes with the benefit of plunging more deeply into the reservoir of God's boundless mercies is my prayer as the study comes to a close. May we experience the love of God revealed in Christ's life and atoning death, possessed through the gift of God, the Holy Spirit, the very presence of the life of God within our very beings. May this revealed and possessed love radiate from our lives in the way we treat our fellow Christians and may it motivate us to speak of the love of God to a world that has lost its way; perhaps it is better stated, to a world that has never found the way.

As I think about the five works of John, I find a certain unity among them; they collectively speak of the centrality and wonder of Jesus Christ. John, to say the least, was very impressed with Him having been in His inner circle of companions for over three years. In the Gospel, John sought to explain the person, claims, and accomplishments of Jesus, whom he believed is the Christ. John tells us at the end of his account that 'these things have been written that you may believe that Jesus is the Christ, the Son of God, and that believing you may have life in His name' (20:31). Jesus, according to John, is the divine, only-begotten Son of God sent to the earth to reveal the character of God and make a provision that we might know God. When the Gospel drew to a close John gave us four additional literary masterpieces (the assumption being that John wrote the Gospel in the decade prior to the Jewish Revolt that led to the destruction of the Second Temple in 70 A.D.).

While the church had spread geographically throughout the empire in the interim years, the embryonic movement had encountered significant opposition from without (the Jewish community and the Roman state, with its ever-increasing panoply of deities that included the emperors), and from within (the emergence of false teachings and teachers that brought disharmony, chaos, and threat). This is the context of John's three letters. The first is John's attempt to assure the Christians in the churches of Asia Minor that they can have certainty of salvation without minimizing or forgetting that regeneration does not cure our natures; that Christ's atoning death answers the sin question for us yet finality awaits the final day, that false teachers are to be expected ('light collects flies' is an apt adage!), and that the apostles' teaching is the true message that Christ brought to us. The second letter of John is likely a circular letter warning the churches of the possible inroad of false teachers itinerating through the churches spilling their destructive venom on the unlearned and naïve. The third letter addresses the importance of itinerants who are teaching the apostles' doctrine; they are to be helped in their ministries to the churches.

The Revelation is set in the context, at least it seems to me, of the troubles that have been occasioned by the growth of false doctrine, as well as the growing hostility of the state that viewed Christianity as culturally and religious adversarial to the health and well-being of society. John writes this final work to explain that we should live in hope, that Christ will triumph over His enemies, and that persecution should not be allowed to hinder our zealous proclamation of Christ.

What cannot be missed in these writings is John's presentation of the person and work of Jesus Christ. Sadly, false teachers continue to abound, certainly in our day, who teach that Jesus was an important and insightful person, but no more than that. Many of our churches have abandoned the apostles' teachings for a Jesus that is an idealized myth or fiction of altruism, merely the grandest of examples of compassion for the economically, politically, socially, and culturally oppressed, Jesus being a symbol rather than a heaven-sent, divine reality. He is the divinely sent anointed one! It is not that Jesus was endued by the power of the Spirit at His baptism, elevating His status and becoming God's representative to humankind. In such phrases as 'the Son of the Father' and 'the Son of God', John would have us know that Jesus is God incarnated; that Jesus (being the Christ) came among us to make it possible for finite, blighted creatures to come into the family of God, the realm of absolute holiness; that Jesus accomplished this for us by becoming for us the atoning substitute, and that it is through Jesus only that sinners can be forgiven! This is the gospel, the only gospel. Any deviation from it, any de-evaluation of Jesus' person and accomplishments, is no gospel at all! I think Brown is quite right when he writes that '...the issue is not that the secessionists are denying the incarnation or the physical reality of Jesus' humanity; they are denying that what Jesus was or did in the flesh was related to His being the Christ, i.e., was salvific' (505).

John would have us know that sin is not a matter to be treated lightly, that we cannot wish it away. The solution is not to deny its existence in us, nor is it in asserting that an encounter with the Spirit after our initial meeting with Jesus, a second work of grace, somehow eliminates the Christian's continual struggle with the remnants of sin's once universal grip on every faculty of our innermost beings. The message of John is this: it is not necessary to deny the presence of sin in our lives, living in the mythic realm of deception and delusion. The apostles' teaching is that Christ's atoning sacrifice addressed the guilt of sin; however, it only guarantees that the presence of sin will be eradicated and that will occur when we get to see Him on the greatest of days. How we deal with imperfection in this life is to understand that Christ is our righteousness, that when God sees us, He sees us through the perfections of His Son. It is to realize the seriousness of sin in limiting our ability to appreciate the Savior as we ought. Sin diminishes our ability to know His beauty, and demonstrates our lack of appreciation for what He has done for us. The normal Christian life is a life of confession, turning to God for restorative mercies and saying, 'I am sorry for dishonoring the Lord who loves me.'

The invisible change that redemption brings through embracing Jesus as the Christ in our innermost being is evidenced by outward, observable alternation in our priorities, delights, and passions. Though the struggle within is an ongoing reality, a lot has changed for every believer. Those changes (the embrace of the truth of the apostles' teachings, obedience to a lifestyle consistent with our profession, and, most particularly, love for God's other children) are evidences that the Spirit of God indwells us, and He is there as the promise and presence of eternal life. The practical importance of this reality is striking. It tells us that profession of Christ without the character of Christ is likely to be a false, empty profession. It is not merely embracing of the historical record of the events of Jesus' life, death, and resurrection that makes one a Christ-follower; rather it is in following Him, in submission to Him, that we have evidence of being in the family of God. A childhood confession of belief, even an adult one, that shows no evidence that a life-change of interests and priorities has taken place is likely a false and merely an outward encounter with the Christian tradition, and not with Christ Himself. Further, it tells us that education in the things of God and a conducive environment that supports Christian faith are no guarantee of the embrace of Christ, however important and necessary these may be. God does not 'grandfather' our children or grandchildren into the family because He has been gracious to us. We must pray for that invisible working of God wrought by the Spirit that would make the Christian faith not only true but also 'real' to our loved ones. We must represent Christ in word and deed to our families until they come to Christ and then continue telling them of the ever-present Savior until we can no longer do so. We can know that we actually know Christ! It is not the result of being perfect in some way; it is in daily recognizing our imperfections and inadequacies and then relentlessly turning to the perfect one for cleansing.

Though it has become less important to be a part of a strong Christ-centered church in our culture, the notion being that Christianity can prosper without church (many recognizing that church-life presents its own set of problems that may be counter to Christian growth), it always remains the God-sanctioned community for the nurturing and cultivation of spiritual vitality. This seems to be an inescapable reality as one reads through the five writings of John. Christ established it, the apostles announced and expanded it, followers have taken refuge in it through the centuries, and God has promised to come for it, and then restore it to the beauty of His divine habitation forever. Yes, the church is not without its failings, being composed of flawed leaders (think of Diotrephes) and communicants (there are even false teachers in it!), but it is the place for true community, growth, and protection.

These letters call us to be discerning when it comes to whom we listen and embrace. All who claim to know the scriptures, all who claim to have been taught of God, all who claim insight from the Spirit of God, all who claim to be His spokesmen simply may not be! It is not in words that truth is found, even when accompanied by the appearance of zealousness, sincerity, winsomeness, devotedness, and care. There is an old adage we all know: 'All that glitters is not gold.' The tests of the right to be listened to are several: Is the instruction consistent with the apostles' teaching both in content and emphasis? Does the teaching cause me to focus on the beauty of Christ or, in some way, to turn away from His character and message? Does the teacher offer promises of spiritual progress and accomplishment devoid of the reality of struggle, some type of instant spirituality? Does a teacher possess credible credentials for the position he/she claims from credible sources (remember Gaius!)? Has the person had a proven, durative ministry? Do they ask for money?

John helps us to understand the nature of true joy. It is found in the embrace of the gospel, as well as by living in the community of those who have that faith-commitment. In the western world where individualism and privitism dominate, it is easy to think that contentedness is found in self-oriented accomplishments. For the Christian, the community has become a new reality. Joy in I John is participating in the fellowship of believers in a common commitment to Jesus Christ and His followers (1:4); in II John it relates to sharing in the reward of participating in the gospel (v. 8); and in

III John blessing is found in sharing in the dissemination of the gospel through supporting those who have been uniquely called within the community to become teachers who travel beyond localized boundaries and thereby participate with them in a worldwide movement (v. 8). John calls us to a life centered first in devotion to Christ through adherence to the apostles' doctrine and then to each other!

I conclude this study by citing an old hymn. It captures the theme of I John rather clearly, the privilege and delightedness we have in knowing God through Jesus Christ. I pray that it will be a progressive and daily reality in each of our lives, putting our fears and frustrations to rest until faith reaches its fullest and complete manifestation when we get to see the longing of our souls. The poem was composed in 1873 by Fanny Crosby and entitled 'Blessed Assurance'.

> Blessed assurance, Jesus is mine!
> O what a foretaste of glory divine!
> Heir of salvation, purchase of God,
> Born of His Spirit, washed in his blood.
>
> This is my story, this is my song,
> praising my Savior all the day long;
> this is my story, this is my song,
> praising my Savior all the day long.

Group Study Questions

I John 1:1-4

1. As you think about the prologue to John's first letter, what is the fundamental theme that the author introduces and becomes the topic throughout?

2. According to John, what is the crux of the message Jesus gave to the apostles to proclaim? How does what John explains to us differ and is consistent with how you and I often hear the claims of Christ presented?

3. Is John describing Jesus here or something about Jesus? What are the implications of your answer?

4. Can you even vaguely imagine what it would have been like to hear and see Jesus? What do you think when you think of hearing, seeing, and being personally in His presence?

5. Why do you think John employs the teaching device of repetition as a characteristic of his writings? What does that tell us in our effort to be effective communicators and how it is that people learn?

6. What does he mean when John employs the word *fellowship*? How does John use the word differently from how it is often used in many contemporary Christian discussions? What are the implications of this in describing the Christian life?

7. Can a person be granted the life of God and not be transformed in their thinking, priorities, and moral attitudes? Can the Spirit of God enter a life and leave no traces of His presence in that life?

8. What is the nature of true biblical joy? Is it an external quality or an internal quality? What is the object and origin of biblical joy?

I John 1:5

1. How can it be said that this is the fundamental, controlling verse in the entire book?

2. In this verse, what is the difference between spiritual light and darkness?

3. If knowing God means the possession of the life of God, and the life of God is the actual character of God, how can it be said that anyone knows God since our lives are neither totally holiness nor darkness?

4. What can you say about the darkness that remains in your life and mine? What does this tell us? How can this be?

5. The greatest insight about Christianity, and the one clearly answered by Jesus and the apostles, is this one: Can a sinner really know God if the criteria of knowing Him is to be like Him? How can this be when redemption does not cure human nature from the entirety of its blight?

6. Is it not amazing that the gospel is about the life of God in us, not merely the transformation that God has brought to our lives? The religious of the world tell us that life is through moral codification, but Christian faith points us away to one who says, 'receive,' receive a gift unearned, unmerited, and perfect. Does this not re-arrange your perspective on the meaning of the Christ message?

I John 1:6–2:2

1. How does the practice of sin differ from acts of sin since no believer is characterized by the former and yet plagued by the latter?

2. What would John say of a person whose life is character-ized by a continual calloused, rebellious attitude toward

God even though they may claim to have met Jesus sometime prior in life?

3. What does this passage tell us about the nature of experiencing the life of God in the soul?

4. If the experience of God does not immediately, nor ever in this life, lead to victory over the blight and scarring effect of sin in human nature, what is the remedy for the believer in Christ Jesus?

5. As you think about this paragraph as a whole, how would you describe the normal Christian life? How does this help you understand the complexities and convolutedness of your Christian experience?

6. There is a question that lies at the foundation of all religions. The greatest of all questions is perhaps this one: How can sinful people come to a holy God if the criteria for coming to God requires possession of the character of God since God only condones what is in perfect congruity with Himself? How would you answer that question?

7. Is not the good news for all mankind that we do not have to become what we cannot become because one has come who is what we are not? Is not the really 'good news' that someone from the realm of God has come to gather us in Himself so that we can enter the presence of God?

8. Have you come to the realization that God is pleased with you because of Jesus, our redeemer and advocate? Are you still seeking to please God or are you seeking to show appreciation for all that God has done as a token of your gratefulness?

9. How is the character and work of Jesus described in these verses? What comfort do these insights offer you?

10. Is the Christian gospel about us or is it about the claims and accomplishments of someone else? How does this insight help you to think about your faith, your duties, and what you say in witnessing?

I John 2:3-11

1. What have you learned from the previous paragraph when you come to read this and later paragraphs that speak of criteria for knowing that we possess the life of God, though imperfectly manifested now?

2. Why do you think that John begins to discuss the grounds of assurance of the divine life in the soul with the characteristic of obedience? What does this say about assurance based on experiential feelings and one's emotional state alone?

3. If moral evidences in themselves (such as kindness, gentleness, and care) are not, in themselves, evidence of the changed life, what makes moral change actual evidence?

4. If Jesus and John placed the litmus test of assurance of the life of God in love of others, what does this tell us fundamentally about how we are to live in relation to others? What does this say about selfishness in our lives?

5. What is the goal of the Christian life as lived out in this life? Is it not interesting that the essence of the Christian life is the development of inward character qualities, not outward actions, though it inevitably leads to outward actions (inward qualities always lead to outward expression)?

6. In what sense do you think that the world is passing away? How is John using this concept?

7. How would John urge us to walk the Christian walk in our struggle with sin? Is he not advocating a basic displacement theory; that we are to fill our minds with good thoughts, not the thoughts that drag us to worldly thoughts?

8. The expression that John uses to elucidate obedience is love. If love is the expression of the character of God, and, therefore, the evidence of the life of God in us, how are you doing with loving the unloving?

9. Though this passage could create fear in us arising from the reality that our lives do not match John's description of the life of God, what in this passage counters that thought?

I John 2:12-17

1. Is worldliness merely the attraction to things or a motive that attracts us to things?

2. Why do you think 'young women' is not a category in John's list of ages or realms of spiritual development? What does this tell us?

3. How is eternal life described in these verses? What can you gather from the various phrases about the assurance of salvation?

4. How are you and I to obey the commandment not to love the world when John tells us in his gospel account that God loves the world? How is the word 'world' being used in each instance and what are the implications for us?

5. What does it practically mean to you not to love the world? There are two realms of enticements, external and internal. It takes an external object and an internal desire to follow the values of the world. What are you doing, or what can we do, to minimize these?

6. We all have our struggles, but they can be reduced to two: desire for inordinate pleasures or misperception of our importance. How would you suggest we combat these in our lives?

7. Have you come to grips with the fact that this world is both a wonderful place and not so friendly a place? What are you doing to recognize the difference?

8. What is the 'will of God' that promises he/she who pursues it will live forever?

9. Do you find hope and comfort in the fact that there will come a day in the great denouement of this world, and

the beginning of the eternal kingdom of God, that our struggles will end forever?

10. What are the implications in our passage (v. 17) that the concept of abiding is not a temporal state of spiritual victory over some sin or circumstance, but a synonym for life in God as a normal experience?

I John 2:18-27

1. Because Christians do not agree on all points of the teachings of the Bible what does it mean that we are to remain in the apostles' teachings? How are we to treat brothers and sisters who do not interpret the Holy Scriptures as we have been led to do?

2. If there have been many antichrists through the centuries, how are we to see the opposers of Christ in our day? Are we to see them necessarily as an evidence of the end of the current age?

3. What can you and I learn from the fact that the false teachers that John is speaking of are those that once were seeming well-meaning embracers with him in the teachings of Christ? How can it be that the faith communities create their own adversaries?

4. Why is it that true believers are not deceived by false teachers? What is the preventative? What is the practical implication of this for those who follow them and is this a ground of assurance for those who do not?

5. What is the essence of the teaching of every false teacher? Can a person know God the Father without knowing God the Son? Can a person deny the absolute deity of the Son and know the Father? What are the implications of this for people who claim to know God but not Jesus as the Son of God?

6. It is clear from Holy Scriptures that God has given us teachers to instruct us in the things of the Lord. However, what does it mean when John tells us that we do not need them?

7. What does this passage tell us about what John's initial readers were facing? Is there any correlation to what we are facing in this regard?

I John 2:28–4:6

1. John makes the point that 'everyone who practices right-eousness is born of God' (v. 29). How do you balance that statement with John's clear teaching that no true believer is sinless in motive or behavior? What does this tell us?

2. How should the hope of the coming of the Lord and our appearance before him serve as a motivation for us in our daily walk?

3. Is it not interesting that practicing sin is defined within the context of a lack of love for others? Can persons harbour hatred for another in the family of God, or outside of it, and have assurance that God has brought a change in their lives from death to life? What does 'practice' mean in these verses?

4. How is love defined in our passage? How was it modeled for us? Clearly it was not in Cain's reaction to Abel!

5. Are there specific ways that you should love that are not mere expressions in words? Are there particular instances that you failed to love in deed but you did seek to hide it with words? What lessons have you learned from such situations that would prove helpful for all of us?

6. While the essence of the meaning of being redeemed is not moral, it is the embrace of the claims of a person, Jesus Christ. Why do you think that conversion invariably causes the invisible to be visualized?

7. If you know that you will be truly righteous and holy before God one day, what are you specifically doing today in order to be like Jesus when He appears to gather you to Himself?

8. Do you allow your conscience to give you unrest, stealing away your peace and comfort? How have you found ways to resist the whispers of your conscience when what God

has said about you in Christ is greater, more truthful, and trustworthy than what your conscience sometimes dictates?

9. A heart in tune with God is one that knows how to ask appropriately, and, when asked, God delights in answering us as any father his children. The condition for answered prayer is love (first toward God and then to one another). Do you find yourself asking God for things and wonder why He does not answer? What can you learn about prayer here?

10. In context, the promise of prayer going unanswered concerns what might be a lack of biblical love for a member or members of the body of Christ. Could this universal gift of answered prayer relate to loving others?

I John 4:7-21

1. What do you think about the tests whereby we can know that God has done a gracious work in our hearts? There is significant overlapping when it comes to obedience, awareness of error, moral purity, and love. What do you think this tells us?

2. How does John define biblical love in our passage? Can a person truly love without knowing God through Christ? How is love distinguished between that of believers and unbelievers? Is it in the act of loving or something else?

3. Are there instances in your life when you have felt that you loved others out of true biblical love? What did that look like for you?

4. What is the gospel message if you could only read the passage we are studying today?

5. Is the state of abiding the same as the state of salvation in our passage? What are the practical implications of this insight for daily Christian living?

6. If all the world will not come to bow in heart-felt love and devotion to the Savior, in what sense is Jesus the Savior of the world?

7. To be a Christian is to know the love that God has for you according to John. It is not the privilege of some Christians; it is the privilege of all. Being a Christian must imply knowledge that God loves us. Do you delight in knowing that God loves you?

8. Is it my or your love for God that casts out fear of judgment or is it God's love for you or me that casts out fear of judgment? Is the gospel message about us or is the beginning and ending point in God? Does the gospel glorify us or God primarily? What are the implications of this as you think about your confidence in God?

9. Is there any reason we should pick who we love in the body of Christ?

10. Abiding in God's love means to be preoccupied in our thought life by God's love for us, not to be led astray by false teachers or the allurements of this world system. What are we to do to abide in God's love since no one can come in and out of God's love?

I John 5:1-12

1. Is it not significant that the final test of assurance is how life in God began for us, in believing? What does this tell us about the nature of the Christian life? How has the Christian life been a life of faith for you? Have there been times when all you clung to was the fact of the object of your faith?

2. Faith, love, and obedience are the valid grounds of assurance. Faith is the greatest with love and obedience being the manifestation of what is invisible. How do you go about evidencing faith in regard to love and obedience?

3. The object of our faith is the one that the Spirit witnessed to and the one to whom he witnesses to us, continually 'crying aloud to us, Abba Father.' How are you growing in your relationship with the object of your faith?

4. Assurance of salvation is a simple matter of trusting, of reliance on the claims that Jesus made of Himself, and

which the apostles declared. Spiritual life and spiritual assurance are inseparable, though distinguishable. How would you say the two are inseparable yet distinguishable?

5. The internal witness of the Spirit is the greatest ground of assurance that you and I can have. Why is this so? What are the implications of your answers?

6. If God requires of us acceptance, trust, and reliance upon His promises through His Son in order to become the recipients of the life of God, how can we say that salvation is a free gift? If Jesus purchased our salvation for us at Calvary, how can we say that salvation is free?

7. In God's opinion His life comes only through His Son. Why do you think this is so other than God said it?

8. Why is entertaining thoughts of a lack of personal assurance an act of trusting our own selves more than trusting God and His revelation to us in Jesus? If God is greater than we are in truth, holiness, righteousness, and justice, why would anyone think that their inner fears should be trusted more that the infinite being?

9. It is worth the pause to think about the phrase, 'God has given us eternal life' (v. 11). Do you find delight and confidence in this statement? What troubles you about it?

10. The mark of the saint is not so much the extent of his obedience and love as it is his struggle to pursue obedience and love. Since we are not perfect people, as of yet, is not the struggle to do right a basis of assurance? If we did not know God as revealed in Jesus Christ, we would tend to think there is nothing wrong with doing as we naturally please.

I John 5:13-21

1. A person who suggests that the life of God in the soul cannot be known to be true and valid personally simply has not understood John's letter. How can you know that you are a child of God? How do you have assurance

when you do things that you should not do? What would John say to us?

2. A knowledge of assurance of salvation, a knowledge that we are the children of God, the experience of the divine life in our very inner being, should and will lead to intimacy with God in conversation as with a dear friend. Is that true for you? What hinders you from the experience of intimacy when God delights for you to come into His presence?

3. What is clear in our passage is that God answers prayer for the restoration of His children. God may delay the answer for reasons only known to Him and the answer may be when a sinning brother or sister enters heaven, but the prayer will be answered. That is the promise of God. Do you have a prayer- concern list that is more than a forum for gossip and that you carry in your heart for others in the family of God?

4. What is the kind of prayer that God will not answer?

5. Is the sin leading to death a particular sin? If so, what would it be? Is the sin leading to death any sin that is habitually, callously, and perpetually engaged in revealing the heart of a person without the life of God?

6. Is this text telling us that we should not pray for unbelievers? Is the fact that we should pray for unbelievers a clue as to what John is actually saying here?

7. How do we understand the three things that we know in this passage (vv. 18-20) in light of the teachings of the entire letter?

8. How has the study of John's letter matured your spiritual growth? How has the study grounded you in greater assurance of life in God though we all remain broken people in many ways? God does ask perfection of us; He asks us to reside in the perfections of His Son, Jesus Christ!

9. What are the idols that we should avoid after reading through this entire letter? What idols are particular to your life that you should put away from you?

10. How are we to put away idols? Is it not by putting better things in our minds to preoccupy us? How would you say we should go about this? What provisions has God made that we can do this?

II John

1. There is no greater delight than to see those you love following the Lord. This was a significant motive in John's work and it should be for us. Do you take special delight in seeing people growing in obedience and love for the Lord? Does this find expression in your home, among your neighbours, in your workplace, in the assembling of God's people? What helpful ways have you found to promote this in these several spheres?

2. It is clear in reading John's letters that he places significant emphasis on love and obedience, while we often find significance in large projects or great endeavours that require enormous energy and time investment. Could it be that we could do more to serve our Lord by doing less? How do you determine when less is better than more?

3. Are the moral characteristics of God known to us, as they are in themselves, or as they are revealed in His providential and benevolent actions toward us? If God is not revealed essentially, being spirit, but through His acts, what does it tell us about the place of our actions in helping people to see the God we love?

4. John would have us know that if the truth abides in us, if God has taken residence in us through, by, and in the Spirit, He will do so forever. This is our ultimate ground of assurance and experience of divine security. Is there any ground for a person who experiences the life of God revealed in, through and by Christ to wonder about eternal security? John provides for us insight into the nature of those who profess faith, claim to teach faith, but do not possess saving faith, being apart from the life of God, denying the incarnation of Jesus, His heavenly origin, and that He was deity manifested in true human flesh. Have you met people who think of Jesus as little

more than a great person or example? What would John have you say to them?

5. If we cannot lose what we have been given (eternal life, abiding in life forever), what does John mean when he speaks of the possibility of some degree or type of loss through the deception of false teachers?

6. A person who once professed Christ, but later finds something or someone more attractive and appealing, is a person who has never actually met him, according to John. Do you know people such as this? What can be said of a profession that only leads later to the rejection of and disinterest in what once attracted them?

7. Are we to actively support those who do not hold to the truth of God and teach error consequently? How are we to show love without such support that we become unwitting supporters of deception? How do we draw our boundaries?

8. There are instances in life where things spoken from a distance or in print should have been handled directly, immediately, and personally. How do you erect guidelines between distance communication and immediate communication?

III John

1. Here we meet a man who is in better spiritual health than physical health. We live in a world that has made an icon of the latter and thinks little of the former, a world that believes the visible is more real and important than the invisible. Do you find yourself falling into that type of perspective of what is real and important? What can be done to adjust our perspective?

2. When people speak of you in your absence, would they express the same ideas and feelings as in your presence? Do you of others? The particular reference is that of care for missionaries who serve the Lord. Do people speak well of you as one who serves the servants of the Lord? Supporting God's servants is worthy of commendation.

3. Have you ever met a Diotrephes-type in your social dealings with other Christians? How should we go about handling people who seek preeminence in the church, who are dominating and self-possessed of their importance, and yet think they are doing what is right.

4. Is Diotrephes an example of a person that operates from a good motive (in this case concern for the damage potential of itinerants), but goes about the concern in the wrong way and manner? Have you found yourself falling into this type of behaviour? If we act in this way, how can we help ourselves?

5. Do you think Diotrephes was a Christian, a follower of Jesus, from what is disclosed about him in this letter?

6. I think in most of our churches we have Gaius, Diotrephes, and Demetrius. They are fixtures. What does this tell us about churches in the first century? Do you think we have improved or retrogressed? Or, is this a witness to the fact that human nature is what it is, human?

7. What can we glean from these two brief letters from John about the churches in the first century? How are they different from churches in our day and time?

8. The letter seems to make the point that truth takes precedence over social relationships when it comes to the family of God. How do we balance truth and love in our relationships as believers? Should we not begin by seeking to discern the difference between truth and truths (what we must cling to even at the expense of what others call a lack of love or what is merely conceived as a strong opinion)?

Bibliography

The following are resources that proved helpful in the preparation of this commentary on the letters of John the Apostle. Each offers greater detail and fuller discussion of the issues relative to interpreting the letters than I reflect. Though not specifically noted in this commentary through the use of copious footnoting, these works have been liberally consulted and their insights employed. You will find these works helpful in the development of your understanding of these books and they have been chosen because of their literary accessibility. Some of these works, such as those of Brown, Bruce, Kruse, Law, Marshall, and Stott are particularly noteworthy.

Akin, Daniel L. *1, 2, 3 John. The New American Commentary.* Nashville, TN: B&H Publishers, 2001.

Bass, Christopher D. *That You May Know: Assurance of Salvation in I John.* Nashville, TN: B&H Publishing Group, 2008

Boice, James Montgomery. *The Epistles of John.* Reprint, 1979. Grand Rapids: Baker, 2006.

Brooke, A. E. T*he Johannine Epistles.* Edinburgh: T. & T. Clark, 1912.

Brown, Raymond E. *The Epistles of John.* New Haven, CT: Yale University Press, 1982.

Bruce, F. F. *The Epistles of John.* Grand Rapids: Eerdmans, 1970.

Calvin, John and Matthew Henry. *1, 2, & 3 John.* Edited by Alister McGrath and J. I. Packer. Wheaton, IL: Crossway

Books, 1998. Since Calvin did not write commentaries on 2 & 3 John, the editors included the works of Matthew Henry to complete the series.

Edwards, Ruth B. 'The Johannine Epistles' (pp. 110-203) in *The Johannine Literature*. Sheffield, England: Sheffield Academic Press, 2000.

Henry, Matthew. *An Exposition of the First General of John* in *Acts to Revelation. Commentary on the Whole Bible*. Vol. 4. Reprint. Mclean, VA: Macdonald Publishing Co., n.d.

Kruse, Colin G. *The Letters of John. The Pillar New Testament Commentary Series*. Grand Rapids: Eerdmans, 2000.

Law, Robert. *THE TESTS OF LIFE: A Study in the First Epistle of John*. Edinburgh: T. & T. Clark, 1909

Marshall, I. Howard. *The Epistles of John. The New International Commentary on the New Testament*. Grand Rapids: Eerdmans. 1978.

Netbible.org is a marvelous website for Bible study. It is free and easily accessible. The numerous footnotes are helpful. It provides access to many other sources of a practical nature to augment any study.

Smalley, Stephen S. *1, 2, 3, John. Word Biblical Commentary*. Waco, TX: Word, 1984.

Stott, John R. W. *The Epistles of John. The Tyndale New Testament Commentaries*. Grand Rapids: Eerdmans, 1964.

Thompson, Marianne Meye. *1-3 John. The IVP New Testament Commentary Series*. Downers Grove, IL: IVP Academic, 1992.

Yarbrough, Robert W. *1–3 John. Baker Exegetical Commentary on the New Testament*. Grand Rapids: Baker Academic, 2008.

Subject Index

Scripture Index